T0354892

A GREAT LIFE

A GREAT LIFE

JOE BURNWORTH

A GREAT LIFE

iUniverse books may be ordered through booksellers or by contacting:

iUniverse
1663 Liberty Drive
Bloomington, IN 47403
www.iuniverse.com
844-349-9409

ISBN: 978-1-6632-6353-7 (sc)
ISBN: 978-1-6632-6354-4 (hc)
ISBN: 978-1-6632-6355-1 (e)

Library of Congress Control Number: 2024910912

Print information available on the last page.

iUniverse rev. date: 09/26/2024

CONTENTS

Dedication

This writing of my memoires is dedicated to my mother, Frances L. Burnworth. My Mother meticulously chronicled her family history as far back as records would allow. She then passed her detailed narrative and photographic findings, with personalized recognition, along to each of her children and grandchildren. Her commitment to establishing our solid family foundation set the stage for my follow up supplemental addition.

Dedication

Foreword

It all began on November 2, 1943, at 708 Neeley Avenue in Muncie, Indiana. In too much of a hurry to enter my new world, I was born in my parents' bedroom less than three miles from Ball Memorial Hospital. I was very fortunate to be welcomed into a wonderful, loving Christian family of four, with expansion plans beyond my control and imagination.

As a few years passed with two more children being born, an aunt, my grandmother and great grandmother added to our nine hundred square foot three-bedroom one-bath home. Cramped as it was, I daily sought solitude outside, studying all the elements Mother Nature had to offer. Additionally, I ingratiated myself to my neighbors, boyhood friends and others to fill my day from sunrise to sunset, staying away from the cramped quarters my parents had created.

Tired of wearing hand-me-downs from my older brother, Dale, at age twelve I took an after-school job selling Downy flake Donuts door-to-door. This first job formed my independence from reliance on my parents so much that I purchased my own clothes and first wristwatch. As I changed and upgraded my employment, I was able to buy my first car and ultimately pay my way through college.

With just two classes to finish my undergraduate degree at Ball State University, I was drafted into the U.S. Army. The escalating war in Vietnam needed fighting soldiers and I was compelled to become one of them. For six months I was assigned to a team designated for search and destroy missions with the 1st Air Calvary. Fortunately, I was chosen "Soldier of the Month," which ended my combat duty and was given the opportunity to serve as the aid to our Battalion commander. As such, I was elevated, promoted and no longer directly in harm's way!

Returning home from Vietnam was difficult! The war was very unpopular, with anti-war protesters, the negative mainstream media reports and stories of U.S. Soldiers killing babies and civilians. With the exception of my mother, Father, immediate family and one close friend, J.T. McCafferty, there was no sense of 'Welcome Home' to me.

Eight months later I met Linda Lou Anderson. She was the most beautiful, articulate, and interesting girl I had ever met. We immediately became inseparable! Approximately eight months later we were married on the "Sweetest Day" October 16, 1971. On our wedding day I saw the most beautiful sight my eyes would ever behold, my bride, Linda, walking down the aisle to me.

My entrepreneurial spirit, supported by Linda, led us from owning a single rental property to purchasing a printing company, opening three disco roller-skating rinks and ultimately developing and building apartments and condominiums across the country.

With our two sons, Neil, and Reid, we became world travelers visiting 18 countries, exploring their underwater sanctuaries and studying the varied above water cultures.

I have been blessed with many successes! Being taught by my giving and loving parents, I was encouraged to share it with others. To that end, I provided financial support to many worthwhile organizations. Linda devoted her life working with some of them and many other philanthropic organizations.

Realizing early on there are no straight roads in it, I have had a Great Life!

Early Years

CHARLES J. [JOE] BURNWORTH

Impatient, that's the description my mother always used when she referred to me! Like a sprinter at the starting block, coiled in anticipation for the loud report of the starter's gun to begin the 100-yard dash, I was excited to launch my life outside my mother's womb. I couldn't wait for my mother to get to Ball Memorial Hospital three miles from our family home, my birth happened right there in the master bedroom of 708 Neely Avenue, Muncie, Indiana on November 2, 1943. Why couldn't she get to the hospital? She didn't tell me and now I can only speculate. Was my father at work, were the neighbors unavailable to help, did I arrive earlier than expected? And who assisted in delivering me, the third child, to this caring and loving family? Our doctor, Dr. Orville A. Hall, known to his friends and colleagues as "Orvie" wasn't there because my birth certificate was signed four days later by Dr. John W. Funk, Delaware County Health Officer.

At the time of my birth the United States of America was in the middle of World War II, which was recognized as the bloodiest war in history where 60 million people perished worldwide. America's war effort was being coordinated by 28,000 military and civilian personnel in the new Pentagon Building located in Arlington County, Virginia. The groundbreaking for the largest low rise office building in the world occurred on 9/11/1941. Forty years later the 9/11 date would become synonymous with one of America's greatest tragedies. The 6,500,000 square foot structure facetiously referred to as the "five-sided foxhole" was completed on 1/15/1943.

During this time rationing of food, clothing, gas, which was at an amazing low price of $.15 a gallon, tires for cars and many other common family items were in short supply.

My Mother, Laura Frances Bickner was born, August 10, 1918, in Como, Indiana, identified only by a sign on either side of an intersection on Highway

1

67 between Muncie and Portland, Indiana. She was the fifth child born to Oscar S. and Nevada May Bickner, farmers of 120 acres of less than favorable soil. Having grown up in the meager dusk to dawn and beyond farming lifestyle, The Valedictorian of her 30 student Gray High School class of 1936 reversed her much preferred first name to Frances Laura Bickner and enrolled at Indiana Business College in Muncie. This two-year educational program promised the opportunity to fulfill her dreams of a better and more fulfilling lifestyle, which was enhanced and realized when she met one of her classmates, John Burnworth.

The two new IBC students, both concentrating their efforts in the growing demand for office workers, were immediately drawn to each other. When they were separated, he was living with his parents in Eaton, while commuting to school in Muncie, daily, wrote each other love letters. Many were sent before the other was received keeping their bag [pouch] carrying home delivery mailmen busy. Soon the correspondence and separation grew too much for them, as young people in love, they were engaged to be married. The short engagement was followed by their wedding, December 4, 1937, in Eaton performed by Reverend E.D. Burnworth, Pastor and Father of the groom.

My Father, John Evans Burnworth was born on July 13, 1916, in Loranger, Louisiana the only child of Edward Davis & Gladys C. Burnworth, who as pastor and wife, migrated first to Pennsylvania and Illinois before arriving in Indiana to serve the Brethren Church. Reverend E.D. Burnworth was the son of a well-traveled Brethren Church Pastor, Reverend John Henry Burnworth, who had served in several towns in Nebraska and Kansas. My Father's parents and grandparents wanted him to be the third generation of the family Brethren Church Pastors. But being more timid and more reluctant to speak in front of others, my father decided he wanted something different for his life. He wished to establish himself in the more growth-oriented position of a clerical office setting. Thus, he enrolled at Indiana Business College in Muncie. After completing his education My Father attempted to serve his country during WWII but, due to poor eyesight, was denied the opportunity.

Shortly after their marriage my parents purchased their first home, a three-bedroom bungalow at 708 Neely Avenue for $2,500.00. My older Sister, Phyllis by three years and my brother Dale, who was two years older, preceded me in occupying our family home. It was ideally located in the northern developing sector of Muncie, available by the city bus and, which I would discover later, walking distance to downtown and Saturday Movie Matinees at the Liberty and Rivoli Theatres. Ball State Teachers college was due west through Schick's Woods, which was great for hunting frogs and snakes, all the things a young boy relishes as he discovers the ever-expanding world in which he lives. Our family church, Riverside United Brethren Church was three short blocks due east from our home. This made it easier for Mom & Dad to take their family at least three times a week to the religious services the church provided.

Just two city blocks further due east from our home were the five great mansions of the Ball Family. Each of the original Ball Brothers, who founded Ball Brothers Company, a maker of Ball food canning jars and lids, with free natural gas provided their business, built their homes on Minnetrista Parkway. Frank C. Ball, one of the original five brothers, still lived there with his wife Elizabeth when My Parents bought their home. However, I don't recall them ever telling me Frank invited them over for dinner. Frank listed his occupation as a manufacturer of glass, paper, Zinc, and rubber. Could he have ever envisioned his company's rise to be a Fortune 500 Company, NASA's contractor to build the first spacecraft, Orbiting Solar Observatory, and supplier of scientific instruments for the Hubble Space Telescope?

In the 1940 U.S. Census my father, waiting for his first opportunity after graduating from Indiana Business College, worked 52 hours a week as a florist and was earning $1,611.00 a year with Cade Flower Company. This was slightly below the national median annual income of $1,725.00 for a 40-hour week. Frank C. Ball declined to list his income.

Directly across the street from our house on Neely Avenue lived Wendell Moore, an art teacher at Wilson Middle with his wife and two daughters. One of his daughters was two years older and the other my age. Mr. Moore had a hobby, an additional income producing practice as a taxidermist. He had several stuffed animals situated in every room of his home and was always working on a small furry or feathered animal for a client. His hobby was fascinating to me, the animals, and the natural way they appeared as they were placed; a squirrel climbing the post of a floor lamp, a rabbit crouched on a coffee table and an owl peering down from bookshelves in his home. My inclination to spend most of my time outdoors looking for anything that moved and didn't bite too hard meshed with the work he was doing so I spent a lot of time at the Moore home.

Mr. Moore also had a nice collection of caged songbirds. Among the variety was a pair of parakeets. As a young boy I was very active, in fact, most would say I couldn't sit still even for a moment, prone to talking when I should be listening but not destructive except to other's peace of mind and tranquil environment. So, as Riverside Summer Vacation Bible School began its annual two-week session, Mr. Moore told me, if I could behave and get a good citizenship report, for the full two weeks, he would give me the soon-to-be hatched baby parakeet. Mrs. Thomas, my vacation bible school teacher, reported she had never seen me so well behaved and even put it in writing. But the parakeet egg didn't hatch! The conversation surrounding the disastrous non-birth of the baby parakeet, as I heard it, was that maybe it wasn't fertilized correctly, whatever that meant. But I had been good for two whole weeks and had nothing but a clean vacation bible school report card to show for it. I wasn't sure if there was a conspiracy between My Parents, Mrs. Thomas and Mr. Moore but I was disappointed and learned the lesson, "There was no reward for being too good for too long."

TELEVISION

While Mr. Moore, even without having lived up to his promise to give me a baby parakeet, was still fun to be with and his many projects held my attention. However, my new most favorite neighbor on our block became the Heltz family. They, the Heltz's, with three young children, Dave happening to be my age, were the proud owners of a new 1950 Admiral Television, the only one outside of a department store I'd ever seen. As soon as they opened their front door to show it off, the Heltz's home became my first choice of places to visit. Their Admiral Television was a floor cabinet model with a 10-inch screen in the center. It had four knobs on the front of the television so they could change the channel to one of the four available stations, three national networks [ABC, CBS, and NBC], and one regional; adjust the volume and contrast the picture to lighten or darken it. The last knob was used to keep the transmitted picture from rolling bottom to top, a frequent occurrence with this new technology. Additionally on top of the television was a set of two ½" diameter metal tubular devices embedded in a rotating base called "rabbit ears" as they looked like such when fully extended. They could be adjusted in length and were frequently rotated toward the best available television reception signal.

A few times each week I would make myself available between 5:30 and 6:00 pm for an invitation to my new best friend Dave's house and watch the latest episode of The Howdy Doody Show. With great anticipation we would turn on the TV, sit on the floor in front of it, not too close as to ruin our eyes, so we were told at the time, and wait for "Buffalo Bob", in his tasseled buckskin cowboy outfit, to come on the screen and say, "Say kids, what time is it?" and we, along with 40 on-stage kids in the "Peanut Gallery" would say, "It's Howdy Doody Time!" At which point, "Howdy Doody" a freckle faced boy puppet [48 freckles, one for each state in the Union] with red hair to match his bandana and plaid cowboy shirt and 11 marionette strings perfectly attached would appear smiling and waving to the crowd as we all sang together the theme song, "Its Howdy Doody time", [set to the tune of "Ta-ra-ra-Boom-de-ay"]. The show had a cast of seven supporting Puppets including Heidi Doody [his sister], Phineas T. Bluster, Mayor of their fictional town of Doodyville and Inspector John J. Fadoozle ["America's number 1 private eye"]. There also were several human characters, most notably the mute Clarabell the Clown, who communicated by honking horns on his belt and squirting seltzer, Sir Archibald the Explorer, Chief Thunderthud, head of the Oorangnak tribe of Native Americans [kangaroo spelled backward] and Princess Summerfallwinterspring. The show was full of fun filled with antics between the puppets and the human characters on stage. It was a half hour of laughing, singing and some trumped up drama, between puppet characters, most notably the pompous Phineas T. Bluster and Inspector John J. Fadoozle with Howdy Doody saving the day.

At the end of each of the three comedic, sing-along or drama episodes an announcer would come on the screen and invite us to go home and tell our mothers to buy Colgate Toothpaste, Halo Shampoo or 3 Musketeers Candy Bars. He would hold up a sample of each and explain why we should buy these products and support Howdy Doody. I bought into the concept of supporting Howdy Doody and told my mother to buy 3 Musketeers Candy Bars.

Another of my favorite shows to watch was the Gene Autry Show. Gene Autry was a singing cowboy, who, along with his sidekick and comic pal Pat, rode his trusty horse Champion from town to town bringing song and justice to the old Southwest. Gene Autry's shows always had the bad guys doing bad things like robbing banks, stagecoaches or taking advantage of defenseless people but, in a showdown our cowboy hero would outdraw the bad guy, shoot the gun out of his hand and turn him over to the local sheriff. After he had completed this task and assured all the offended parties involved, they were once again safe, he would ride off into the sunset singing one of his favorite songs, "I'm back in the saddle again out where a friend is a friend."

The lesson I learned from Gene Autry and other cowboy shows with sidekicks, Hop-Along Cassidy, and Roy Rogers, was you always wanted to be the hero. They got all the adulation while their sidekicks generally bore the brunt of the situations before our cowboy hero stepped in to create the happy ending.

One day when Dave's parents were gone, our curiosity about the television and its inner workings got the best of us. We really wanted to see for ourselves just what it would take to create a moving television picture on the front of a wood cabinet. So, as young boys do, we carefully moved the television out from the wall and peered into the back of it. Beyond the pressed wood back cover, we could see the conical shape of the television tube that projected the visual images to the front.

We then observed several odd sized bulbous glass tubes, some longer and thinner while others were shorter and fatter, many had little pinnacles on them like the top of a Dairy Queen ice cream cone. They were sticking up from a platform type board, which appeared to be connecting all of these strange items together. When we turned on the television the filament in them glowed like a series of light bulbs, some brighter but all were lit. This was a really intriguing sight and we wondered if we could inspect the inner workings a little further. But instinctively we knew Dave's parents could come home at any time and we'd be in serious trouble if we were caught dissecting their most prized possession. So, we slid the cabinet back to its original place and hoped no one would discover our inspection.

However, a few days later I noticed a truck parked in front of Dave's home. On the side of the truck, painted in clear bold letters, was the name and telephone number identifying Dave Elder's television repair company. Nothing about the television repair or service man was ever discussed between Dave and I, probably for fear the walls could hear us.

The programming offered by the television industry continued to evolve, enticing more people to watch a larger variety of shows timed to increase their audience and creating a swoon in the advertising industry. The door was wide open for this new phenomenon, the television, and the future for it was bright but not yet as clear as a cloudless sky.

As the popularity of television grew, so too did the market for them. Many new companies were started, to offer better televisions with larger screens. Some TVs were designed to be set on existing tables; others included radios and phonographs in a combination cabinet. There seemed to be no limit to the size and variety offered to the person who could afford to buy their product.

To enhance the signal sent to the television owners and entice more people to purchase them, large antenna towers were built in populated cities, and some were placed on tall buildings in major metropolitan areas. With these new Eiffel Tower looking devices added to our horizon, the snowy-grainy quality of the pictures on the screen became clearer and the rolling of it ceased to be a problem. The post WWII changing culture found more families firmly entrenched inside their homes enjoying this new form of entertainment. But still the price was over 10% of my father's income so it would be years before my frugal parents with their expanding family would own a television.

Grandparent's Farm Visits

Several times a year my mother would announce, "We're going to the farm!" This was my absolute favorite place in the whole wide world. Going to the farm meant I would be able to run free, like a puppy off his leash, covering as much of the 120 acres as I could in a day. The fence around its perimeter was my boundary, which applied only if my mother had visual sight of me.

On the way to the farm my mother would turn on the car radio, probably to drown out the noise created by her now five children, press the selector button to WLBC, Muncie's only radio station, or WOWO, Ft Wayne, whichever one was playing her favorite song and sing along. She loved to sing! My Mother had a clear soft well trained soprano voice. She would sing along with the music on the car radio and could feel like she was performing at Carnegie Hall.

In the back seat my older Brother Dale and I would play visual games created by looking out the car window saying, "I spy!" Then the other would have to find it and say, "I see it too." The game would go on as we discovered every curious new item on the horizon and challenged each other until there was nothing new left to discover or we just became bored.

One of our favorite things, while riding along, was to see if there were any new Burma Shave signs on Highway 67. The pioneering white on red signs were

6

small 2' X 8' ' billboards sticking up on a post stationed along the fence row next to the highway. There were normally six of them with some humorous or rhyming poem promoting America's Favorite Brushless Shave Cream. One sequential version was, Big Mistake...Many Make...Rely on Horn...Instead of...Brake... *Burma Shave*. While we were passing them, we'd read along and then when we came to the final one, we'd shout out, with booming mimicking voices, "Burma Shave!" Then we'd laugh at our antics and wait for the next big distraction.

Our Grandparent's Farm was on a long gravel road connecting several similar farm families from Como to the intersection at Gray High School. The Bickner Farm included a two-story white with red trim house, a large faded red wood plank barn, chicken coop, grain bin, milk house, and storage-maintenance-repair building.

A large cloud of dust from the gravel road signaled our arrival long before the car was in sight. Our grandmother was at the side of the road when our car came to a stop.

As my mother unloaded the car and brief, Hellos, and hugs," were given to our grandmother, my brother Dale and I, with our younger brother Rick, trying to keep up, ran across the gravel road to the huge double doors at the front of the Big Red Amish Style Barn. The faded and peeling paint on the century old building was an exhibit to the desperation my Grandparents felt on a daily basis as they were forced to lead a patch work life on the unforgiving infertile soil of Jay County. While they raised or grew almost everything, they needed to be physically self-sufficient. The farm ground itself was a most unreliable source of income and created a most abysmal situation resulting in the stunted growth of investment in modern farming machinery. But as curious happy young boys we were oblivious to these circumstances and only saw the sunshine shimmering on the barn, the biggest play toy ever.

With the big doors of the old barn closed we teamed up and braced our shoulders to the edge of one and together rolled the squeaking wheels along its rusty track until it opened enough so we could slide through. Then, looking around the interior, we would find the vertical stairs to the hay mow and clamor hand over hand hoping with each step there would be enough bales of hay to build an impenetrable fort, at least to girls.

Dale, Rick & I would then create a battleground and play Cowboy and Indian games where it was more fun to be the guy who got shot. Because, when the big blast from the make-believe gun occurred, the Cowboy or Indian who was shot, with great vocal inflection, would grab their chest and dramatically fall from the top bale of the fort into a fresh pile of hay.

We tied ropes to the hand-hewn beams supporting the old barn's skeletal system and created Tarzan styled swings where we would go back and forth but ultimately dropping off into that new pile of hay. We put an old tire on one rope, sat on it and pushed it off from the beam to swing until we dropped into the pile

7

of hay. Anything we could do to create a game involving bales of hay and falling into the pile we did.

When we tired of the haymow Dale, Rick and I went down to the creek, which was the length of a football field from the house. The creek was so narrow at this point in the stream my brother Dale and I could hold hands in the middle of the hip high water and touch the sides of the bridge over the gravel road. Before heading down to the creek, we stopped by the house to get a few quarts sized Ball Jars. These open mouth glass containers, normally used for canning fruits and vegetables for the long winter months, served our purpose in catching the monster sized fish we would most certainly encounter from the creek.

The three of us would take off our pants, strip to our underwear and with Ball Jars in hand enter the murky water of the creek in search of the elusive fish that lived in our pristine watery playground. We moved very slowly trying not to create too much sediment and scare our prey. When a fish bobbed to the top of the water, we would spot it and move to where we thought it would surface again. Gently we submerged our glass jars filling them with just enough water to create a vacuum for the unsuspecting fish. When the fish surfaced again, we would release the vacuum and the fish would be sucked into the ingenious trap. Then we'd screw a lid, with punched holes in the top so the fish could breathe, onto the jar and we'd get ready to catch another monster.

After filling several of the quart jars, each with one fish, we'd put our massive catch gently, so as not to break any of the glass jars, in a large two handle burlap bag. Dale would grab one handle and I would take the other and off we'd go to show our day's catch to all we encountered. At the house we would implore Mother to filet the fish so we could have them for dinner. But she politely demurred, consoled us with her observation they were baby monster sized fish and she and Grandmother had already planned our evening meal. She said we should take the fish down to the creek, release them, hurry back, wash our hands and get ready for lunch.

Disappointed, we moped our way down to the creek's edge, unscrewed each perforated lid and gently lowered the glass jars into the murky water. As they disappeared, we each muttered, under breath, about our lost opportunity to be the family providers at the evening dinner table, secretly hoping the next time we caught the fish they would be meal size bigger. Then Mother would have to agree to filet and fry them for us. We never had fish from the creek for dinner!

As Mother had suggested we hurried back to the house for lunch. The Bickner Farmhouse was the typical farm home of the time, a two-story beaded clapboard sided dwelling. But, unlike most others we saw, theirs was weather-beaten so bad places showing usually concealed black felt paper were exposed through the exterior side walls. The red window trim and white siding paint was so faded it almost blended as one washed out color, gray.

The downstairs of the farmhouse contained a front bedroom, living room and kitchen. The upstairs consisted of two bedrooms. The living room had a wood burning pot bellied stove used to heat the whole house. There was no duct work from it to any of the other rooms so in the wintertime, with no insulation in the side walls, we could see our breath in any room except the kitchen, where Grandma always kept her oven stoked.

Hanging on the wall in their living room was their only communication with the outside world, a 1920 Kellogg Telephone. Unlike the one we had at our house, which was black, had a rotary dial for selecting the number we wanted to call, a one-piece handle to listen in and talk out and sat on the lamp table. Theirs was made out of brown wood and was about 10 inches wide and 18 inches high.

The wall telephone had a small hand crank on the right side to activate the calling out system, a receiver hanging on a hook on the left side so they could hear what was being said, a mouthpiece on the front to talk into, and two metal disc bells at the top that rang, to alert them, when they were receiving a call. When they wanted to call someone, they turned the hand crank on the side of the rectangular shaped box. The motion of the hand cranking generated an electronic signal to a telephone operator sitting in front of a magnificent switchboard device, servicing as many as a hundred telephone customers, many miles away.

The telephone operator, usually a woman, was in charge of receiving, connecting and monitoring all area phone calls. When she got the cranked electronic signal, the operator knew who was calling by the small light activated on her switchboard. She was courteous, referred to them by name and would ask with whom they wanted to speak. Then systematically connect the designated plug to the correct portal on a board in front of her containing numbers, names, and lights.

In the late 1940's and early 1950's my grandparents phone was of the party line variety. This meant they shared their phone service with several other families. In order for them to make a phone call, first they had to pick the receiver off its hook and listen to hear if anyone was talking. If they heard someone they would politely hang up and wait for the line to clear. However, with so many people using the same line that could take a while so they would have to pick up several times to get a clear call out line. Of course, if they waited too long without the other people getting off the phone or if the other parties felt they were being imposed upon, unkind words were exchanged. Sometimes, when they picked up the receiver and listened, they knew who was talking and interrupted to say, "Hello!" then ask them how long they were going on the phone. Occasionally they would get a neighborhood three-way conversation to catch up on all the latest news. Emergency situations, as frequented by the farming community, always took precedence over social calls.

After a quick lunch of peanut butter and jelly sandwiches, washed down with a glass of milk my brothers and I would grab a couple of the Ball Jars and head back down the gravel road. Just a few feet past the culvert over the creek where we were forced to release our biggest catch of the season was, "The Gate!"

The metal tubular gate was the embarkation point for us to enter 40 wooded and grassy acres of trails, pathways and unexplored territory even Davy Crocket hadn't seen. It had milk weeds, thorn bushes, and trees twice as big as my grandparents house, a pond with frogs and turtles and a dried-up creek bed perfect for fossil hunting. It was the ideal place for adventurous, curious, and fearless young boys to explore until the last secret of the woods had been discovered. As we hiked one leg at a time over the gate, we were keenly aware this was going to be a great day to catch a frog, snake, field mouse or find a giant dinosaur skeleton.

Our first stop was always the pond to see if we could catch a frog or turtle. They were always so elusive! It was almost as if someone had warned them, we were coming. The turtles would sense our presence, roll off a log where they were sunbathing, submerge under water, and swim to the middle of the pond, rarely to be seen again. When we spotted a frog, one of us would circle around and sneak up behind it and try to catch it before it could hop away out of our grasp. We always gave it our best effort, taking off our shoes, rolling up our pants legs and getting plenty muddy trying to out fox and coax the frog into the little traps we would set. And while we could see it, the frog could see us, and it continued to remain out of our reach.

After our futile attempts at the pond, we would venture off to find much easier prey, one that could be cornered on dry ground and more easily trapped. In the woods there were always small fallen tree limbs or a random piece of wood siding, the perfect place for a garter snake or field mouse to hide. Being the quickest and most daring of the trio I would position myself where I would consider to be the escape hatch for our unsuspecting prey. Then I would put a cotton glove on my right hand and be at the ready when Dale & Rick exposed its hiding place.

When they raised the board, I leapt into action pouncing on whatever animal had just been revealed. If it was a snake or mouse I'd hold it in a soft non-threatening manner, at least to me, and wait for it to stop fighting and squirming to get out of my grasp. Then I would hold out my glove encased right hand and let the snake or mouse bite it. Once the captured animal realized it couldn't hurt me and I wasn't going to hurt it, I would place it in a jar with a perforated lid along with some leaves and grass. This was the temporary home for our newest pet until I presented it for show and tell at school the next day.

Our Mother didn't mind us bringing home any of our normal catches for a short visit, with a stern ultimatum for release date given. But one time when we couldn't catch any living fast moving animals, we found a Praying Mantis egg case attached to a milkweed. We removed it from its resting place, put it in a lidless glass jar and took it home. Oh yeah, we forgot to tell Mother about this catch! A few days later, much to our absolute amazement, there were at least two hundred, half inch long Chartreuse Green Baby Praying Mantis in our bedroom.

They were everywhere, on the curtains, all over our beds, on the walls, in our closet. There wasn't a square inch of our common quarter bedroom that didn't have one of these cute little prayerful creatures. Our parents were aghast at the sight! They ordered us to keep the bedroom door closed so the baby praying mantis couldn't penetrate the rest of the house. Of course, my brothers and I enjoyed the whole scene and tried to think of two hundred names for our new friends, but fell woefully short. Finally, in desperation, knowing they would either escape or die, we took the screen out of our bedroom window and coaxed a few of them to safety. That was the last time we left The Farm without first being frisked.

While we were in the woods our mother, grandmother and our older sister, Phyllis, were preparing for our evening meal. My sister and grandmother went to the garden, walking its many rows choosing from the wide variety of vegetables she grew which included seasonal favorites, green beans, peas, tomatoes, okra, onions, potatoes, turnips, radishes, and sweet corn. To enhance the flavor of the menu a variety of fruits were available from the plum, apple and pear, cherry and peach trees surrounding the house. If something wasn't in season or couldn't be picked fresh from the garden or plucked from the trees, there was always a stored jar of whatever they needed to complement the evening meal.

When we were having chicken for dinner, we would cut our afternoon in the woods short to help catch the chicken our mother would then kill, pluck and clean. Dale and I would play a little game of Reaux Sham Beaux, better known as rock, paper, and scissors to see which of us would catch the chicken. When a winner had been decided Mother gave the victor a 4' long sturdy piece of wire with a curved hook at the end. The victor then became the stalker looking in the backyard for a chicken he could outmaneuver while getting the hook around the lower part of the scaly inflexible foot of the chicken.

The white chickens, with the fleshy red protruding caruncles on their head and throat flopping ceaselessly during the chase, like quicksilver on a desktop, were always quick and elusive. It could take a few minutes of chasing, staying low to the ground, swiftly moving to the left and right, singling one out of the group before the eluder could be hooked. After the unlucky barnyard fowl was caught both feet gathered together, body and head dangled down swinging helplessly on its way to the chopping block.

Mother, now in charge, would lay it down across the wood stump and quickly swing the shiny sharp-edged hatchet down to cut off the unsuspecting chicken's head. A French Guillotine couldn't have made a smoother severance! Once cleaved the body of the chicken would flop headless around the yard splattering blood in all directions. We backed away from the decapitated carcass, not wanting to catch any of this sanguine fluid on our clothes as it flailed its wings and feet searching aimlessly for its now severed head. When the chicken finally lay lifeless our mother would pick up the scarlet mottled body, dip it in a bucket of boiling hot water and begin plucking the yard bird's plumage.

While Mother was preparing the chicken our grandfather appeared from the field he'd been working, to the same gate we used to enter our enchanted forest. There he would meet his patiently waiting milk cows. His tall lean frame with a white shock of hair streaming from under his six-inch-tall sun protecting cap created a striking solemn vertical figure among the seemingly dwarfed horizontal wide hipped milk cows.

Every afternoon at five o'clock and every morning at six, 365 days a year the milk cows would be waiting at the gate for someone to open it and let them travel up the gravel road to the barn. When the remaining eight of the original twenty Holstein cows reached it, they, through the rote learning method of having done this routine time and time again, they would amble to the rear small door to the milking room.

Then one foot at a time the cows would step onto the concrete floor and plod, carefully negotiating the narrow trench which would serve as their inside bathroom, to their designated stalls. Once they stuck their heads between the two metal bars they were confined in place. My grandparents would place shackles on their hind legs to prevent them from shuffling and kicking over the milk buckets. When completed my grandparents, each with a small three-legged stool and pail, would position themselves next to the cow's hindquarters and massage the udder to check the volume of its contents.

Then, avoiding the cow's fly swatting tail, with a gentle downward motion, they squeezed two of the four teats at a time guiding the milk into the waiting galvanized container. My grandmother, in her considerate nature, would tenderly hum one of her favorite songs as she relieved her donor of its precious cargo and would periodically direct a stream of milk to the patient ever vigilant feral barn cats.

After the milking was completed and the cows were taken back to the pasture, my grandfather, wearing his rubber thigh high boots and employing his broad scooped shovel, bailed the animal excrement out of the narrow trench onto the big heaping pile at the rear of the barn. The manure would later be used as fertilizer for the fields. This was recycling at its best. Nothing was wasted at the farm!

After dinner Mother would go into the living room to play the only luxury my grandparents owned, a beautiful pristine 1894 Estey Pump Organ. The seven-foot-tall brown wood cabinet was ornate with carvings, engravings, and spindles. It regaled the room with its great pomp and circumstance. My Mother casually sat down on the colorful cushioned stool facing this magnificent looking apparatus, folded the hinged top back exposing the keyboard and nine push-pull pistons that adjusted the tonal quality of what she was about to play.

She then pumped her right foot on one of the two pedals near the floor to fill the bellows before she began to play. Her left foot gently moved downward on the other pedal close to the floor adjusting the volume while her fingers began to glide across the keyboard. She played as if she were the organist at an old-time religious revival. Mother's selections always included our grandparents favorites, "The Old Rugged Cross, "Holy, Holy, Holy" and "Amazing Grace.""

As my grandparents sat in their wooden rocking chairs listening to their talented daughter play these wonderful timeless hymns and watching their now quiet grandchildren, a sense of relaxation softened the wrinkles on their weather-beaten faces. They softly sang along momentarily forgetting their many hardships.

When my mother's private concert concluded the sun was setting on the fields. It was time for us to head back home. But before we could embark on this short journey, she insisted we relieve ourselves because there would be no suitable place for us to stop until we got to our own front door. In order to fulfill this request, we had to exit the rear door of our grandparents house, turn left and follow the grooved dirt path 20 feet to the only building on the farm without a foundation and unlisted on the County Assessors records.

The four-by-four square and seven-foot-high structure had several 6-inch-wide vertical planks held together by two diagonally crossed boards serving as its entry door. A foot long length of rope extending through the portal with a small piece of beveled wood on either end functioned as a duo handle, with the bonus feature of serving as an occupied sign. The other two visible sides of the small structure had horizontal planks with the never to be seen rear wall possibly of a herringbone design.

Inside it was dark! There was no window, no lamp, just some penetrating light emanating through a few small seams in the side planks. There were spider webs at every corner, flies, mosquitos, centipedes, and an assortment of other creepy crawly creatures inhabiting the small edifice. At the top of the rear wall a board connecting the sheet metal shed roof was missing, replaced with a strategically located small strip of wire mesh, the building's only source of ventilation.

A short step inside exposed a wall to wall two-inch-thick wood board, thigh high, with a ten-inch circular well-worn one size fits all hole in the middle. This was the business class seat. A roll of single layer toilet paper stood vertical at the side of the opening. Then there was the "Long Drop ", a three-foot plunge from the top of the plank's opening to the dark cavernous layer of accumulated decomposing pee and poop below.

The odor emanating from the stool droppings permeated the surrounding intrinsically clear air, wafting in the direction of the daily breeze with such brazen force the mint bushes, strategically planted on three sides of the wooden temple, were barely noticed.

When it was my turn to use my Grandparents Outhouse, I would cautiously approach the throne, gingerly and butt first, slide over the front edge of the seat board. It was far better to endure some slight potential posterior defacement than enthusiastically approach the chasm and land in a V-shape position, butt down with legs and head up. If that happened, I would get stuck! How would I get out? Who would come to my rescue? Would I slide down into that wretched abyss? If that happened my brothers and sisters would squeal on me, and I'd become the laughingstock of the neighborhood. No! Better to use the cautious approach than chancing the mockery of the Earth Closet's Black Hole.

While we were all making our separate treks to the family's privy one holer, our mother was busy catching two unsuspecting chickens for their one-way ticket to her frying skillet. To my younger sister, Jonetta's, everlasting chagrin, Mother would throw the clucking, feathers flapping everywhere, chickens into the trunk of our car.

Jonetta was mortified at the thought that her mother would decapitate our next Sunday's dinner in the backyard of her home. Her next-door neighbor and best friend Susan, looking at this domestic massacre, wouldn't be able to contain herself. Jonetta knew a detailed account of the backyard carnage and archaic method of food processing would be revealed to her classmates at school. People would never look at her the same. How was a pretty young girl to have a "Coming Out" if her mother's killing, scalding and plucking chickens in public? Oh, the infinite humiliation of it all!

On the ride home Mother would ask if we'd all been good at the farm and stayed out of trouble. Of course this was a ruse! How are five children going to answer a question like that? Trumpeting in unison we would say, "Yes Mother, we did!" With that, she would announce, since we had been so good, we would be stopping for a tasty treat at St John's Frozen Custard Store in Albany.

As our car rolled to a stop in the gravel parking lot of the 'walk-up, stand in line, order, and wait' custard stand, we excitedly bounded out to look at the small cone special of the day. Jonetta kept looking over her shoulder to see if any of the Albany Little Leaguers waiting in line would notice the muffled clucking coming from the trunk of her mother's car.

Educational years

Academics in the form of scholastic achievement and bestowed establishment recognition were not my strong suit. Rather commitment, endurance and hard work would become the mantra for what became my extended trek toward my pursuit in the world of higher education.

Emerson Elementary School was walking distance, five city blocks, from our home on Neely Avenue. Each school day of my first year at Emerson my older siblings, sister Phyllis, and brother Dale, would escort me to the corner of Ashland Avenue and Pauline Avenue, where the educational three and a half story square red brick structure stood waiting to receive its energetic young pupils. With its gravel strewn playground, the fenced compound encapsulated a full city block.

This palace of primary instruction contained a maze of rooms all branching off the main hallway with two staircases at either end connecting the replicated levels in this labyrinth educational operation. Each classroom seemed to be a clone of the others and was equally enhanced with a full-length black chalkboard at one end, with the alphabet, a through z, displayed in both small and capital letters spaced evenly above it.

The black chalk board was used for full classroom instructional purposes. When our First Grade Teacher, Mrs. Wilson, wanted to show us how to write a letter, number or series of words or numbers, she would scratch the white chalk across the black chalkboard leaving some tracing residue behind relating the lesson she wished to convey to her young eager students. Once the lesson was completed and finished, she would wipe away the letters, numbers, and words from the board with a fabric-based rectangular hand sized eraser.

The better classroom students, and teacher's pets, would daily be temporarily dismissed from her class to go outside and clap the dust filled erasers together, cleaning them for future use. This was rarely one of my tasks!

Mrs. Wilson's desk faced our twenty individual tabletop chairs where, dutifully seated, we were encouraged to learn our letters, numbers and how to behave in a disciplined manner. The only noticeable difference in our room from the others in this educational warehouse was the teachers' name plate and grade number, next to the entrance door.

Twice a day we had what was called a "recess!" This was a 15-minute break from our classroom when we, weather permitting and not otherwise interred for some minor infraction of the yet to be published school rules, were ushered, in an orderly manner, down the hallway and outside into the gated gravel playground area. When we reached the exit door, like monkeys escaping from a zoo, we burst from the gray matter developmental factory, toward our favorite playground toys and equipment. Each liberated neophyte raced to their favorite, jungle gym, merry-go-round, monkey bars, teeter-totter, swing set, tether ball, basketball court and hopscotch, calorie burning, fun producing and brain boosting areas.

My favorite play station was the jungle gym. The galvanized steel, geometric dome structure with its many web-like connecting bars created an intricate maneuvering puzzle which required the physical dexterity of a chimpanzee. We would play, "Tag, your It" and scamper all over the geo framework chasing each other or create our own, "bet you can't do this" routine. Energy was burned off, muscles were stretched, bumps and bruises were indiscriminately doled out, but fun and laughter always prevailed.

When it became too crowded on the jungle gym, I would look for some other outlet for my pent-up energy. One day a classmate, John, who was twice my size, as were most of the other boys in my class, lured me to the teeter-totter. John enticed me to sit on one end of the balanced board while he sat opposite facing me. I saw him smile as he pushed off with his feet and went up a foot then down with his bottom on the ground and I projected six feet into the air.

The object of the seesaw was for one person to push with his feet going up in the air while the other went down then the person on the ground would push off creating a replication of motion where each person gets the benefit of feeling they were part of a high-flying circus act.

But John had his own idea of merriment and sat laughing, me elevated and stuck. With legs flailing like a puppet on a string, I was helplessly pleading to once again get down on the ground. After a few moments he tired of teasing me and quickly slipped off the end of the fulcrum sending me pummeling rapidly to the hard ground. As I crashed, he stood beside his vacated end of the teeter-totter laughing at me. My butt hurt! And so did my pride. John had just taught me a valuable lesson on weight and leverage, and also to catch myself with my feet instead of using my diminutive butt.

As recreated students we procrastinated leaving the playground when the bell sounded for our "recess' ' time to cease and sluggishly plodded back toward our internment center. The teachers too were equally disappointed with our separated time to conclude. Like nap time for little babies, they needed that 15-minute interval away from us to re-energize, go to the teachers' lounge, have a cup of

16

coffee, a bottle of coke a cola, or smoke a cigarette. So, they too trudged back to the classroom to resume the process of educating the future leaders of America.

Four times a year our teachers charged us to take a "Report of Progress" to our parents so they would be apprised of our advancement, or lack of it, in their classroom. The front of the bi-fold manila report card stated our name, grade, number of days present and absent, times tardy to class, height, weight, teacher, and school principal's name.

On the inside cover were the details of our academic accomplishments. At the top of the cream-colored folio was, "Subject Matter Achievement" including Reading, Language, Spelling, Writing and other assorted standards for progressive educational evaluation.

Below those categories in bold letters was, "Citizenship." This section included such areas of social interest as; Is interested in his [not gender neutral] work, does neat work, obeys rules of classroom and school, Respects rights of others, Works and plays well with other children, has good posture and a few other similarly evaluated topics.

At the bottom of the judgmental document was, "Meaning of Marks," S, is making normal progress, T, tries hard, but work is below standard, U, is not making satisfactory progress.

On the opposite page, front and back were, First, Second, Third and Fourth Quarter, Teachers Comments, Parent's Comments and Parent's Signature.

The marks on my quarterly student evaluation were all, S, with an occasional S- for such minor institutional infractions as; Does neat work, and mostly keeps well occupied, Obeys most rules of classroom and school.

Each quarter my first and second grade teachers, Mrs. Austin and Mrs. Wilson made comments such as Joe is an all-around good child, he is an interesting child to our room, But! There was always a but to every comment they made. But he has been a little careless with a few classroom rules, but he talks during quiet times and plays in the halls, but he handles his books a little roughly. But, But, But!

My Mother never sent a comment back. She just signed and returned each "Report of Progress" card. She could've defended me and sent back supportive comments such as "Did the other students enjoy the Garter Snake he brought to your room? Or "Did you let his classmates touch the field mouse he brought for show and tell?" How about, "He spent a whole afternoon stalking and catching a chipmunk for bring-a-pet day."

My teachers didn't acknowledge my unique contributions to our classroom and my mother didn't remind them of my special living gifts to the urban neophytes. None of my extra circular efforts seemed to matter and thus they went unnoted in my "Permanent Record."

At the end of my second year at Emerson our family moved to Springfield, Ohio, where our father had accepted a career promotion. We lived there less than a year so my third grade at the local elementary was in a strange and forgettable environment.

The following year we migrated back to Muncie. The move away and back to our hometown had not been a successful venture, so instead of our family relocating to our former white collar, manager and professional, neighborhood, where property values had increased, they purchased a less expensive home in the blue collar, labor and industrial, district of the community at 1924 East 21st Street.

My new school, Stevenson Elementary, was a three-story brick institutional structure similar, front door entrance, back door out to playground, in almost every way to Emerson. It was also exactly five city blocks from our home and now I was older, in the fourth grade, so I meandered, skipping, zigzagging, stopping to observe the latest Mother Nature had to offer, unescorted along the graveled edge of Mock Avenue to school each day.

On one of my daily solitary strolls in the general direction of Stevenson I met another ambling boy, David Carl Thomas. He was one the biggest, most athletic boys in fourth grade, while I was, by far, the smallest kid in my class. I learned, shortly after our relocation to 21st Street, the children and neighbors had a little rougher way of acting and talking toward each other than I experienced on Neely Avenue. So, walking to school and hanging out with "Big Dave" offered "Small Timid Joe," some leave this kid alone, he's my friend credibility.

Dave and I became "Best Friends." We got into young boy mischief together. We climbed utility line poles, built snow forts, and peppered cars with snowballs as they drove by, then ran like scared rabbits when we saw their tail lights go red. We performed stunts on our bikes, riding backward, standing on the seat with no hands on the bars, always trying to one-up the other with minimal personal physical damage. We became nemesis to mutual neighbor Wilmer Jack, as his yard was the gateway connecting our two homes. Wilmer would do his best verbal saber rattling when he saw us traverse the well-worn path between our houses, and then would put his challenging demeanor aside when we volunteered to help him pick red raspberries and sweet corn from his garden.

One day Dave and I were watching a cowboy and Indian show on television when the two main character sworn enemies concluded to make peace forever. They raked a knife over the palm of their hands, drawing a stream of blood, then clasped them together becoming, "Blood Brothers", a lifetime bond never to be broken. Dave and I decided to become "Blood Brothers" as well but lacked the courage to do the full slice the palm of our hand with a knife ritual. Rather we pricked the tip of our first finger with a needle and waited patiently until enough blood oozed from the puncture to blend together and held our hands high pledging eternal allegiance to each other.

Dave totally shocked me when he invited me over to his house while his parents and sister were gone. He secretly guided me into the off-limit area of his parents' bedroom, opened one of the dresser drawers, took out a large envelope and proceeded to spread several photographs on the bed. I was astonished to see his mother and father in the 3" X 5" and 5" x 7" black and white stills, posing naked, totally without any clothes, not even socks. There was absolutely nothing left to my wholly undeveloped immature imagination. Breasts, bush, and erections fully exposed, were displayed in several vertical and horizontal positions standing next to and lying on the theatrically staged recliner. My emotions and senses were unexpectedly heightened in a way I'd not previously experienced.

My curiosity was aroused, and I was uncomfortable, embarrassed staring at these naked pictorial models, but soon, ever so shyly I looked away. Prior to this graphic display, the only breasts I had ever seen were on the front cover of National Geographic. Wow! I would never be able to look at Dave's mother and father the same innocent way again. After he returned his parent's personal pornography back to the dresser drawer, I went home and wondered if that was how Superman saw men and women when he used his X-ray Vision!

When Dave and I would arrive at Stevenson, he would venture off to one of his athletic sports of baseball, basketball, kickball, anything ending with a double LL as the last two letters in the game's name, leaving me to find a less competitive way to bide my time. One of my favorite fewer physical activities became the game of marbles.

A marble, Greek for shining stone, is a ½" to 1" spherical ball usually made of agate or glass. The aggie style of marbles came in various solid colors with unique brilliant exterior patterns. Another vogue orb was the Cat's Eye, with a central eye-shaped colored insert, enhancing the clear glass surrounding and a favored prize in any player's collection.

There were two ways we would play the game, one was "chase." This contest rendition involved one person throwing or pitching their marble a few feet away, usually in a low grassy area, and the next person following in pursuit. Once both had thrown their marble it was "open Season" and the first person to hit the others got to keep it and add it to their collection.

The second, and the one in which I was most adept, was the "ring." This most notable game involved using a small stick or index finger to draw a 12-inch circle in the dusty gravel area at the edge of our playground. Once done we would each put a like number of marbles in the center of the ring. Then we would lag a marble toward a straight line a few feet away to see who would be the closest to the groove and thus get the first shot at the pot.

Once done we would select our favorite and most accurate "shooter" cradle it in the bend of our front finger, set it at the edge of the ring and flick it with our thumbnail toward the quarry of our choice. When a direct hit was made and the target marble was knocked out of the ring the momentary victor collected the "keepsake," placed it with their other gems and prepared to shoot again. The object of the contest was to end up with more of the magnificently colored globes than we had individually placed in the ring.

Before I began to take my turn, like any serious competitor, I would stretch my thumb back toward my wrist several times. Then I would rotate it clockwise, reverse the motion and go counterclockwise several times to insure it was loose and flexible. Finally, I would flick it quickly, with intentional focus, starting at my little pinkie and progressively moving up to the game winning front finger. I needed to ensure my two most critical digits were strong, flexible; the adrenalin was flowing, and I was psyched up ready for action. When I placed my prized aggie possessions in "the ring" I had to be prepared to get them back with dividends.

I became so good at the game of marbles instead of them being a few small, rounded bulges in my pants pocket; I purchased a leather pouch for my amassed trophies. After each of my successful triumphant ventures, I would set my bag of treasure a little roughly onto the top of my desk, which noisily announced to my classmates I was the "king of the ring."

Twice a week we walked four blocks from Stevenson north on Mock Avenue to Industry United Brethren Church for Bible Study. There we were subjected to daily scripture readings and all the goodness the church and God created in our lives. It was a good, unique experience and one class for which we were not graded.

Halfway between the church and school was a wooded five-acre horse farm with four beautiful full-grown horses, a small stable barn with a wood fence surrounding the perimeter. Dave and I were magnetically drawn to the concept of our favorite television cowboys on their trusty steeds and frequently, during our school lunch break, snuck across Mock Avenue to check out these most amazing equines. We smuggled apples from our home's fruit bowl, placed them in the open palm of our hands, stuck the temptations through the open rail fence gate, and talked gently as we coaxed them close enough to eat out of our hands.

Dave was feeding an apple to one of the bare back unbridled mares when I quietly climbed the fence, reached the top rail, lifted both legs over and placed them quickly mounting the back of the unsuspecting animal. This uninvited occurrence shocked the horse. My friendly ride into the sunset on my trusty steed turned into a rodeo bronco busting foray into the woods where my once gentle mare turned into a wild bucking mustang.

Within five seconds the frenzied charger found a low branch of a tree it could clear sans its rider. There were two loud thuds as I was immediately and unceremoniously sent sprawling from the bronco's back, one when the tree limb struck my midsection and the other when I hit the ground. Dave couldn't hold back his bend-over laughter at my discomfort and humiliation, nor would he hold back every single detail of my wayward adventure to our classmates. No more apples were given to those unappreciative horses!

When I was in the fifth grade I was placed in a combined class with sixth graders; Mr. Everett Zirkle was our teacher. He had an incentive-based program where he offered a Clark Bar [popular candy bar] to the student who could answer one of his difficult problems or questions. One day he asked his sixth graders which number was larger, .005, .05 or .5.

They all guessed .005 and were stymied when the mathematically challenged students realized they were incorrect. To make his point that a fifth grader would know the correct answer, he asked me which one I thought to be the biggest equation. I answered .5 and he said, "Correct" and lauded my accomplishment to the whole class. But he didn't reach into his desk drawer and give me a Clark Bar. No Clark Bar? I couldn't believe it! That slight ranked right up there with the unfertilized parakeet egg.

My biggest drawback at Stevenson Elementary School was not the rough kids or foul language but my Mother. Shortly after we moved to our new home on 21st Street, she accepted a position as secretary to the Principal of Stevenson, Mr. Lyell Bussell. Now, she saw my report card before I had a chance to explain my transcribed misdeeds.

She knew my every mischievous move, and most were brought to her attention by my most eager tattletale classmates. They would run up to her in the hallway and say, "Mrs. Burnworth, Mrs. Burnworth, do you know what Joe just did?" From a safe distance I could see her roll her eyes back in her head as if to say, not again!"

At home, my mother frequently answered our phone with the familiar phrase, "What did Joe do now?" It seemed to me she took the position of Stevenson just to keep a closer eye on her young mischievous son.

When I began to attend Blaine Junior High School in the seventh grade, my mother packed a peanut and butter jelly sandwich in a brown paper bag and sent me walking on the 17-city block trek to my new academic institution. At Blaine, our assigned place to eat was the cafeteria where most students purchased their lunch and many quizzically gazed at my strange culinary selection. Not only was I eating a home packed lunch in the cafeteria; I was wearing my older Brother's thread bare hand-me-down outdated clothes. I was undersized, underdressed and humiliatingly nourished.

At home, my mother's parents moved from their failed farm to live with us until they relocated to her brother's home in Jacksonville, Florida. A year later, after the death of their spouses, my father's grandmother, mother and briefly his aunt, moved into our three-bedroom one bath 900 square foot home. With five siblings and five adults living under one roof our housing quarters were cramped and could have been subject to the Fire Marshall inviting some of the brood to relocate to the garage.

My grades at Blaine were slipping and I began to care less about my academics than my own creature comfort, peer prestige and personal survival. So, at age 12, I got a job selling Downyflake Doughnuts.

Each day after school I jogged a few blocks to 12th Street, stood along the side of the road, stuck out my right thumb and hitched a ride two miles straight to Madison Street. There the Downyflake Van was waiting in front of their retail store for five additional urchins to go door to door selling their product.

As we clamored into the mobile sales operation, we were given a Tomato Peck Basket with six clear cellophane bags of cake doughnuts: three each of Chocolate, Carmel, Cinnamon and Powder and a one dozen bag of Glazed Yeast doughnuts. The chauffeur, manager and overseer of our individual personal enterprise operation drove us to a neighborhood where we would disembark to canvas each street, knocking on every door, pitching our carney-like spiel, hawking the fresh, delicious, world's best Downyflake Doughnuts.

The cake doughnuts sold for $.49 a dozen and the yeast were priced at $.55 a bag. With my biggest cherubic smile, I barked out my well-planned presentation with great success. As my happy customer sorted through their change my smile held long and strong and I lingered with pleading eyes to ensure they didn't really need the penny change from their $.50 in collective coins. When I added the penny and sometimes a nickel as a tip from a sale of the yeast to the $.05, I made from each sale; I could end the afternoon with as much as $1.00. This amount could be doubled on a full Saturday shift.

From my early doughnut selling proceeds I was able to purchase a bike, so I didn't have to hitch a ride to work, wore new store-bought clothes and sported a 17-jewel wristwatch, a status symbol piece of jewelry very few children my age possessed. I no longer brown bagged my lunch to school, rather ate at a nearby sandwich shop. With this added personal wealth my self-esteem improved as did my grades. I was no longer the hand-me-down looking runt of the class, just the small well-dressed kid.

At Blaine I finally discovered a game ending in double LL in which I could not only play, but became one of the best in my class, Dodgeball. We played this game of elimination on an indoor basketball court with the center line being the separation point for two equal numbered teams of student targets. Each team was given three large balls and encouraged to fling the solid leather well inflated spheres and hit, as hard as we could, each other. This stinging, welt raising game was the bully's and want-to-be athlete's opportunity to hit and hurt other students without being sent to the Principal's Office. It was a sanctioned on-court gym class fight.

When a player was hit, unless they or a team member caught the ball before it touched the floor, they were eliminated. If the thrower's ball was caught by the opposition, he was eliminated. The team with the most players on the floor when the bell rang, or the gym teacher tired of the action, was the winner.

I was small, agile, elusive, and quick, so my forte was to get as close to the center court dividing line as possible and bait the opposition into throwing their scalding accelerating fastball at me. I gauged the hostile pitchers to know the intensity of their arm strength and the precision of their accuracy. Then I stealthily positioned myself in a region on the floor where I would dodge; duck, or dive to avoid the impending body smasher they threw my taunting direction. When they missed, and they usually did, my teammates would applaud my efforts. If I caught one of their errant or weak efforts, I would give it to one of the bigger athletic players on my team, thus ingratiating myself to future classroom and hallway protection, without payment.

Proving I was one of the best front-line dodgeball players greatly enhanced my gym class profile. So, I was always the first or second player selected when teams were chosen, and our teacher wanted to observe and subject his students to some physical form of retribution.

Orchestrating one of my more memorable Junior High experiences was fellow classmate George Coyne with Oscar Mossberg, a long-time woodworking shop instructor, his unassuming foil. Mr. Mossberg's classroom was set with him perched on his desk, legs dangling down, at the front of the room. On the wall above his head was a large electric clock, chrome rim, white background with distinctive numerical black hour, minute, and secondhand ticking.

There were six bulky wood top desks each with four workstations, a student sitting on top at their assigned spot, eye level with Mossberg, all positioned toward him and the front of the room. At the rear of the spacious area were the bandsaws, planes sanders, and other necessary shared tools needed to shape our rectangular pieces of pine into functional gradable projects.

Mr. Mossberg, a bit of a crusty sort, slightly overweight, white hair in a short burr cut, tenured some thirty years earlier and rigid in his classroom decorum. He became easily unhinged when we were heard talking, whispering, or noticed us not paying attention during his daily redundant project update presentation. His spiel could last as long as 30 of our 50-minute class time.

Being a carpentry specialist, he had shaped several 2" cubes of wood, placed them within reaching distance, and would fling them at any of us he felt was not paying attention to his verbal presentation. Many found their target.

George, a very bright student, was certain woodworking or any project requiring a hammer, nail, saw or plane, was not in his future. He was bored and a bit inept with trying to produce any fact simile Mossberg required each student complete as their semester class project. Added to his lack of interest in the mandatory class was the fatigue of listening to the ad nauseam 20–30-minute discourses by Mossberg. This drum rolling daily dialogue also cut into George's compact crafting time. It was most difficult to get started on his shared tool design before the class changing bell alerted him it was time to put his rough-hewn work away for yet another day.

Weary of Mossberg's digressions and needing a distraction of his own,

George developed a lottery. His not-for-profit game of chance was limited to the members of Mossberg's class, wager was a penny per minute, with the time randomly drawn between 10:00, the time class began, and the moment Oscar stopped talking. Each of us would give George a penny before entering class; he listed our names next to our "lucky minute" and we all glanced with anticipation at the clock ticking away above the yammering Mossberg's head. Periodically a slight moan could be heard as the second hand reached 12, clicked off another minute, and a disappointed gambler watched his bragging rights drift away.

After two weeks of running the highly successful and riotously amusing lottery, Mossberg closed his extensive daily dialogue with the comment, "The Bookie can cancel all bets!" The gig was over!

We were having so much fun with this exclusive classroom guessing game, someone let it leak out and the word spread like wildfire through the school. Many of the other students enjoyed their passive participation in the contest and crowded in the hallway outside of Mossberg's class to celebrate the announcement of the daily winner. This game of chance became too large to conceal.

When the lottery was exposed and eliminated, we were once again subjected to Mossberg's daily spiel. But we all continued to glance, with amusement, at the clock above his head knowing we'd escaped his inane discourse for two full weeks.

On Tuesday, the day after the Labor Day Holiday Weekend in September 1958, I walked out my front door, crossed 21st street then Mock Avenue and waited patiently at the Southeast corner for the Number 9, Industry Willard City Bus. The soon to be overloaded, standing room only bus took me, along with 50 other apprehensive and anxious young students, downtown to the corner of Jackson and Walnut Street. Once the cigarette smoke filled, the sweltering hot congested bus stopped, we exploded like rats out of a flooding water pipe from our cramped mobile transport. Disheveled, we departed and walked two short blocks to Muncie Central High School.

This imposing edifice to higher education, the ultimate aspiration by most, was a three-story full brick square building, which covered the entire downtown city block, from High to Franklin and Adams to Charles Streets. There was not a playground, no outdoor activity center, or green space, just this overwhelming structure with cars parked bumper to bumper adjacent to the sidewalk surrounding it.

All 2,400 plus students were given a sheet of paper designating their class schedule, curriculum, times, and room numbers. Sophomores like me entered Muncie Central High School holding these slips of paper wondering where, in this enormous chamber of hallways and rooms, were we to find our designated space. This giant above ground ant hill had no apparent directional signs, except the "one way" staircase symbols.

Occasionally a naive disoriented sophomore would ask an upperclassman if he knew where his classroom was located, only to be told it's on the fourth floor. Then the unsuspecting novice would be directed to a sign-less closed door and told to wait for the elevator. Eventually there were two or three neophytes waiting in line for the 'lift' when the janitor would come by, open the door to his broom closet and the novices would be exposed to their first high school prank.

The MCHS building was overcrowded. The sardine-can, like school, had classrooms brimming to overflowing conditions. The beginning and ending classes as well as lunch times were staggered and seniors, with enough graduation credit hours, were encouraged to attend school half days.

Muncie was a post-World War ll industrial boom town, so along with many other undecided curriculum students, I was sent half day to the Muncie Trade School for more skilled manufacturing production type training. There we were to learn trades such as wood working, sheet metal, printing, and various machine operations.

In my sheet metal class, I learned to cut, bend and weld metal. One of my mid-year projects was to make a coffee table out of 1/4" round metal rods to be used as legs and 1" angle iron to hold a decorative Formica top. On two separate occasions, during the course of this four-month class, after welding two pieces of my future coffee table together, I shut off my Oxy Acetylene Torch.

Then systematically, I removed my gloves and face shield to assess my progress. Erroneously, while suffering a mental lapse, I proceeded to pick up the once fiery red-hot, now turned black, still scorching metal rods. Each time the palm of my hand was seared like a steak on a grill. The branded swollen wounds would ultimately vanish but with each painful mistake, it was becoming clearer to me, working with sheet metal and torches was not going to be my future vocation.

My machine shop class harbored even worse personal physical results. The semester project, given us by our teacher, was to reshape a solid rough piece of, 2" X 4"X 1", rectangular metal bar into a smooth highly polished product, finished within a tolerance of .005". The final stage of the reshaping process was to use a surface grinder; a vertical high speed solid sandpaper like wheel spinning perpendicular over a horizontal surface.

To meet the final grade worthy finish, I frequently shut off the surface grinder and immaculately rubbed the piece of metal and the base plate of the machine to meet my instructor's expected product precision. I would then make a very minor adjustment to lower the grinder wheel closer to the base plate with my unfinished product between them.

As I was getting to my final degree of tolerance, I had a brain wave interruption and forgot to shut off the grinding wheel. It was still spinning as my hand went into the product polishing area and ground one of my fingers down to the bone. This appendage damage was permanent!

The whole industrial environment, teachers, machines, and mangled body parts was not for me, so I opted out of Trade School.

When my senior year began, I was given the opportunity to be in the Distributive Education Program, a version of an Internship, where students are assigned a position to a potential future employer. My job began as a minimum wage, $.75 per hour, stock boy at Haag Drug Store, a regional chain of neighborhood pharmacy and retail outlets.

With this new opportunity I was able to say goodbye to my post donut sales job of delivering, except Sunday, daily afternoon newspapers door to door. Now there would be no more bitter cold, rainy, hot, and sweaty, dog chasing me, days carrying those heavy bags filled with rolled up newspapers, winging them right and left from my bicycle, aiming, and successfully hitting the 100 plus miniscule concrete front porches for me. I would be underroof protected from the environment working in a clean, safe, and more professional atmosphere.

Upon graduating from high school in 1961, my class ring read the same regardless of which way I put it on my finger, I began working full time at Haag's Drug Store earning $.80 per hour. This was less than 1/3 of the average annual income of $5,315.00, but still enough for me to buy my first car, a 1956 white Ford convertible and keep it filled with $.27 a gallon gasoline.

Within a year at the drugstore, working 60 hours a week, with no extra financial consideration for overtime, I became the Floor Manager of the store. In addition to my regular duties of overseeing the shelves were stocked correctly, orders placed for new inventory and items priced accurately, I assisted the pharmacist in filling medical prescriptions.

The pharmacists wore clean white tunics, worked in a somewhat sterile environment, were respected by doctors and customers alike and paid far better than even the store manager. I began to gravitate toward this better lifestyle when Bernie Young, one of the full-time pharmacists, announced I had assisted in filling enough prescriptions and gained enough medical knowledge to become an Apprentice Pharmacist. He ceremoniously awarded me a framed, state numerically certified, piece of parchment attesting to my new status.

Bernie educated me with his knowledge of a single drug action or interaction with other drugs on the human body, basically the effects both beneficial and harmful they possess. He had a keen wit and sense of humor, which were on full display to customers and employees alike, including my fellow floor manager Ron Gegenheimer.

Ron had a habit of going out drinking too much alcoholic substance on Friday night and coming to work Saturday morning with a hangover, begging for immediate medical relief from Bernie. The weekly request for hangover aid finally became tiresome so Bernie decided to attempt a psychological remedy for Ron. Upon Ron's next request Bernie scoured a shelf of rarely used bottles of medication, gave him a nice small easy to swallow pill and waited patiently for his follow up reaction.

Ron soon went to the bathroom to relieve his system of some of his excess

Friday night fluids and let out a ghastly scream from the men's enclosure. He emerged a little pale, frightened and exclaimed his urine was "bright blue." Bernie looked at me with a little wry wicked smile and winked at his successful little chicanery. We had a good laugh at Ron's expense, one episode of a large Friday night outing he wouldn't soon forget.

Bernie enamored me with his many college stories and encouraged me to attend Purdue University to get a pharmaceutical degree. I decided, with his reassurance, to attend Ball State Teachers College, in my hometown Muncie, take the basic biology and other preliminary courses necessary then, after two academic years, transfer them and myself to Lafayette, Indiana, home of Purdue University.

Two and a half years after graduating from high school I began attending Ball State Teachers College on a part-time basis, taking two classes, while continuing to work full-time at the drugstore. My academic path for the next few years was unfolding in a calculated and methodical fashion. What I lacked in college preparation skills, writing, reading for comprehension and good study habits were made up for in sheer determination to succeed at this endeavor.

My first two classes at BSTC were 20th Century World Civilization and Flag Football. The world civ class was the normal; purchase the book, attend class, take notes, study for the exam, and make an offering to the Intellectual Test Gods. But the flag football class was on a whole different plane.

The flag football instructor, also the school's football coach, Jim Freeman, believed all his male students had the athletic capabilities to tackle, block and scrum over the inflated oblong leather most prized possession of his livelihood. And it was his intention to bring this skill out of his students, on the field of engagement, the easy or the hard way.

According to my Selective Service Card, the U.S. Federal Government required Draft Registration for boys at their 18th birthday; I was 5'8" and weighed 110 pounds. Now at age 20, I added, maybe, another 15 pounds but had rarely ever participated in any physical, competitive, contact, athletic activity. Physical competition was not in my DNA!

However, my size or lack of it didn't have any sway over Jim Freemen assigning me to the offensive line of our randomly selected flag football team. My primary responsibility was to keep the defensive man from stopping our running game or hitting our team's quarterback.

The defensive man opposite of me going to create this disruption in our offensive game plan happened to be Oscar Lubke, the former" First Team All-Conference Offensive Lineman" for the "Fighting Cardinals," switched to defense for his one credit hour college requirement. Oscar was 6'3" tall and weighed 245 pounds. It was David versus Goliath, but I had no weapon!

When we went to the line of scrimmage, Oscar would look at me, smile "Cheshire-like," as I struck my most serious, stout pose bracing for his impending aggressive attack at my weak offensive, actually defensive, position. Each time the ball was snapped he would play cat and mouse toy with me, like I was his personal amusement plaything. Undaunted, each time I would face him straight up; try to push him to the right or left, with a new maneuver. He'd seen all my pretentiously deceptive moves before from opponents twice my size. So, nothing I could ever do would phase or disrupt his athletic intentions.

My only success came when he made a concession on a meaningless play. Coach Freeman must have been amused at my unwillingness to capitulate to the "Behemoth Lubke" as I, along with several bumps and bruises, received a "B" from his flag football class.

In the winter of 1965, the same year Ball State Teachers College transitioned to university status to become known as Ball State University, I quit my management job at Haag's Drug Store, sold my absolutely beautiful blue, eye-catching, 1963 Pontiac Catalina muscle car and enrolled as a full-time student. My grades were above average, my academic confidence had grown, and I was ready to move my life forward at a more rapid pace.

My ambition to become a pharmacist, upon completion of my basic prep courses, took an about face in 1966 when, after comparing my part time income to my housing, tuition, auto, living expenses at BSU versus what they would be at Purdue, I decided I couldn't afford to make the move. Added to my potential financial deficit and the additional year needed to complete the pharmacy program at Purdue was the reality of the escalating War in Vietnam.

In 1966, more than 382,000 men were drafted by the Selective Service into the military in preparation to serve the United States war effort in Vietnam. This was approximately five times the number drafted in 1962. Each male student attending college was given deferments from the draft for four years. Once the student had used his four deferments, he was automatically subject to immediate call up to serve two years of active military duty.

By 1966, I had used two of my four deferments, but still needed 2 ½ additional years of academic studies, in my new major in Business Management to complete my four-year degree. The race was on to complete it prior to being drafted and hoped for a professional critical job deferment or the termination of the Vietnam War. I did not want to go to Vietnam!

In the 1960's a long running theatrical cartoon show, "The Road Runner '' became more relevant to me. The Characters of the 6–9-minute laugh filled side slapping shorts, parody to a cat and mouse scenario were The Road Runner [Boulevarous Burnupus] and Wile E. Coyote [Dogus Ignoramus].

The animated Road Runner, a ground running bird, was depicted as sleek, vertical, purple, and light blue with a plume on the top of his small beaked head and two yellow rapidly, sometimes spinning like a top, legs. Wile E. Coyote was cast with brown scraggly fur, malnourished appearance, sporting a white dining bib, a knife in one hand, a fork in the other with a red panting tongue hanging from his mouth as he, too vertical, was perpetually chasing his elusive prey.

The settings for their many lure trap and escape misadventures were an open desert with long winding dirt pathways strewn with boulders, cactus and tumbleweeds and a Grand Canyon like scene with rocky cliffs, ledges, valleys with a stream running through it.

The flighty fun fast paced situational background music filled cartoons each chronicling several attempts by Wile E. Coyote to deceive, snare, trap, to ultimately catch and subsequently eat The Road Runner were frequently aided by complex and ludicrous devices from a mail order company, the fictitious 'Acme Corporation'. They ultimately failed in improbable and spectacular ways with Wile E. ending up burnt to a crisp, squashed flat or at the bottom of a canyon, always with a failed disbelief look on his face forced to listen to the mockingly victorious "Beep Beep" of the unscathed Road Runner.

The Road Runner and Wile E. Coyote were the two characters of my most prized speech in my "Fundamentals of Public Speaking" class. In my classroom pedestal presentation, I characterized myself as The Road Runner, while Wile E. Coyote was depicted as the Villainous Draft Board at the Selective Service. Like The Road Runner I was trying to avoid being caught, drafted, sent to war, and possibly killed in action. While the Indiana Draft Board was measuring my time at BSU, ringing their collective hands together, waiting for my deferments to expire, thus making me eligible to fill their monthly quota of men being demanded by the U.S. Federal Government.

My professor and fellow classmates loved the humorous analogy! I received an "A" on the speech, but no additional deferment.

On October 16, 1967, Specialist 4, Ray N. Gribble, a high school classmate and all-around fun-to-be-around-guy, volunteered to leave his secure, well deserved rear job and rejoin his undermanned Fighting Black Lion Battalion. The next day his unit was lured into a well-designed ambush by the North Vietnamese Army. Ray was killed! He left his wife behind.

On April 3, 1968, My Best Childhood Friend, Staff Sergeant David Carl Thomas, "believed in never leaving a soldier behind" was killed in Vietnam while trying to recover the bodies of two of his fallen squad members. David was my Blood Brother! My hero! Now he was dead, leaving his wife and young son Danny behind. I was shaken!

On May 25, 1968, 1st Lieutenant Roger Moore, whose family lived next to our church, Riverside EUB, husband and father of two young children was killed in Vietnam.

The war in Vietnam was Real!

In August 1968 I was denied an additional deferment to finish my last two classes at BSU. Two weeks later I boarded a Greyhound Bus, along with 40 other young potential inductees, to Indianapolis for a physical examination to assess our personal fitness to serve in the military. I passed the exam.

. In October 1968, at age 25, I received a formal letter from the Selective Service Draft Board requesting me to report for induction into the military service. On December 5, 1968, I reported to the Selective Service Office in Muncie, was sworn into the military service, bused to Indianapolis, where I was ordered to serve in the U.S. Army and then bused to Ft Campbell, Kentucky for basic military training.

Wile E. Coyote had caught The Road Runner!

Vietnam War

The Vietnam War beginning on November 1, 1955 and extending unendingly through to April 30, 1975 had a major impact on my life, the lives of my contemporaries, our country's [United States of America] standing in the world, the culture of our society, the anguish and pain felt by the families directly affected and the emphatic bitter embattled division the Vietnam War created among the citizens of the United States of America. For these reasons I'm writing first about the Vietnam War, then about the effect it had on our country, The United States of America, and finally, the Vietnam War from my perspective.

War is an organized and often prolonged conflict carried out by states or non-state actors. It is generally characterized by extreme violence, social disruption and an attempt at economic destruction. War is an actual intentional widespread armed conflict between political communities and is defined as a form of collective political violence or intervention.

War may be an inescapable and integral aspect of Human nature inevitable under certain socio-cultural ecological circumstances. There are human societies in which warfare does not exist thus humans may not be naturally disposed for warfare.

Wars include small-scale raiding parties to major allied conflicts. Between 3,500 BC and the late 20th Century approximately 14,500 wars took place, during which 3.5 billion lives have been lost. There have been only 300 years of peace in the last 5,500 years.

The largest aggregate number of casualties in a war is most frequently the unprotected civilian population, which includes women, children, and the elderly. These innocent war bystanders are brutally and unmercifully subject to dislocation, disease, starvation, physical abuse, such as rape and torture, and accidental as well as intentional death. While statistically these innocents are historically listed as killed or casualties of a conflict many are, in fact, "MURDERED!" The synonyms frequently used to conceal these horrible atrocities, killed or causalities, tend to undermine the genocide, butchery and frequent criminal actions taken directly against the innocents. The word "Murdered" should be listed in these historical accounts as well.

In World War I, historically listed, there were 7 million Civilian Casualties versus 10 million military personnel. In World War II, historically listed, 38-55 million Civilians died of war related events including disease and famine, compared to 22-25 million military killed. The total number of people, civilians and military personnel who died in WWII accounted for 3% of the world's population. The Korean War resulted in an estimated, historically listed, 2,500,000 killed or wounded civilians and 2,312,067 military dead or missing.

Wars have an implicit yet definitive degree of Autocratic Evil to them. The Vietnam War was no exception!

The Vietnam War, as it relates to the United States and its minimally involved allies, started on November 1, 1955, and ended April 30, 1975. During the approximately 19 1/2 year war, historically listed, there were 2 million Civilian Casualties and 1,812,000 military soldiers killed in action.

In 1950 the Soviet Union and the People's Republic of China, both Communist countries, recognized Viet Minh's Democratic Republic of Vietnam based in Hanoi, North Vietnam, as the legitimate government of Vietnam. Ho Chi Minh, leader of the Viet Minh coalition and former WWII U.S. ally was the Vietnam government's leader. However, at that time Vietnam, Cambodia and Laos were still at war with the French.

In 1954 the French were soundly defeated in the Battle of Dien Bien Phu. A summit was held in Geneva where the French negotiated a cease fire with the Viet Minh and independence was granted to Vietnam, Cambodia, and Laos. One of the stipulations of the Geneva Conference was that Vietnam was divided at the 17th parallel establishing two separate countries, North and South Vietnam, until unifying elections could be held in 1956. The unifying elections never occurred.

According to the U.S. "Domino Theory" of that time, if one state i.e., Vietnam, Cambodia, Laos, Thailand, or the Philippines fell to the Red Tide of Communism, the other states may follow as well. Therefore, the possibility of South Vietnam falling to the Communists of North Vietnam was counter to the U.S. containment policy and must be prevented.

The Vietnam War, which in part included Cambodia and Laos, began on November 1, 1955, when President of the United States, Dwight D. Eisenhower sent 3,500 military advisors to South Vietnam in support of its recently elected President Ngo Dinh Diem. The U.S. government viewed American involvement in the war as a way to prevent the Communist takeover of South Vietnam, preventing the spread of the dreaded Red Tide of Communism.

The North Vietnamese government, centered in the capital city of Hanoi, and National Liberation Front, a.k.a., Viet Cong, energized with support from the countryside villager's population living in South Vietnam, were fighting to reunify Vietnam under communist rule. The North Vietnamese and Viet Cong viewed the conflict as a "colonial war" fought against America, which regarded South Vietnam, whose capital city was Saigon, as a U.S. "puppet state."

In 1958 the Viet Cong, with behind the scenes support from North Vietnam, actively started the revival of the Civil War in South Vietnam. In 1960 the Communist Party of North Vietnam formally bestowed it's blessing on the Viet Cong and called for the liberation of the South from American Imperialism.

In 1960 John F. Kennedy, the first Catholic President of the United States, succeeded Eisenhower. In his inaugural address, President Kennedy made the ambitious pledge to, "pay any price, bear any burden, meet any hardship, support any friend, oppose any foe to insure the survival and success of liberty."

Like Eisenhower before him, President Kennedy believed failure on the part of the United States to gain control and stop Communism expansion would fatally damage U.S. credibility with its allies, and his own personal reputation. Kennedy was thus determined to "draw a line in the sand" and prevent a Communist victory in South Vietnam.

Kennedy followed up his promise to "support any friend" by tripling troop levels sent to South Vietnam in 1961 and again in 1962. His policy toward South Vietnam rested on the assumption that Diem, the President of South Vietnam, and his forces had to ultimately defeat the Viet Cong Guerillas on their own.

Diem, a stanchly devout Roman Catholic, was elected President in October 1955, in a rigged poll supervised by his older brother, Ngo Dinh Thuc, giving him 98.2 % of the vote including 133% in Saigon. Diem was fervently anti-communist, nationalist and socially conservative. His domestic policies toward the Buddhist and countryside peasants had a huge impact on his ultimate inability to succeed as a leader in the Vietnam War.

The majority of the Vietnamese people were Buddhist. They were alarmed by actions such as Diem's dedication of the country to the Virgin Mary. Discontent with Diem's religious preferential policies exploded in 1962 in the city of Hue Phat Dan when nine Buddhists were shot protesting against the ban on the Buddhist flag on Vesak, the Buddha's birthday. This directed hostile action against the Buddhist's resulted in mass protests against the discriminatory policies favoring the Catholic Church and its adherents.

Buddhist pagodas were reportedly being demolished by Catholic paramilitary, and on August 21, 1963, ARVN troops loyal to Diem's brother, Thuc, raided pagodas across Vietnam, causing widespread damage and destruction and leaving the death toll estimated to be in the hundreds. Diem refused to make concessions to the Buddhist majority or take responsibility for the deaths.

Also, the class relations of the countryside population became a major disruptive and actively contentious force for Diem. The vast majority of the population lived in the villages in the countryside where land reform was the key issue.

Earlier the Viet Minh had purged the landowners, executing 172,008 "landlords" during their "land reform" "rent reduction" campaign and leased the land to poorer peasants. When Diem was stuff-ballot-box elected to president he brought the landlords back to the villages in the south. Under his government's rule, the peasants who were farming their land for years now had to return it to the original owners and pay back rent. The rent collection on the former land farming peasants was enforced by the South Vietnamese Army [ARVN]. This action resulted in 75% of the once peaceful supportive countryside peasant villagers backing and, in many cases, actively joining the Viet Cong forces.

The ARVN were led in battle by Diem's most trusted general, Huynh Van Cao, commander of the IV Corps. He was a Catholic who had been promoted based on his religion. Cao's main objective was to preserve his forces to stave off the growing number of coups against Diem. In Washington policy makers had begun to conclude Diem was incapable of defeating the Communist and may even make a deal with Ho Chi Minh.

Behind closed doors, U.S. officials began discussions of a regime change. The State Department was generally in favor of a coup, while the Defense Department was in Diem's corner. The Central Intelligence Agency [CIA] was in contact with ARVN generals planning to remove Diem. They were told the United States would not oppose the move, punish the generals, or cut off aid to them. On November 2, 1963, President Diem was overthrown and executed along with his brother, Thuc.

President Kennedy had not approved this unauthorized solitarily directed action by the CIA and was 'shocked and dismayed' when told of Diem's death. However, approving of the coup, Henry Cabot Lodge, the U.S. Ambassador to South Vietnam told President Kennedy, "The prospects are now for a shorter war."

General Paul Harkins, the commander of U.S. forces in South Vietnam, confidently predicted victory by Christmas 1963. The CIA was less confident, however, warning "the Viet Cong by and large retain de facto control of much of the countryside and have steadily increased the overall intensity of the effort."

Twenty days later, on November 22, 1963, President John F. Kennedy was assassinated.

Lyndon B. Johnson, Vice President, was sworn in as President, aboard. Air Force One, the presidential plane carrying the former president's body from Dallas Texas, where he was slain, to Washington D.C. It is the only time in U.S. history when two presidents were on Air Force One at the same time.

On November 24, 1963, President Johnson said "the battle against communism…must be joined…with strength and determination. The pledge came at a time when the situation in South Vietnam was deteriorating. While Kennedy had been positioning the U.S. for a withdrawal of troops, President Johnson, with his own agenda, was interested in expanding the war.

On August 2, 1964, the USS Maddox, on an intelligence mission, along the North Vietnamese border in the Gulf of Tonkin was allegedly fired upon by some North Vietnamese patrol boats who had been stalking it. Two days later a supposed similar incident occurred involving the USS Turner Joy.

The second attack led to retaliatory air strikes, prompted Congress to approve the Gulf of Tonkin Resolution, which gave the president the power to conduct military operations in Southeast Asia without declaring war. Immediately Johnson publicly pledged, "he was not…committing American boys to fighting a war that I think ought to be fought by the boys of Asia to protect their own land."

Correspondingly, with Diem's suppression policy toward the countryside villagers the strength of the Viet Cong, with support from the North Vietnamese, had risen from 5,000 in 1959 to approximately 100,000 by the end of 1964. Gaining momentum, the Viet Cong were attacking and destroying hamlets friendly to the government at an alarming rate, 7,559 by early 1965. They took control of the countryside voluntarily and by force when necessary.

The number of U.S. troops in South Vietnam had risen from 2,000 in 1961 to 16,500 in 1964.

Following an attack on a U.S. Marines barracks in Pleiku, and to attempt to fracture the support of Viet Cong from the North, on March 2, 1965, the National Security Council recommended a three-stage bombing strategy of North Vietnam, Cambodia, and Laos. The bombings were intended to strike the industrial sites manufacturing military ordinance, airport runways, rocket launching sites and supply routes to the south, which included railroads, highways, roads, and trails. The military personnel and supply transportation routes referred to as the Ho Chi Minh Trail were circuitously woven through North Vietnam, Cambodia, and Laos with the trailhead in South Vietnam.

During the next three years, millions of tons of bombs were strategically and randomly dropped on North Vietnam, Cambodia, and Laos. Chief of Staff of the United States Air Force, Curtis LeMay, long an advocate of this massive, saturated bombing, stated, "We're going to bomb them back to the Stone age."

Factories, bridges, and highways were destroyed along with many civilian casualties. The air invasion had an intended direct destructive impact, but it only strengthened the North's resolve and more unified the Minh forces against the U.S.

The massive bombing raids resulted in a reciprocated increase of Viet Cong directed ground attacks on several bases housing U.S. Air Force bombers. The ARVN troops protecting these bases were ineffective in protecting the American planes landing strips and their crews. So, on March 8, 1965, 3,500 U.S. Marines were dispatched to South Vietnam to protect the air force bases, thus beginning the American ground war.

In a reactive statement Ho Chi Minh warned, "If Americans want to make war for twenty years, then we shall make war for twenty years. If they want to make peace, we shall make peace and invite them to afternoon tea."

The initial Marines' assignment was defensive, but the war, taking on a life of its own, was inevitably escalating and shifting to an obvious offensive mode. U.S. commanders in South Vietnam, after witnessing several ARVN battle losses, desertions, and their plummeting morale, considered them incapable of winning the war. Thus, they committed to increasing the role of American involvement. By December 1965, there were 200,000 U.S. troops in South Vietnam.

General Westmoreland, head of Military Assistance Command, Vietnam [MACV] stated," I'm convinced U.S. troops with their energy, mobility, and firepower can successfully take the fight to the...Viet Cong." With his aggressive recommendation he moved the American troops to the forefront of the war and sidelined the ARVN.

General Westmoreland outlined a three-step plan to win the war:

Phase 1. Commitment of U.S. [and other free world] forces necessary to halt the losing trend by the end of 1965.

Phase 2. U.S. and allied forces mount major offensive actions to seize the initiative to destroy guerilla and organized enemy forces. This phase would end when the enemy had been worn down, thrown on the defensive, and driven back from major populated areas.

Phase 3. If the enemy persisted, a period of twelve to eighteen months following Phase two would be required for the final destruction of enemy forces remaining in remote base areas.

The plan was approved by President Johnson and marked a profound departure from his previous public position that the government of South Vietnam was to defeat the guerillas. Westmoreland confidently predicted victory by the end of 1967.

The new change in U.S. policy depended on matching the North Vietnamese and Viet Cong in a contest of attrition and morale. The opponents were locked in a cycle of escalation and the idea that the government of South Vietnam could manage its own affairs was shelved. The complex situation was beginning to appear as a Medusa with too many heads and too few helmets to cover them.

The U.S. media, favorable to the South Vietnamese struggle for independence, was not told of this aggressive change in policy by the Johnson administration. Rather President Johnson, his staff and military representatives employed a policy of "minimum candor" in its dealings with the U.S. media. Military information officers sought to manage media coverage by emphasizing stories that portrayed progress in the war.

On January 31, 1968, the NVA and Viet Cong broke the truce that traditionally accompanied the Tet [Lunar New Year] holiday by launching the largest battle of the war. The Tet Offensive deployed over 85,000 NVA and VC troops in the hope of sparking a national uprising. Over 100 cities including 36 of the 44 provincial capitals, five autonomous cities, 72 district towns, General Westmoreland's headquarters and the U.S. Embassy in Saigon were attacked.

To date most of the war had been fought in the countryside and rice paddies, now the North supported forces focused on the more populated larger city urban areas. The U.S. and South Vietnamese forces were shocked by the synchronized broad magnitude and number of the TET surprise attacks. They were unprepared for the new urban concentrated yet widespread offensive.

The longest and bloodiest battle of the lengthy Vietnam War was fought in the former capital city of Hue. The combined NVA and Viet Cong troops captured the Imperial Citadel, most of the city then executed and massacred over 3,000 unarmed Hue civilians.

The fierce and brutal month-long predominately U.S. counter offensive pushed back slowly but progressively against the occupying enemy house by house, building by building and block by block to recapture Hue. The Americans ultimately were forced to employ their superior firepower that left approximately 80% of the city in ruins.

Across South Vietnam 4,100 American and allied troops, 4,900 ARVN, 20,000 NVA and Viet Cong, and 14,100 civilians lay dead. In every sense of military conflict, the Tet Offensive had been deadly, destructive, and utterly devastating.

The American media, which had, until the Tet Offensive, been largely in support of U.S. Efforts, turned on Westmoreland and the Johnson Administration for what had become an increasing 'credibility gap'. The daily televised reports streaming into the living rooms of American families showing, in real time and graphic color, detailing the brutality of the war had a profound emotional and distasteful effect.

Although the Tet Offensive was a significant victory for allied forces, in terms of casualties and control of territory, it was a major public relations defeat. It led to an immediate and irreversible decline in public support and the turning point in American involvement in the Vietnam War.

The Tet Offensive additionally became a political victory for the Communist forces because it ended the career of President Johnson, who, with plummeting approval ratings, charged with the loss of 30,000 American Men during his administration, declined to run for re-election.

The magnitude of Tet Offensive had contradicted the claims of progress made by the Johnson Administration and his military advisors. It was seen by the American public that the Tet Offensive constituted an intelligence failure on the scale of Pearl Harbor. That vivid oversight costing so many American lives would not soon be forgotten.

On May 10, 1968, despite low expectations, peace talks began between the United States and North Vietnam in Paris. Negotiations stagnated for five months until; Johnson gave orders to halt the bombing of North Vietnam.

The chess pieces were beginning to move, but like the game itself, would be a long protracted, drawn out strategic resolute negotiated process. This "Domino," Vietnam, had fallen to the Communist. It was just a matter of time before the checkmate was conceded.

Vietnam was the major political issue in the presidential elections held in 1968. The American public was fraught with angst over the whole Vietnam issue and voted Richard Nixon as the fourth President of the United States to be involved in this conflict.

Severe Communist losses during the Tet Offensive allowed President Nixon to begin troop withdrawals. His plan, the Nixon Doctrine, was to build up the ARVN so they could take over the defense of South Vietnam. The policy became known as "Vietnamization."

Within fifteen months after his election, Nixon withdrew 150,000 troops from Vietnam. He, along with General Creighton Abrams, changed the strategy of the war moving most of the troops from the border areas where the majority of the fighting took place and redeployed them more to the interior and coastal areas.

The U.S. bombing of North Vietnam continued, and at times escalated as it became one of the few pieces of the 'peace puzzle' Nixon had at his disposal. North Vietnam invaded both Cambodia and Laos and used their border areas for training, supply routes and combat staging grounds for their continued aggressive efforts in South Vietnam.

On September 2, 1969, Ho Chi Minh, longtime leader of the movement to reunite North and South Vietnam under Communist rule died.

His legacy was solidified in the commitment by the senior members of his party to see his vision through to completion.

In May 1970, U.S. and ARVN forces launched an incursion into Cambodia to combat NVA and Viet Cong bases, interrupt their supply routes and rout them from the area. The mission was to not advance more than 100 miles into Cambodia, so the North Vietnamese and V.C. retreated from the border until the U.S. troops abandoned the mission.

The Vietnamization of the ARVN continued as they launched Operation Lam Son in February 1971. The aim of the offensive action was an attempt to cut the Ho Chi Minh supply trail from Laos. The action precipitated by the ARVN was met with such resistance they retreated in a confused and chaotic rout.

U.S. planes were forced to destroy their abandoned equipment, including tanks to prevent them from falling into enemy hands. The operation was a total fiasco and represented a complete bust and failure of the Vietnamization program.

The military blunders were numerous and monumental. Many of the top officers tutored by the Americans and trained in the U.S. for ten to fifteen years were clueless, unable to direct their forces in an authoritative and organized military manner and actually were first to leave their post. Still the U.S. could not give up on the Vietnamization concept as it was the only way out of Vietnam for the Americans.

In 1971 the U.S. troop count was further reduced to 196,700 with a deadline to remove another 45,000 by February 1972. Most of the allied forces had left Vietnam in 1971.

Vietnamization was again tested by the Easter Offensive in 1972 when the NVA led a massive conventional invasion into South Vietnam. The NVA and Viet Cong quickly overran the Northern provinces and threatened to cut the country in half.

Once again, American airpower came to the rescue and halted the invasion's advancement. However, it became clear that without the supporting American air power the south could not survive.

The peace talks in Paris were moving at a slow pace, with both sides unwilling to concede until Nixon, showing support for South Vietnam, ordered Operation Linebacker II, a massive bombing of Hanoi and Haiphong December 18-29, 1972. The air offensive destroyed much of the remaining economic and industrial capacity of North Vietnam.

Simultaneously President Nixon pressured South Vietnam's leader of five war torn years, President Thieu, to accept the terms of the peace talk's agreement. Thieu was told if he continued to balk at the war ending agreement, Nixon would reach a bilateral peace deal with the North Vietnamese and cut off American aid to his country.

On January 15, 1973, Nixon announced the suspension of offensive action against North Vietnam. The Paris peace accords on "Ending the War and Restoring Peace in Vietnam" were signed on January 27, 1973, officially ending direct U.S. involvement in the Vietnam War.

A cease-fire was declared across North and South Vietnam. The agreement guaranteed the territorial integrity of Vietnam and called for national elections in the North and South.

The remaining U.S. ground troops were withdrawn by the end of March 1973 and U.S. prisoners of war, being held in North Vietnam, were released.

Elections were never held in North or South Vietnam; rather, sensing a weakened South Vietnamese resolve, North Vietnam and the Viet Cong began a systematic strategy to consolidate the country under one Communist government.

With the bombings of North Vietnam suspended, highways and bridges connecting the Ho Chi Minh trail were rebuilt and the North Vietnamese along with the Viet Cong mobilized their forces to wage a three-year dry season offensive push into South Vietnam's major provinces, which, they projected, would end in the 1975-76 dry season.

The North Vietnamese and Viet Cong were well organized, highly motivated and well-funded by the Communist bloc countries. Although they possessed 1/3 less artillery, ½ the number of tanks and 50% fewer fighting troops than South Vietnam, they had 'determination of purpose' on their side.

During the dry season offensive of 1973-74, the NVA and VC proved superior in all aspects of military maneuvering and sent the ARVN fleeing every battle, showing little resistance.

The NVA and VC increased their military pressure and will on the south and progressed faster to their ultimate reunification goal than previously projected. With U.S. aid to South Vietnam cut by at least 30% and a Congress refusing to support any further funding, the country found itself in the precarious position of rallying its own resources to survive or fall to the Communist.

As the 1974-75 dry season approached the NVA and VC readjusted their aggressive military tactical approach to reunify Vietnam in two rather than three years. On December 13, 1974, The NVA and VC attacked Phouc Long Province and seized control of its capital, Phouc Binh, in just 24 days.

On March 11, the NVA and VC attacked Dak Lok Province and captured its capital, Pleiku, one day later. The NVA opened a siege surrounding the town of Hue on March 22 and it fell three days later on March 25.

The North Vietnamese forces were moving so fast their supply line resources were having trouble keeping pace. The ARVN were collapsing, demoralized, leaderless, leaving their weapons behind, and assimilating with fleeing civilians.

The cadence-like falling of province after province led to the final offensive against Saigon, South Vietnam's Capital City. The operational plan for the Ho Chi Minh campaign called for the capture of Saigon by May 1. They wanted to force the South Vietnamese to capitulate before the oncoming monsoon season began, which would prevent any redeployment of ARVN forces.

After one last gasp of a two-week stand, April 7-21, at Xuan Loc, 40 miles east of Saigon, the ARVN were once again defeated. The North Vietnamese march toward unification was now insured.

In the United States, South Vietnam appeared to be doomed. On April 23, 1975, the fifth president of the United States to be involved in the Vietnam War, Gerald Ford, declared an end to the war and all U.S. aid.

On April 27, 100,000 North Vietnamese troops surrounded Saigon. On April 29, "Operation Free Wind", the largest helicopter evacuation in history began removing diplomatic, military, and civilian personnel from the grounds of the U.S. Embassy. In the early morning hours of April 30, the last U.S. Marines were evacuated from the roof of the U.S. Embassy.

On April 30, 1975, NVA troops entered the city of Saigon and quickly overcame all resistance. An NVA tank crashed through the gates of the Independence Palace at 11:30 am and the Viet Cong flag was raised above it. The Communist reunification effort of Vietnam was complete!

Eisenhower's predicted "Domino Theory" was validated with the fall of Cambodia to the Communist Khmer Rouge on April 17, 1975. A few months later, in December, Pathet Lao overthrew the royalist government of Laos. The region of Southeast Asia had, as feared, systematically fallen to the Red Tide of Communism.

The United States of America for the first time in its almost 200-year history felt the humiliation and sting of defeat. The democratic country had lost its first war!

The United States Vietnam War

The Vietnam War, involving the United States, a country based on the democratic principle of government, began as a limited involvement conflict to contain the international growing threat of communism, an ideology supported by the Union of Soviet Socialist Republics [USSR], commonly referred to as the Soviet Union or Russia and the Republic of China.

The democratic system of the United States and Russia's political programs were based on opposing ideological principles. They hypothetically seemed to share the "power to the people" philosophy. In practice, however, the two systems of government structure, the economic and political fabric of their society, were woven in markedly different ways.

In the economic sphere, communism calls for the government to take control of all capital and industry in the country in an effort to rid its people of financial inequality. On the other hand, democracy respects individuals' right to own property and means of production.

The political landscape is very different in democracy vs. communism as well. In a democratic society people are free to create their own political parties and contest in elections, which are presumably free of coercion and fair to all contestants. In a communist society, however, the government is controlled by one political party and dissent is not tolerated.

Neither democracy in the United States nor communism in the USSR operated perfectly, as the ideological principles are projected, but the main differences were there, nevertheless.

After World War ll the Western Bloc of European countries including the United States, and the Eastern Bloc of European countries, led by the USSR entered into a philosophical and economic contest for world leading supremacy. Both groups acted in extremist, protective and often aggressive fashion leading what was from 1945 until 1991 called, "The Cold War."

Sides had been drawn and the concern of an 'Atomic Bomb War' was the catalyst to major international tension.

For a time, the people of the United States acted with paranoia thinking there was a communist under every rock in the country, plotting to emerge and create a people's revolt from within. These fears came to define-and, in some cases, erode the era's political future. Labeled the "Red Scare," the spreading anxiety was real and being played out in the hyper-suspicious atmosphere of the Cold War.

On October 1, 1949, in China, the Chinese Nationalist Party was overthrown by the Chinese Communist Party.

On June 25, 1950, the North Korean Army, supported by the Soviet Union and the new Communist China, invaded the democratic country of South Korea. The United States and its allies supported South Korea in its defense against their invaders until an armistice agreement between the two countries was reached, July 27, 1953.

Four days after the United States announced their intention to introduce artificial satellites to survey our outer space system, the Soviet Union, on August 2, 1955, responded with their own space program. The Soviet Union announced they intended to send unmanned satellites to the Moon, Mars and Venus, and human space flight in low Earth orbit. The Space Race between the two competing countries was on!

In August 1961, the Soviet Union built the Berlin Wall cutting the city of Berlin, Germany in half, essentially separating the communist controlled East Germany from the allied and democratic supported West Germany. Families and citizens of the country were physically separated, and people trying to cross the border from the communist east to the democratic west were shot.

In October 1962, The Soviet Union was discovered building nuclear missile bases in Cuba, just 90 miles off the coast of Florida. President Kennedy established a military blockade around Cuba to prevent further armament of the nuclear missile sites. For 13 days a chess match, the magnitude of which never before could have been conceived, between Soviet leader Nakita Khrushchev and President John Kennedy, played out on television world-wide.

It was the closest the Cold War era came to escalating into a full-scale nuclear war. To resolve the stalemate between the two nuclear superpowers, The Soviets agreed to dismantle and remove their missiles from Cuba and the U.S. agreed to do likewise, with their here-to-fore secret nuclear missile sites in Turkey and Italy.

The stage for an escalating confrontation between the supremacy of the two ideologies was set, but the place for the actual conflict was yet to be determined.

When President's Eisenhower and Kennedy initially sent advisors, then followed up with a small supportive troop base, for the democratic government of South Vietnam, their intention was to stop the now growing international threat of Communism. They felt the strong democratic government of South Vietnam, with some assistance, could hold its position against the communists of North Vietnam.

The general consensus of the anti-communist American public was supportive of the U.S. limited involvement in Vietnam. The citizenry bought into the concept of Eisenhower's, "Domino Theory" that if one Indochina country fell to the communists then they all could as well, ultimately ceding the whole region to "the Commies".

The journalistic news media was supportive of Vietnam's anti-communist, Catholic regime of President Ngo Dinh Diem, ignoring his despotic tendencies. From Hong Kong and Shanghai, they were writing of progress being made against the communist by the South Vietnamese Army [ARVN].

However, the death of civilians in a coup against President Diem at the end of 1960 started to change how Vietnam was viewed by the media and, by extension, the American public. As a result of the reported atrocities by Diem, the New York Times sent their first reporter to Saigon, the capital of South Vietnam.

Murderous situations, tragedies and wars always draw media attention and soon other journalists from magazines, Time and Newsweek arrived in South Vietnam.

The basic policy governing how the U.S. mission in Saigon handled these reporters reflected the way the administration of President Kennedy conceived the American role in the war. Under that framework, the United States' role in South Vietnam was only to render advice and support in that nation's war against the Communists.

In January 1963, the illusion of South Vietnam being able to defend itself against the communist of the north changed dramatically when the ARVN were soundly defeated in the battle of AP BAC. Immediately President Diem began receiving harsh criticism of being a weak leader, corrupt, bigoted, and violent toward the country's Buddhist majority population. Many Americans began to believe the best solution for the U.S. was to get rid of Diem or take direct control of the war.

On November 2, 1963, President Diem was assassinated by the Central Intelligence Agency [CIA] of the United States. Twenty days later, President John F. Kennedy was assassinated by Lee Harvey Oswald, a pronounced communist.

As the nation mourned the death of the charismatic and highly popular President Kennedy, the former Vice-President, now President Lyndon B. Johnson was plotting his more aggressive strategy for Vietnam. On November 24, two days after JFK's assassination Johnson stated, "the battle against communism…must be joined…with strength and determination."

Johnson would later announce that, "he didn't want to commit American boys to fight a war the boys of Asia should fight to protect their own land," but that was all for public consumption. In private President Johnson was organizing his plan to get the United States more directly involved in Vietnam.

In January 1964, a Gallup Poll of the U.S. population indicated two out of three Americans agreed that South Vietnam would never form a stable government and four out of five Americans felt the communists were winning the war. Few, however, wanted a unilateral withdrawal and 50% believed that the

U.S. was obliged to defend independent freedom seeking nations from communist aggression.

Every war needs a trigger, a horrific incident, to get the conflicting countries to engage in battle. World War l was declared after the assassination of Archduke Franz Ferdinand and his wife, Sophie. World War ll was triggered by the Japanese surprise attack on Pearl Harbor and the Korean War ignited when the Communist Chinese backed North Korea invaded South Korea.

On August 2, 1965, the USS Maddox, a Navy destroyer engaged in collecting signals intelligence in the Gulf of Tonkin, inside North Vietnam's territorial limits, was attacked by three North Vietnam Navy torpedo boats. One supporting U.S. aircraft was damaged and one 14.5mm round hit the destroyer, but there were no U.S. casualties. Two days later, on August 4, another similar incident involving North Vietnam Navy torpedo boats attacking the USS Maddox was reported.

The outcome of these two incidents was the passage by Congress of the Gulf of Tonkin Resolution, which granted President Lyndon Johnson the authority to assist any Southeast Asian country whose government was considered jeopardized by "communist aggression." The resolution served as Johnson's legal justification for deploying U.S. conventional forces and the commencement of open warfare against North Vietnam.

President Lyndon B. Johnson had baited and provoked the North Vietnamese into a military confrontation and ultimately orchestrated the war he wanted in Vietnam.

As President Johnson escalated U.S. involvement in the Vietnam War so too did the media covering the conflict. The number of correspondents quickly rose to more than 132 American members of the press corps.

Initially, the reporters were spoon-fed reports meted out to them by the Military Assistance Command; Vietnam (MACV) under Johnson's program formerly "Operation Candor" renamed "Minimum Candor," which favored his policies. The MACV meetings, with the media, soon became known as the Five O'clock Follies, as most correspondents became steadily more convinced they were being lied to, manipulated by the MACV as well as the Buddhists and the communists.

At home, in the United States, some critics of the war had begun to question the government's assertion that it was fighting a democratic war to liberate the South Vietnamese people from Communist aggression. A small movement against U.S. involvement in the Vietnam War began among peace activists and leftist intellectuals on college campuses.

Originally deemed communist sympathizers, the movement gained national prominence in February 1965, after the United States began a full scale and highly publicized bombing campaign against North Vietnam. Anti-war marches and other protests, such as the ones organized by Students for a Democratic Society (SDS) began attracting a widening base of support.

The increasing number of peace marches and protests, with more widespread support, were generating national media attention. This coverage was beginning to feed the frenzy and stir the public's sentiment in the burgeoning peace versus war controversy.

President Johnson needed troops to fight his war and the number of American volunteers wasn't adequate to fill the demand by the military leaders in Vietnam. So, he activated his most accessible resource for military manpower, the Selective Service.

At the time all males, within 30 days after their 18th birthday were required, by law, to register with the Selective Service and make themselves available to serve the military. This potential obligation, at the discretion of the government, to the U.S. would continue until the registries' 26th birthday. The only exceptions to the service requirement were those deemed incapable of serving for medical or psychological unfitness.

During the Vietnam War years between August 1964 and February 1973, some 1,857,304 young men were drafted into the armed forces through the Selective Service program.

While this conscription method of filling the needs of the military leaders in Vietnam was necessary, it became a major point of contention between the war protestors and the government as an estimated 500,000 men, approximately 25%, "dodged" the draft, as it was called, through methods both elaborate (fleeing the country) and mundane (simply refusing to respond to conscription notices).

As the war was escalating in Vietnam, so were the number of protests and protestors against it in the U.S. After being accused by one senator of having bamboozled the American public with the fabrication of the Gulf of Tonkin incident; in a 1965 private conversation President Johnson asserted, "For all I know our Navy was shooting at whales out there." This was an incendiary comment!

The war in Vietnam was the first "television war," the first "living room war." The singular family television brought us the "horror of the war" night after night, on the evening news.

Most families, fathers, mothers and even children were glued to the TV broadcast bringing them the daily updates of the events in Vietnam. They all had sons, brothers, cousins, uncles, friends, or neighbors either directly involved in the war or expecting to be called into active duty.

My college roommates and I, comfortably seated 8,841 miles from Saigon, anxiously watched the televised war being played out in front of us wondering if, how, when or whether any of the action we were watching would occur in our lives. We each silently held our own private thoughts on being drafted out of school and what our individual reaction to it would be.

In the daily TV broadcasts reporters and their camera crew, uncensored, would transmit live color action filled video footage of soldiers firing their weapons in defense of their position or as they advanced on the enemy.

Their reports were very graphic showing combat troops in jungle entrenched fighting, the sound of enemy AK-47 automatic rifle fire crack, crack, cracking overhead with the return fire of the GI's M-16's. Outgoing artillery shells blasted as they left the huge barrels of their ordnance, then GI's, in unison, yelling "incoming" when the enemy responded in kind.

Soldiers with authority were heard shouting orders of engagement. Huey Helicopters buzzed through the sky bringing much needed replacements, ammunition, and food, returning to their base camp with the dead and wounded.

Video footage was shown of American soldiers, with Zippo cigarette lighters setting fire to thatch hutched villages suspected of supporting the VC while the hamlet's peasants vacantly stared at the proceedings. Hundreds of action scenes and images, intended to capture the gravity and success of the war against the communists were transmitted nightly into our living rooms.

The television networks, concerned about their audiences' sensibilities, kept most of the "horrors of the war" off the screen. However, approximately 25% of television coverage showed blood and gore images of dead and wounded soldiers.

The sensitivities were skewed when it came to showing the numerous mangled and disfigured dead communist enemies versus our bloody bandaged or body-bagged American warriors.

Propaganda style war updates were frequently given by the TV camera friendly and twice Time Magazine's "Man of the Year," General William Westmoreland on the success of our troops in Vietnam.

Every Thursday evening all three major television stations, ABC, CBS, and NBC, broadcast the weekly casualty report. Included were the number of enemy dead or wounded comparing them to those of our American troops. Statistically the numbers seemed in our favor, usually ten enemy dead for every American soldier killed.

Televised, the lost warriors' flag draped coffins were shown arriving at Air Force bases close to the hometowns of the fallen soldiers. As the months of active fighting dragged on, our dead soldiers began arriving with greater frequency and in larger numbers. More American families were grieving as their sons were delivered to them for burial.

Stress in the American public across the United States was growing as were the number of protests by many disbelieving, disenfranchised and scared draft age citizens. The battle plan of General William Westmoreland, asserting we would win in Vietnam through the "war of attrition" was backfiring on him and the leaders of our nation who supported his program.

The television stations broadcasting the war each day, charging their advertisers for the number of viewers tuning in to their station, increased their revenue. The military, always ready for a war, were receiving notoriety and rapid promotions, Lieutenant to Captain, Captain to Major, Major to Colonel, etc. Finally, the suppliers of all of the ordnance used to fight a war were foremost in placing money in their banks. Everyone was doing well except the poor soldiers assigned to physically fight the Vietnam War.

The numbers of protests against the Vietnam War at home were spreading like out-of-control wildfires across the United States. Many were well organized and drew large numbers of protesters while others were a flickering flame waiting for the flash point that would set their kindling size protest ablaze. There appeared not to be a place in the country that wasn't in some way protesting against the war.

Finding a new way to spread their message and appeal to the national audience, the Vietnam War Protest leaders played to the television cameras with creative, imaginative and in sometimes both brutal and illegal methods.

In 1965 there were approximately 26 protests against the war. Among those protests was one in Oklahoma where college students sent out thousands of pamphlets with pictures of dead babies in a Vietnam combat zone to portray a message about the brutal battles taking place. Another protest in Berkeley California included several hundred people carrying a black coffin. The most gruesome of 1965 was Norman Morrison, father of three, who doused his complete body, head to toe, with kerosene and set himself on fire, as a protest to the war.

Leaders of the protest marches, with bullhorns blaring, stirred the crowds with antiwar messages and chants such as "One two, three, four! We don't want your fucking war!", "Draft Beer not boys", "Hell no, we won't go", "Make love not war" and "Hey, hey, LBJ, how many kids did you kill today?"

The antiwar demonstrations originally were predominately a "youth movement" as the draft age boys targeted to fight the war, were joined by classmates, their older siblings and girlfriends in the protests. They were intended to be vocal, peaceful, "Free Speech," demonstrations meant to bring attention to what they felt was an illegal and immoral war.

The youth of America were supported by many national celebrities, singers, and song writers as they too joined in the anti-war movement.

Among the celebrities supporting opposition to the war was Cassius Clay, U.S. Olympic Boxing Gold Medal Winner, reigning World's Heavyweight Boxing Champion and considered to be the greatest boxer in the history of the sport. He embraced the religion of Islam, changed his name to Muhammad Ali and refused, based on his religious principles, to be conscripted into the U.S. Military. For this action he was sentenced to five years in prison but was released on appeal by the United States Supreme Court. Muhammad Ali did not spend one day in prison.

The Smothers Brothers, Tom & Dick, had a weekly television variety show, which included openly suggestive antiwar messages in their back-and-forth bantering exchanges and comedy skits. Their program was extremely popular, with one of the largest viewer audiences in the country, but also was the one whose original content received the most government censorship.

"War," written by Norman Whitfield and Barrett Strong, sung by Edwin Starr was an anthem for the antiwar movement and a cultural milestone. Its lyrics included War, what is it Good For, Absolutely Nothing...Oh, War, I Despise because it means destruction of innocent lives. War means tears to Thousands of Mothers Eyes when their Sons Fight and lose their lives...War, it ain't nothing but a heartbreaker...War, friend only to the undertaker-Oh war it's an enemy to all mankind...War has shattered many a young man's dreams, made him disabled, bitter and mean, life is much too short and precious to spend fighting wars. War can't give life, it can only take it away...War...What is it good for, stand up and shout it, Nothing.`

The televised support for the protestors emboldened many young draft age men to publicly burn their draft cards as a sign they would rather go to jail than Vietnam. Many did!

Then the "top blew off the tea kettle" on January 31, 1968, when 80,000 NVA and Viet Cong troops invaded 100 towns and cities in South Vietnam in what is known as the Tet Offensive. The up close and personal, door to door, minute to minute, televised bloody brutal fighting of the 60-day Tet Offensive changed the way Americans viewed the war.

At home we watched General Nguyen Ngoc Loan, Chief of National Police, shoot a bullet through the head, publicly executing Viet Cong officer, Nguyen Van Lem. We wretched with, both empathy and sympathy for the innocent fleeing, traumatized and now homeless, residents of errant U.S. bombing raids.

Horrifically, we viewed, with angst, the photo of the naked 9-year-old girl, Kim Puc, running toward the camera on a country road crying and screaming, as the skin on her back was burning from napalm on her body. And, we witnessed the total destruction by U.S. forces of Hue,the royal capital of the country.

These isolated events along with the daily barrage of television footage of the bloody disfigured body strewn streets and bombed out buildings left in the wake of the Tet Offensive just flat out hurt our eyes.

The Vietnam War had become a psychological and public relations battle, one of which the communist forces now had the upper hand.

Divisions over the war received increasing television airtime and the anti-war movement, which had been vilified as Communist inspired in the early years, was now being accepted as a legitimate political movement. Ambitious politicians found this movement to be a platform on which they could gain national prominence, a catalyst to building their careers and exposing it to their benefit.

As the war escalated so too did the frequency of protests, both for and against the war. Those against the war were referred to as, "Doves," while the war supporters were called, "Hawks." The two polarized ideologies clashed in the media and during protests on the streets.

The rhetoric and violence began to escalate, which created a growing interest in public safety. Out of concern for their communities, many city leaders began denying permits for all organized marches whether they were led by Doves or Hawks.

In August 1968, the Democratic National Convention to select their candidate for President of the United States was held in Chicago, Illinois. Mayor Richard J. Dailey, the autocratic style leader of Chicago, intended to showcase his city's achievements to Democrats and the national media. He repeatedly stated; "No thousands will come to our city and take over our streets, our city and our convention" and refused to grant permits for people to legally gather in protest.

To ensure illegal protests would not disrupt the Democratic convention Mayor Dailey enlisted 5,000 National Guardsmen, 5,500 Federal Troops and 12,000 Chicago Police, for a total of 22,500 law enforcement officers. They were strategically located around the convention center area to keep small groups of demonstrators from assembling.

To coincide with the Democratic National Convention, the National Mobilization Committee to End the War in Vietnam and the Youth International Party [Yippies] were planning a "Festival of Life." They were not alone as other groups such as the Students for a Democratic Society [SDS] would join them to total 10,000 rallying in Chicago.

Three days before the DNC, in satirical fashion, the Yippies, led by Jerry Rubin and Phil Ochs, held their own presidential nominating convention with Pigatus, an actual pig, as their candidate.

When they paraded their candidate in front of the convention center all six of the candidate's supporters, along with Pigatus, were arrested. Pigatus became an immediate national photographic figure and media hit, but the tone for control of the streets of Chicago had been set.

On August 28, the third day of the DNC rioting broke out between the police and the assembly when a young man in Grant Park, across the street from the convention center, began lowering the American Flag. The police, incensed at this perceived act of disrespect, severely beat him with their clubs, dragged his shattered body to an ambulance and sent him to a hospital.

Witnessing this unnecessary brutality, the peaceful weaponless onlookers started throwing rocks and bottles at the police. This reaction against the police unleashed a reactionary uncontrollable rage of charged-up anger against the youthful unlawful gathering. The police began recklessly and randomly swinging their clubs, chasing down defenseless protestors and for hours beat bloody anyone not wearing a uniform.

This avoidable antagonistic incident incited what would later become known as the "Police Riot."

Strategically, Tom Hayden, one of the leaders of SDS, encouraged his group of followers to leave the tree-filled Garfield Park for the open area of the public streets. This would ensure the threatening police brutality toward his unarmed participants would not be hidden from the media and would be recorded in full public view.

His group and the other supporters chanted, "Why not give peace a chance?" moved to the streets and into the waiting strategically ranked squads of police. They had been ordered to curtail any act of civil disobedience. As the police shifted to disburse the gathering crowd, they used mace, tear gas, randomly and willfully clubbing all who did not heed their bull-horn messages to disburse.

The former "Festival of Life" peaceful group changed their chant to, "The whole world is watching" as the police continued to brutally attack them in front of the television cameras. The protestors refused to disburse and for five long barbaric days they sustained the barrage of beatings meted out by the police.

After the "police riot" in Chicago was over, 400 protestors had been treated for exposure to mace and tear gas, 1,100 were treated for injuries and one person was killed. Additionally, 36 journalists were injured covering the prolonged skirmish, with one, Dan Rather, being attacked by police inside the convention center.

Watching this brutalization of young American citizens disgusted me in a way I had never felt about our government before. I was fearful these cruel and inhumane actions in Chicago were an embryonic stage to the hatching of a national uprising, which could lead to Civil War.

The actions in Chicago set the stage for the Vietnam War protests. They held several hundred rallies and protests in many cities and at university campuses, (none at Ball State University) across the United States.

The protestors held sit-ins, took over control of administration buildings, daring police to take action and always making sure the television cameras were in attendance. Some protest rallies swelled to over 500,000 participants. At one protest rally over 30,000 former Vietnam veterans joined the ranks of the protestors stating they had lost a lot of their buddies, and the war was senseless.

At another protest rally National Guardsmen were dispatched to protect property and preserve peace. They were armed with rifles and stood shoulder to shoulder along the street where protestors were legally marching. In a symbolic gesture several young college age girls placed long stemmed daisy flowers down the barrels of the National Guardsmen's rifles sending their message of peace.

These Vietnam War protests and rallies became muted to me as my attention had been forced elsewhere.

In September 1968, I received news that my good friend and former roommate James T. [JT] McCafferty had been gravely wounded in Vietnam. JT was a 6'2" all-around athlete, handsome guy, [the girls loved him], and had a great quick wit sense of humor, which kept us laughing even after he had left the room. His father didn't have many details, but told me JT's injuries, still unknown at this time, were not life threatening. However, they were still so severe he had been flown from Vietnam to Japan for extended treatment and possibly some rehabilitation.

I soon discovered combat related traumatic battlefield injuries, like JT's, meant the soldier, once recovered, would be sent back home to the states. JT's fighting days in Vietnam were done.

About the same time, I received a letter notifying me the Selective Service had denied my request for a deferment. My recently petitioned three-month educational extension would have allowed me to finish my final two classes and graduate from BSU.

The government process to engulf me in the war effort was now in full motion. A few days later I received a notice to meet at the Selective Service office in Muncie and take a bus to Indianapolis for a physical examination. A few weeks later I received a formal letter from the Selective Service informing me I was deemed, 1-A, physically fit to serve. Another letter followed shortly thereafter notifying me I was to report for induction into the U.S. Army on December 5, 1968.

During the Vietnam War, like most other wars, there were boys/men who patriotically volunteered to serve their country but were scared and those who were drafted and terrified of their outcome but went anyway. Then, there were a few refusing to serve, cowards, who looked for ways to avoid being conscripted.

These unpatriotic rebellious young men, shirkers, could volunteer in many non-combat ways, but refused to support their country in any manner. I knew three such cowards who found various ways to avoid serving and thus lived their life with this major character flaw.

I will refer to them as the Three Stooges, Larry, Curly, and Moe

The first was my early childhood next door neighbor, Stooge number one, Larry. When he graduated from college, instead of finding a way to support the country and its resources that had educated him, Larry fled the United States to Canada. The Canadian immigration policy was lax, so Larry was able to find refuge in this safe haven and avoid deportation.

Another of my college classmates, Stooge number two, Curly was highly creative in avoiding his potential military obligation. Intentionally, he sought out a female student, we'll call her Clueless, who was majoring in speech and hearing. While they were dating, Curly persuaded Clueless to train him how to fail the hearing test segment of the Selective Service physical examination.

She cooperated by placing him in a soundproof booth, engaging her hearing test equipment and alerting him to the types, pitches, and tonal notes he could expect at his examination. Curly failed the hearing segment of his Selective Service Physical thus he was awarded the status of 4-F, unfit to serve. When he was assured, there would be no recall of the examination, Curly stopped dating Clueless.

Stooge number three, Moe, another college classmate, enlisted the support of a doctor to aid him in avoiding conscription. The only child of overprotective parents, Moe and his family found an anti-war and sympathetic doctor. They paid him to write a letter stating his patient, Moe, suffered from chronic Asthma and it was his opinion Moe would be unfit for the rigors of the military. Once the letter was submitted, Moe was deemed 4-F, unfit to serve.

Unlike the Three Stooges, Larry, Curly and Moe, my personal character, love and respect for my family and commitment to my country meant more to me. I would not avoid the draft and would, with some personal reservations, serve the United States of America.

My Vietnam and Cambodia War

In November 1968, three months after being severely wounded, JT McCafferty returned home to Muncie. Fully clothed he looked the same as before he'd left for Vietnam. But, when JT took his shirt off, his exposed back revealed the deeply scared and pockmark discolored stitched remnants of irregularly shaped metal shrapnel. He had been struck by a targeted mortar projectile.

JT told me his fighting unit was engaging the enemy when he heard the thump of a mortar bomb being shot from its tube. Instinctively he knew it was the enemy's and needed to take swift action in the few seconds he had before the mortar's projectile landed. Not knowing where it would hit, he took refuge next to a tree. JT said the exploding projectile must've struck one of the branches in the tree exploding and spraying the hot detonated shrapnel on him in his defenseless position. The next thing JT remembered was waking up in a hospital. A few days later one of the doctors told J.T., he was being evacuated to Japan for additional surgery, after which he'd be sent home and discharged from the Army.

Now in Muncie, JT was looking for a place to live and knew I had received my orders to report for the December Draft. He asked if he could take my bedroom in the home where I lived with four of our mutual friends. In January, JT told me, he was planning to return to Ball State and finish his final year of school. Of course, I said!

He then reminded me we were both business majors and it would be helpful if I would let him use my classroom books, which he would keep for me. With nothing to move or mess with, again, I said, yes!

In the early morning hours of December 5, 1968, my mother and Father drove me, their 26-year-old son, to the Selective Service Office in the 400 block of South Walnut Street in Muncie. My Mother embraced me and gave me a misty-eyed hug! I received a firm handshake from my father. They both stepped off to the side to watch the short formal proceedings, which were about to take place.

We, the apparent inductees, stood around looking at each other waiting for the next thing to happen. Some of the guys were smiling because they had volunteered while others, draftees like me, were a little dour and less enthusiastic. As our names were called, we were lined up shoulder to shoulder, ten future military men, in two rows. A man, with obvious authority, read a formal statement loud enough for all to hear. We, the objects of attention, were then asked if we accepted the call, in my case the demand, to serve our country. If so, we were, ceremoniously, to take one step forward.

Unlike Muhammad Ali, the World Heavyweight Boxing Champion, who refused the advancing step and was arrested, in staggered unison, we all moved forward. From that moment on, as far as I could envision, my body and life belonged to the United States Army.

With the brief ceremony over, we were ordered by a man in a U.S. Army uniform to get on the Trailways Bus waiting at the curb. One by one we stepped through the door of the bus, which was already half full of future army soldiers.

We were then driven to Indianapolis, offloaded, and ordered into a large two-story brick building with a gymnasium the size of a basketball court. Our bus group was led to a corner of the gym, identification was checked, records were confirmed, names were called, and smaller groups were formed.

My group, of approximately ten men, was ordered down a hallway where we met with 30 similar deer-in-the-headlight men and escorted to board another Trailways Bus. This one, we were told, was taking us to Fort Campbell, Kentucky, wherever that was, for basic training.

After approximately four hours the bus slowed, made a right-hand turn, and went past two brick pillared stanchions hosting a large sign, "Fort Campbell." Our bus drove past row after row of cloned two-story white wood planked buildings. It seemed they extended well into the horizon.

The bus finally stopped at a large warehouse type building where we disembarked and were ordered to walk single file through its front door. Once inside we recognized it as our U. S. Army uniform distribution center. One by one we were herded along a waist high counter, giving our clothing sizes to the supply soldier opposite us. Shirts, pants, socks, underwear, towels, several of each, one jacket and a dress uniform, all in the U.S. Army's favorite color, 'Olive Green.' They, along with two pairs of black boots, were placed on the counter as we moved along the distribution assembly line. The final item we were given was a large heavy duty cloth bag with a shoulder carrying strap.

We were told to put all our new similarly matched clothing and uniforms in it and step outside the door. That would be the last time in the near future we would be told, in a reasonably sounding human voice, to do something.

When we emerged from the distribution center there were four soldiers with stripes and patches noting their rank on each of their uniforms and Smokey-the-Bear style hats. In loud, shouting profanity laced voices never seemed to take a breath, like they had been genetically modified.

The "Drill Sergeants", as they referred to themselves, ordered us to line up shoulder to shoulder in two rows as they verbally dressed us down as being the lowest form of human life they'd ever seen. They continued swearing at us stating, with the miserable pieces of shit they were looking at, we were surely going to lose the war.

The drill sergeants then ordered us to pick up our duffel bags, hold them in front of us, hug them like the girl we'd left back home and run with them. Out of order and out of breath, we were channeled to one of the cloned white two-story wood planked buildings, the barracks, our new home, for the next six weeks.

During this half mile double-time run, which is between a fast walk and slow jog, the drill sergeants got in each and everyone's face calling us all kinds of insulting names, noting our every weakness, stating you're too fucking fat to survive pretty boy. You are nothing but a miserable weak bunch of candy asses, none of you shit cases are going to make it.

They went on spewing profanely based comments connected to every identifying statement. We see nothing but a bunch of rosy cheeked momma's boys, fucking cry-babies and lifelong losers. Jody, your best friend, is already making it back home with your girlfriend. Now, you don't have anything to go home to. The Army is your new best and only friend.

On and on the drill, sergeants shredded each of us with their insulting rants until, at last, we were ordered to stop, form up in orderly ranks and enter our barracks. We were then assigned one of the many equally spaced and parallel arranged bunk beds. At the end of each of our beds was a wooden box approximately 2' X 4' X 18", referred to as a footlocker. In it all of our clothing would be neatly folded, properly spaced, perfectly aligned and specifically located. There was a small space allocated for our shaving supplies and letters from home.

Barking out the direct and specific display of the proper way to make our beds and arrange our footlockers, our newly assigned platoon drill sergeant told us what to wear the next morning and left.

We were expected to empty our duffel bags and perfectly align our clothing as he had instructed. Our platoon of 30 new army soldiers shared confused and frightened glances, across the barracks as we set about to conform our beds and foot lockers to meet his unachievable high expectations.

At about 4:00 am the lights in our barracks flashed on and our drill sergeant began verbally attacking our lazy sleeping asses demanding we get out of our beds, stand at attention next to them and prepare for an inspection of our footlockers. He reviewed each one, dumping several into the middle of the barracks floor, berating the soldiers who had disobeyed his orders, misaligning their specific spacing and folding instructions. His unintelligible but recognizable ranting performance lasted for 30 minutes. As he left, he ordered us to rearrange our footlockers and prepare ourselves to form up outside at 6:00 am for roll call.

At 6:00 am, as ordered, we were standing in formation outside our barracks when a single bugle blaring through our area loudspeaker system played "Reveille."

We snapped to attention and saluted the raising of the American Flag. This was the Army's official notice it was time to start the day.

Our drill sergeant bellowed that we had 60 minutes to return to our barracks to shit, shower and shave and be ready for breakfast. At 7:00 am he ordered us out of the barracks and double timed us to the indoor eating area referred to as the mess hall. There was never any strolling, meandering, or walking allowed in the company area.

As our platoon stood in formation waiting for our turn to enter the mess hall our drill sergeant took this opportunity to inspect his troops for a clean shave. If someone, and there always was a victim, didn't shave close enough they were ordered to double the time it back to the barracks to get their razor.

While the unlucky soldier was retrieving his shave gear, we, the remaining troops, were told how unfit we were for letting our fellow soldier fail his inspection and thus were forced to do push-ups until he returned. Once back, the stubble faced soldier was compelled to dry shave, which was very humiliating, a little painful, with no mirror and positioned facing a plastic soldier sized dummy.

After breakfast we returned to our barracks and were told there would be a full inspection in 30 minutes. During that time, we were to make our beds, buff the floors and clean the shower and bathroom area referred to as the latrine.

When our drill sergeant returned, we were all standing at attention next to our beds and footlockers. He let it be known to us that this was his house; it was his perfect palace, the best castle in the world and not a shit hole like the one we had come from. He held up a large metallic coin and bounced it off one of the beds. When it didn't spring back to him, he tore off the blanket, pillow and sheets and threw them all in a heap.

He then looked at the floor in disgust when he couldn't see his reflection in it. In several places he purposely scraped a black mark on the vinyl floor with his boot. Then he went to the latrine where he found a water spot on the floor. He was incensed and further berated us as he filled a bucket of water and threw it all over the shower and stool area. When he was through further disfiguring his former perfect palace, we were ordered to give him 50 pushups and get his castle back to his regal standards.

This form of harassment and intimidation by our drill sergeant was designed to teach us discipline, cohesion, teamwork and accept a level of responsibility for each other's actions. These strict unrelenting and droning lessons we are learning today may well save our lives in the future.

While our drill sergeant's language and boisterous actions were unsettling to me, I was not affected by it as much as most of the other new recruits. Being 26 years old, having lived outside my childhood home and worked for several years, I wasn't as easily intimidated as were many of the younger soldiers. Also, my brother-in-law, Bruce Russell, had recently finished basic training. He explained to me what I could expect and why.

When our drill sergeant returned, we were formed up outside our barracks and double timed to the first or our many classrooms of the day. In each class an officer instructed us on the U.S. Army way of doing things. We were told, and expected to memorize, the Army Core of Values-loyalty, duty, respect, selfless service, honor, integrity, and personal courage. Additionally, the six Articles of the United States Military Code of Conduct; legal guide for behavior of military members who are captured by hostile forces, was drummed into us, and tattooed in our brain.

Before and after lunch our drill sergeant found time to engage us, his new recruits, in many forms of physical training. We had regular scheduled times on the exercise field where we were required to run a mile for time, do a double set of hand over hand monkey bars, a series of 50 set-ups, 50 push-ups and low crawl, like an alligator for 25 yards. Additionally, and at his discretion, he would make us walk like a duck while inspecting a parking lot for litter, or bark at us to do more push-ups, because a soldier's boot lace was untied, a proper salute to a passing officer was not rendered or the sun was in his eyes and we had not reminded him to bring his sunglasses.

At the end of our first day, we returned to our barracks and stood outside in formation and at attention while a single lone trumpet solemnly played "Taps." Simultaneously the American Flag was lowered signaling the end of the day.

After a rant similar to the previous night our drill sergeant left us to get our boots spit-polish shined, so he could see his face in them, get his castle in order for his next inspection and write a letter home to let our loved ones know we were in the best hands, his, in the U.S. Army. "Lights out at 10:00," he ordered and left.

The next morning when "Reveille" sounded I realized we had actually slept through the night without one of our 'drill daddies' surprise inspections. I slowly and painfully got out of my bed and gradually onto my feet. The first day of basic training had taken its toll on my 26-year-old body. My arm, leg and abdominal muscles were sore, my knee joints inflamed, my eyelids ached and even my toenails throbbed. Every square inch of my physical structure amplified my previous torturous day.

There's no way I thought I could physically make it through another day like yesterday. But I had no choice! There was nowhere to run to, nowhere to hide. So, I slinked my clothes over my exhausted and overtaxed body, laced and tied my heavy cumbersome boots and gingerly started my second day in the U.S. Army.

During the next six weeks our drill sergeant pushed us to our physical limit but began to let up on his rants as we gelled into the cohesive and disciplined unit he relentlessly demanded. We continued to rote learn our classroom lessons, frequented the rifle range to hone our shooting skills, precisely pull the pin and, with careful accuracy throw hand grenades, skillfully climb 50 foot towers and rappel down them, navigate obstacle courses designed to engage and extend every muscle in our body and learn how to execute close quarter ceremonial drills.

58

The final week of basic training, unceremoniously, we were individually given triplicate printed copies of our orders, which included our designated MOS [Military Occupational Specialty], next duty station and date to report. My U.S. Government formally issued a sheet of paper to notify me I had been designated Infantryman [11B] and was immediately and without further notice to report to Fort Polk, Louisiana. This destination was the training station for Vietnam bound soldiers. I was not a happy man!

The next day I boarded a bus, along with 30 other dour-looking soldiers headed for Fort Polk. We understood it was uncomplimentary designated as Fort Puke since it was the last stop for most soldiers before going to Vietnam. When we arrived, I noticed the military base looked eerily like Fort Campbell, with all the barracks aligned neatly in order, but when I stepped off the bus there was a noticeable difference. It was hot!

Fort Polk was at least 30 roasting degrees hotter, with visible steamy penetrating humidity. When I took my first steps, sweat instantly formed on my brow then began to stream down my cheek, flowing to my neck, and cascading down my chest. It was immediately quite clear to me; we had arrived in simulated Vietnam.

We were met by a single drill sergeant, donning his signature, Smokey the Bear Hat. In his most scowling dictatorial bullhorn voice, he berated his new neophytes while simultaneously ordering us into his barracks. He copiously barked out his orientation message, assigning us bunks and wall lockers, and like our former drill sergeant, without seemingly taking a breath.

Sometime during the early morning hours, our new drill sergeant repeated the same dog and pony show we previously encountered by our former drill daddy. Well before reveille, he flashed on the lights, ripped up a few beds, knocked a few lockers on the floor, displacing bedsheets and clothing and swore at us using many of the same profanity-laced recognizable words we'd heard before.

However, this time we, as a group, were not intimidated by his overbearing and domineering actions. Our drill sergeant wanted to firmly establish his command of his new troops. Message sent and received. We knew his end game was to mold us into a cohesive fighting unit, one where each of us, in any given situation, could count on the other to fulfill, to the best of his ability, his responsibility to the team.

The training at Fort Polk was infinitely more defined in its intent, focusing on minutiae details involving multiple styles of fighting techniques, the variety of weapons we would be using, and situational survival skills. The intense preparation was for real!

We rote learned hand to hand combat, as well as coordinating squad, platoon, and company deployment personnel, while engaging the enemy. Tirelessly, repetitiously, and systematically, for time, we practiced taking our weapons apart piece by piece and reassembling them.

One survival skill session was composed of a two-person 24-hour exercise, using a map and compass, a single canteen of water and a live chicken. We were to navigate the terrain, and using the sun, moon, and our compass, locate our assigned safe destination without coming into contact with one of the staff drill sergeants, posing as the enemy.

At every classroom session, whether physical combat, specific weapon orientation or individual survival training, before taking our seats, we were commanded, in a loud unified voice, to state, "No mission too difficult. No sacrifice too great. "Duty First!"

The mental psychological preparation of becoming a surviving combat soldier was directly and subliminally being honed into us several times a day. The indoctrination that we were fighting a justified war against a criminalized enemy was supplanted in the cadence of every marching step, physical fitness exercise, hand to hand combat drill and targeted bullet fired.

Like Greek Gladiators, but with rifles instead of swords, we would enter the arena of war and only one would survive. This was the redundant message repeatedly being sent to us. Survive and thrive. Don't and die.

In our fifth week, the full company of four platoons, three similar to ours, each with their own drill sergeant, were ordered to formation on our parade grounds. Directly in front of our perfect parade formation, the assembled cadre was our company commander. He was standing on an elevated white plank board fenced platform shuffling several sheets of meticulously organized paper carefully positioned on his podium.

He ordered us to stand at ease and succinctly relayed his purpose for our presence. In his hand, he stated were the orders for our next duty station. Our company commander prefaced his roll call by declaring, all soldiers under 18 years of age were legally ineligible to be assigned to war zone Vietnam. A few others, he stated, would serve as replacements at our military bases in Korea and Germany, leaving a small glimmer of hope for a lucky few.

As he called our names, alphabetically, a compassionate sarcastic cheer would be raised, by all, for each Vietnam bound soldier. When one of the under 18's, Korea or Germany directed soldiers' names were announced a loud, envious "Boo", followed their selection. At the end of this brief notification, we were given triplicate copies of our orders and dismissed for the day.

In 1957 an epic movie, "The Bridge Over the River Kwai" won the Academy Award for Best Motion Picture of the year. It was based on a novel written by Pierre Boulle, about a World War ll Japanese prisoners of war camp in Thailand.

At the POW camp the British and American prisoners were ordered, under penalty of torture and possibly death, to build an expansion bridge over the river Kwai. The bridge was designed to accommodate trains carrying war supplies for their enemy, the Japanese troops. There was much discord among the POW's as to the moral validity of their actions in building the bridge, but they did so anyway.

As they daily marched to do their captors bidding, the music in the movie,

"Colonel Bogey March", was played in the background. The simple tune started with a high-pitched whistling Fife, timely joined by a cadence marching snare drum interspersed with a resonating trumpet. It was a catchy and memorable tune.

The morning after we received our orders for Vietnam our schedule was to march three miles to the rifle range for some additional target practice. Upon leaving the company area our drill sergeant started calling his usual marching cadence. I was in the middle of the platoon when my rebellious nature took over and I started whistling the fife's part in "Colonel Bogey March." At first it was my quiet lone singular sound. Then it resonated familiarly with one another Vietnam bound soldier, then another until soon the whole platoon was whistling in unison.

Our drill sergeant initially looked back around his platoon searching for the musical culprits. But as everyone joined in the frivolity, the whistling soon replaced his cadence, and he had no choice but to go along with his still precisely marching troops. After all, what could he do, we were already, against many of our personal private protests, being sent to Vietnam!

During my eight weeks at Fort Polk I was selected, along with six other soldiers, to represent the U.S. Army at three formal military burial ceremonies. Each service was for a solitary young soldier killed in Vietnam.

Outfitted in our full-dress uniform, we traveled to three regional Louisiana communities to carry out the Army's well-rehearsed solemn symbolic ritual for fallen soldiers. At each cemetery we were charged with removing the American Flag draped casket of the deceased honorable soldier from the hearse, carrying him to his gravesite, resting it on the burial casing, firing the 21 Gun-Salute and listening to the lone bugle play "Taps" in the background.

The outpouring of grief of the parents, loved ones and friends at each ceremony over the unexpected loss of their young hero soldier man, whose life was dramatically and tragically cut short, left me with an enormous emotional void.

This same vacant feeling had washed over me April 3, 1968, when my best friend, Sergeant David Carl Thomas, killed in Vietnam, was laid to rest. I was completely cognizant of what lay before me, and potentially my family, as I completed my burial detail duties.

When we left Fort Polk, we were given a 30 day leave and ordered to report to the U.S. Army Vietnam dispersion headquarters in Oakland California. It took me longer than 30 days to get there.

When I returned home, I had four things I wanted to accomplish before I left for my anxiety laden journey, into the abyss of the unknown in South Vietnam.

The first item on my list was easy. Meet with family and friends, get their well wishes and allay any fears they may have for me as I was mentally and physically prepared as well as I could be.

The next matter involved going to my favorite clothing store, selecting a nice suit, and having it altered to fit me perfectly. Then, I made an appointment with

Peoples Studio to have my photograph taken. If I didn't return from Vietnam, I wanted my parents to have a nice lasting color portrait of me.

My third piece of my business was to meet with an insurance salesman and purchase a life insurance policy. I carefully reviewed the policy presented to me to insure there was no "killed in war" exclusion clause. I assigned the $25,000.00 life insurance policy to include $5,000.00 to each of my four brothers and sisters and $5,000.00 to my parents. As a family we didn't have much money and, at the time, $5,000.00 would make a big difference in their lives.

The final detail on my agenda was to extend my leave from the Army for an unauthorized six additional days. My brother-in-law, Bruce Russell, preceded me in basic training, went to officer's candidate school, and a few other special training courses. He was scheduled to be home a few days after my assigned departure date, and I specifically wanted to say goodbye to him. He would soon be going to Vietnam as well and this could be a final goodbye for either or both of us.

When I arrived in Oakland, the U.S. Army agents were full of consternation at my late arrival. They said I would receive an "Article 15", military penalty, when I landed in Vietnam. However, nothing was ever said about my late arrival issue again as the Army was happy to have another ready, able, and trained soldier to fight in their ongoing war.

Our airplane went dark as we approached then began to descend into Bien Hoa Vietnam. I was sitting next to the window and was astonished at the volume and numerous viewable fighting positions below sending out tracer rounds. With every fifth bullet tipped with a pyrotechnic red charge, the sky below me looked like a vast streaming scarlet laser light show. There was no doubt I was about to enter the intense violent Vietnam War Zone.

As we disembarked, wire mesh protective windowed buses were waiting to transport us to our new divisional headquarters. On the tarmac, we formed up as a group and our individual names were called.

When I heard my name, it was assigned to the 1st Calvary Division [Airmobile]. This special elite fighting unit, I was to discover, used helicopters for air assault in search and destroy missions in dense jungle areas. The assignment was a major revelation to me. I didn't know if being in such an aggressive fighting unit would be good or bad for me. In either case I had no choice in the matter.

At the 1st Calvary Division Headquarters, we were told we would have a three-day orientation and survival training program, assigned our weapon and necessary equipment. We would then join a fighting unit in the field of combat.

The first night at divisional headquarters, after watching a movie, I decided to walk around the well-guarded, secured open area and think through the survival techniques I had learned that day. It was swelteringly hot, muggy and I labored to breathe.

At dusk I saw a lone solitary figure approximately 50 yards away from me walking directly and with intent toward the dining mess hall. He was the filthiest, most unsightly person I had ever seen in my entire life. His uniform was almost indistinguishable from enmeshed red clay, grimy dirt and all stained with dried sweat. He looked like he'd been wrestling with pigs! His camouflage helmet cover was torn, pieces loosely hanging and crusty with muck. The soldiers' face was unrecognizable from dripping sweat, dirt splotches and stubble beard. His rucksack caused him to be hunched over from its weight and his M-16 rifle was slung on his shoulder.

The grimy soldier attempted to open the mess hall door, but it was locked. Seeing an interior light glowing at the far end of the building, he plodded in that direction. He tried the rickety screen door, locked again. He pounded on it and got the attention of the cleanup duty cook. He told the cook he was hungry. I could hear him say he'd been traveling all day, without food and wanted something to eat. The cook told him the mess hall was closed and he needed to return in the morning for breakfast.

The dingy soldier argued with the cook that he wanted to eat, now! The cook continued to refuse to feed him, and the conversation heated up to the boiling point. The soldier became very profane and animated in his gestures. With no concession from his adversary, he leveled his weapon, pointed it at the cook and told him, point blank, you either fucking feed me or die, where you're standing. At this point, the cook acquiesced, let the soldier in the door and fed him. Nobody messes with a hungry grunt!

Little did I know that within a week I would not only look like the mangy soldier but would be similar to him in many unexpected but deliberate actions.

Two days later I was assigned to Charlie Company in the 5th Battalion of the 7th Calvary Regiment, made famous by the imprudent Lt Colonel George Armstrong Custer. I was given a rucksack filled with necessary survival gear, supported on an aluminum frame; heavy enough to make me hunch over like the hungry soldier at the mess hall.

Among the items given to me were a trip flare and a claymore mine. The trip flare was a small metallic device with a flexible thin wire extending from it. At ankle height, a few feet away, the wire would be attached to a stake in the ground. When the wire was crossed it pulled the trigger pin of the flare causing a small firecracker like pop and red flash powder light. The trip flare was used to signal a breach in our perimeter.

The claymore mine was a directional anti-personnel device, which contained about 700, 1/8-inch steel balls, propelled by C-4 explosive. The mine was remote controlled by a handheld clacker. When squeezed together it created a small electric charge detonating the destruction of anything in its patterned kill zone.

Within 30 minutes of receiving my equipment, including an M-16 rifle, I was aboard a resupply helicopter full of food and ammunition heading out to my combat unit. About an hour later when the helicopter landed, I immediately realized I was in machete penetrating dense green jungle. There had marginally been enough room carved out of green bamboo, vine engulfed entrapment for a lone helicopter.

I followed the food and ammo to the waiting Charlie Company Commander. He briefly greeted me, stated how much they needed some replacements and had his 1st Sergeant include me on their roster. Once signed in, the 1st Sergeant pointed me in the direction of my concealed platoon. I was about 25 feet from meeting my waiting platoon leader when I heard the pop of a trip flare. Approximately three seconds later I heard the blast of a claymore mine. I saw my platoon leader instinctively dive for the ground and I did likewise.

Immediately following the detonation, our machine gunner began spraying the area of the claymore blast with a systematic traversing field of impenetrable M-60 bullets. At least two enemy soldiers returned automatic fire with their Russian made AK-47 rifles. The distinctive rapid staccato crack, crack, crack of their bullets being fired filled the air, penetrating the dense jungle foliage around us.

Pinpointing the enemy's general location, two of our men, positioned with the machine gunner, returned fire with their M-16 rifles. The markedly different pop, pop, pop of the M-16 bullets clearly signaled the violent difference in our missions.

After about five minutes of the close-range firefight, the overpowered enemy disengaged. They left behind one dead Viet Cong soldier and a never to be followed blood trail, designating a wounded guerrilla fighter had fled the battle.

When I saw orderly movement being restored in our area, I shakenly reported it to my platoon leader. I had been on the ground in Vietnam for less than an hour and already had hot enemy bullets blazing over my head.

During my brief orientation, my platoon leader told me they had encountered the Song Be area Viet Cong at least once a day in short but sometimes deadly hit and run confrontations. He said, due to the continuing threat in this location we were on hyper alert status. Obviously, I thought!

An hour later we were ordered to move out about two hundred meters to some higher ground and set up our camp for the night. As we approached the top of the hill we inspected, then passed four freshly constructed, well camouflaged Viet Cong bunkers. They overlooked a small narrow valley below. Their sturdy overhead construction and multiple well placed firing ports made me cringe with the thought that it's a good thing we had not taken the low ground and walked into their trap. Each bunker was sized to fit two to three enemy VC's, giving me an idea of the extent of force we may have been and could actually be up against.

I was a little confused why; given our recent conflict with them, the bunkers were abandoned. Perhaps, I thought, they were waiting for reinforcements or maybe they had decided to pull out of the area.

My puzzlement of the situation was quickly answered when the crack, crack, cracking sounds of several AK-47's filled the air. The enemy had circled around us and assaulted our rear-guard position. They had caught us as we were setting up for the night and our perimeter had not yet been secured. No trip flares. No claymores. They were in control of the battle.

Our M-60 machine gun and several M-16's immediately returned their fire, and the exchange of volleys was under way. The pop, pop, pops were answered by the crack, crack cracks, with long barrages from our machine gunner.

Fortunately, our company commander had called in our night defensive position, so our battalion headquarters had our exact longitude and latitude map coordinates. Within five minutes we heard the blast of our strategically located 105 mm howitzer artillery ordnance landing close to our rear-guard position. At least 20 rounds landed, boom, boom, and boom. Overpowered, the enemy disengaged and fled.

Once the turmoil surrounding the fight settled, we prepared our night defensive position by digging a foxhole, approximately 6' long 2' wide and 2 ½' deep. The one night only trench would provide defensive protection for three of our squad members. Simultaneously, we positioned a trip flare and claymore mine approximately 40 feet directly in front of our foxhole.

As I was clearing a few feet of the jungle floor for my personal sleeping space my squad leader told me I would have night guard duty from 2-4 am, at his foxhole. It was located 20-30 feet directly to the left of ours. The nightly perimeter protecting sentry assignment began at dusk, 8 pm and extended to dawn, 6 am.

At 2:00 am someone shook my shoulder and told me it was time for guard duty. Crawling on our hands and knees he led me to the assigned foxhole and disappeared into the dark of the jungle night.

I sat motionless on the rim of the foxhole extending my senses to hear any movement, see any shadow or smell anything that might alert me that something could be amiss. There was nothing! I strained to ensure my judgement of the surrounding environment was accurate. No movement, none, just the serene calm of a tranquil jungle night.

Two hours of the gentle silence later another soldier told me he was relieving me of sentry duty, and I could go catch a couple hours of sleep.

I started my hands and knees crawling back to my foxhole, using my inner compass as my only navigation device. The canopy of the jungle created an in penetrable condition so devoid of any natural light I could barely see the outlined figure of my hand in front of my face.

I had crawled, seemingly, 15 to 20 feet in the perceived direction of my foxhole when I seized up and stopped. I couldn't see anything. There was no path to my hole, no string to follow, no visual or physical hint I was going in the right direction. I sensed I was close, but nothing. I strained my eyes to see any reference point I could trust.

The tiny glint of phosphorus from decomposing vegetation on the jungle floor gave me hope there would be some path back to my hole. But it too showed no significant pattern to offer me security in my direction. I felt the ground around me for loose dirt from the digging of my foxhole. Again, nothing!

Not knowing where I was, I couldn't call for assistance. The enemy could possibly hear me and begin shooting in my direction. If I moved further, I could find myself in a crossfire between the possible VC positioned beyond our trip flares, and the guard on duty at our squad leader's foxhole.

After thinking through my options, I decided there was too much risk to take a chance and move further in any direction. So, I calmed myself. Remembering an old instructor's message, "Be Calm, Be Cool and Be Collected," I sat stationary breathing quietly and waited for daylight.

When enough light filtered through the jungle canopy I gazed to my right and saw my foxhole a mere three feet from me. I said nothing as I moved an extra five feet to gather up my sleeping gear and prepare to begin my second day in the combat zone of South Vietnam.

As we prepared to move out, I groaned as I slung the aluminum framed rucksack up on my back. Hoisting the 85-pound weight, life necessity rucksack, with a moan was one of the reasons we, the infantry, were referred to as "grunts".

Our point man, the first person in our column, chopped, hacked, and pushed aside the dense jungle vegetation as we moved slowly, cautiously looking for signs of the enemy. After about two hours we stopped to take a break. I watched as the men around me systematically lit a cigarette, took off their rain and sweat soaked camouflaged uniforms and burned embedded leeches from their body. This leech cauterizing activity would occur two to three times a day.

After two more days in the Song Be area without finding any major enemy encampments, we were told we'd be deployed to another more active location. The next morning four helicopters landed one by one to lift us off to another remote jungle site.

For the next 18 days we combed the jungle terrain, beneath the concealing canopy, an abandoned NVA hospital, a troop training site, and a few other vacant enemy facilities. The NVA sentries knew we were coming and alerted their men. The inhabitants of their interspersed encampments were most frequently gone by the time we arrived.

After 21 days our company was airlifted from our jungle deployment to Quan Loi, a semi secure South Vietnam 1st Calvary base camp. There I was able to get my first real shower, not one provided from the daily rain, in over three weeks. It felt great! I was able to wash almost a month's build-up of filth, muck and sweat from every appendage, digit and crevice of my body with a bar of soap. Not one inch of my physique was missed. I shampooed my matted hair and shaved my sun blotched face. Then I got a full clean uniform, including socks, a grunts very important necessity. If I hadn't been in South Vietnam, I would have thought it was Christmas.

However, I was still an infantryman, and this was not a three-day vacation. It was just a less stressful situation. By day I was put to work doing odd jobs such as filling sandbags and cleaning weapons. At night, our unit was required to guard the perimeter of Quan Loi, a relative benign assignment since there had been no enemy activity there since the Tet Offensive in February.

On July 20, 1969, three squad members, Ted, Ronnie, Jerry, and I were ordered to the night guard duty on a large perimeter protecting bunker. It was about the size of a one car garage. The bunker was built using 6" X 6" wood posts, covered with durable sheet metal and topped off with three layers of sandbags. It was a total contrast to our dirty foxholes. The strategically built bunker had an open-air top level to view the large expanse in front and on either side of us. The bottom, half underground dugout cellar like room, was constructed with firing ports for close in fighting. It also had four rope strung bunks for sleeping.

The semi-permanent structure's armament included several clackers for the many claymore mines in front of us, a few hand grenades, an M-79 Grenade launcher, an M-60 machine gun and our four M-16 rifles. It was well fortified, adequately manned and facetiously referred to by a hand painted sign, "Phase One of the VC Obstacle Course".

Four days earlier, on July 16th, I discovered the Apollo 11 Astronauts, Neil Armstrong, Buzz Aldrin, and Michael Collins had lifted off from Kennedy Space Center heading for the first ever Moon landing. I was really excited about the space race between the Russians and the Americans. To think we could do the previously considered impossible miracle of putting a man on the Moon was something I someway had to witness.

So, I borrowed a squad member's small transistor radio, acquired some used batteries from our platoon RTO man and jerry-rigged them together. I wanted to be able to listen to as much news coverage of the Moon flight as possible.

It was a beautiful clear sapphire blue star filled night on the bunker in Quan Loi, hot but comfortable. I gazed through the protective concertina wire strung in front of me while I listened to the narration of the hour by hour, segued to minute-to-minute progress of the Apollo 11 spacecraft's mission.

My bunker guard mate and squad member, Ted, was becoming annoyed with my enthusiastic pronouncements of the moon landings progress and began to argue with me. He religiously argued that if man were meant to be on the Moon, God would have put him there. He pressed his point, saying the Moon landing will be a failure because God doesn't want man on the moon. He wants man to stay on the Earth.

I responded that if God didn't want man on the Moon, he wouldn't have given him the knowledge and tools to get there. Arguing my position further, I said, the Russian's are trying to do the same thing; we are just beating them to the punch. Adding, we would not waste the time, money, and materials if we didn't think we could achieve this goal of putting a man on the Moon.

The more the progression the radio broadcasted; the more aggressive Ted fumed over his belief. He became loud and animated to the point I felt he may lose his self-control and it could become a physical confrontation. With all the killing weapons within arm's reach of us I felt it was better to extricate myself from this argument. So, I went below in the bunker and had one of the other guys relieve me.

Around 6:15 am, July 21, 1969, in South Vietnam, I heard Neil Armstrong say, "That's one small step for man and one giant leap for mankind." A man had indeed landed on the Moon. I was extremely excited to have been able to listen to that famous historical event. I would never forget where I was when man first landed on the moon!

The next day four Huey helicopters air lifted us out of Quan Loi to some remote indiscernible jungle destination to continue our assigned search and destroy mission.

On the morning of September 7, our squad leader told me it was my day to walk point! With a machete in one hand and an M-16 in the other I began the day slowly and laboriously hacking and wending my way in the direction I was given.

Around noon I came to an opening in the jungle terrain. I took a few steps into it and realized the area in front of me had recently been used as a night defensive position by another U.S. Army unit. There were a few foxholes strategically located to my front which expanded to both sides of the small open space. I stealthy moved forward two or three steps to more closely survey the area for anything unusual. The opening expanded as I moved, and I could now see where a company sized unit within the past week had dug in for the night.

As I silently moved, I sensed something in front and to the right of me. I froze! I focused on the area and saw some subtle motion in the opening. Then in the distance three NVA appeared. They seemed to be actively searching the area for signs of the previous army's activities. They were close together moving in our general direction. I hand signaled two of my squad members to stay low and join me. They crawled to my position. I explained there were three NVA soldiers approximately 50 yards from us and pointed in the direction they were located.

I told them on my command we would rise up together, site them in and open fire. When we rose up, an anxious quick fire by one of the guys alerted the enemy. We followed with several more shots in their direction, but they scattered into the nearby foliage eluding our contact.

As the sound of our gunfire echoed through the once silent jungle our squad and platoon leaders radioed each other giving details of our brief encounter with the enemy. Our Charlie Company Commanding Officer frantically radioed our platoon leader reading him the riot act for allowing us to force contact with the enemy. He demanded to know if we had killed anyone. We were confused!

Our C.O. raised hell with our platoon leader, who then sent the message forward to us that Ho Chi Minh, the Communist leader of North Vietnam, our number one enemy, had died a few days earlier. In order to allow the North Vietnamese time to honor his passing, a three day ceasefire had been mandated.

He further stated if we had killed any of the enemy we could have been charged with Murder.

Murder! What the hell did they mean we could have been charged with Murder. If there was a three day ceasefire to commemorate the death of Ho Chi Minh, why were we moving in a free fire zone? Why hadn't we been told of the three-day ceasefire? Why weren't we sitting in place having tea? We were pissed!

After about an hour of heated and confusing discussion I was told one of the other guys was taking my place to walk point. Our C.O. told us we were going to move about two meters, which in this dense area would take approximately four hours. Then we were going to set up for the night.

As we were establishing our night defensive position, digging our foxholes, and setting out our trip flares and claymores, we received a startling radio message. The rear platoon had not posted a sentry and an NVA soldier, who had been following us, inadvertently walked inside our perimeter. There was so much confusion with the situation, seeing an enemy soldier in our midst; he had run away into the brush unscathed.

An hour later I had just finished setting out our night defensive trip flare and claymore when, in the distance, I heard the 'Thoomp' of a large 81-millimeter mortar bomb being fired. There was no mistaking the distinctive bellowed sound of the enemy's large projectile weapon. I had five to ten seconds before the high-arching trajectory round would make a vertical descent and find its target.

I scurried to our fox hole to find it only half dug and two of my squad members, Jerry, and Ted knee high already in it. There was no room for me, the third person. So, I splayed myself flat on the ground becoming a minor exposed ridge in the dirt around me.

A few seconds later the mortar bomb projectile splashed down with a roaring 'Boom' inside our company's perimeter. It landed about 75 feet behind our half-dug foxhole but close enough to rattle the area around us. The enemy's forward observer, perhaps the one who had wandered into our perimeter, now knew he had correctly pinpointed our night defensive position.

The NVA forward observer communicated the successfully located landing of the first bomb projectile back to his attacking unit, who then engaged two more 81-millimeter mortar bomb weapons in our cross haired direction. Within two minutes of the first exploding projectile hitting us, I heard the scary most petrifying sound of 'Thoomp,' 'Thoomp,' 'Thoomp'! Now, three enemy mortar bomb projectiles were heading our way. A few short seconds later there were three loud 'Boom,' 'Boom,' 'Boom's and the first volley landed within a 50-foot radius of the earlier fiery hot shrapnel exploding projectile.

The enemy, satisfied with their forward observer's zero in report, now fully engaged in their firing mission. They loaded and fired their targeted deadly mortars in a more rapid succession. The three synchronized 'Thoomp,' 'Thoomp' 'Thoomp's, were now being repeated before the three 'Boom,' 'Boom,' 'Boom's landed inside our perimeter. They were firing as fast as their team of 15-20 men could reload the three tubes.

We were totally defenseless against the continuous successive volleys of the three enemy mortars. We were at their mercy, with no quarter to be given. We were forced to wait out our relentless enemy's offensive barrage.

The search and destroy hunters had themselves become helpless targets!

After about 30 to 35 aerial projectile explosive bombs had been fired from each of the three tubes, one for each of the one hundred men in our company, the attack suddenly stopped. The sun had set; the shelling had ceased. It was now dark inside our perimeter. Some beams from flashlights switched on and the multiple cries for medics broke the brief eerie silence.

The mortar bomb attack had been directed to the rear of our foxhole position. However, two exploding projectiles had struck a large tree within 20 feet to the right of our position and shrapnel had sprayed down all around us. We each asked the other, "Are you ok? Shaken but luckily, we were. No medical attention would be needed for the three of us.

Our company of 100 men carried one 81-millimeter mortar tube as an offensive weapon, with a five-man support team carrying two-three projectiles each. We had ferociously been attacked by three 81-millimeter mortar bomb weapons savagely dispersing approximately 100 projectiles.

The speed with which the NVA had organized and launched their attack, bringing three mortar tubes with 100 plus projectiles, with its surgical accuracy, was astounding and almost incomprehensible. We had stumbled into a major NVA military offensive operation.

This enemy was systematically coordinated, well trained, fully prepared, fast acting and overly aggressive. The search and destroy hunters were now being surgically decimated.

The enormity of the force used against us meant we were, prior to the attack, outnumbered at least three to five men to one. But, given the presently unknown number of dead and wounded from their fierce attack, the ratio of us versus them could even be worse.

We needed to prepare for a follow up ground attack, which, given their strength in numbers, I felt was imminent. We had one claymore in front of us and I felt I needed to add at least one more. I didn't want the enemy to overrun our position. I did not want to become a casualty of this engagement.

So, I grabbed another claymore and decided to locate it close to the one I had placed a short hour earlier. It was pitch black dark. I couldn't see anything in the jungle entanglement in front of me. Resourcefully I used the wire from the clacker as a guide to help me locate the other claymore.

I slowly and carefully crawled on my hands and knees feeling my way into the deeper jungle darkness using the claymore clacker wire as my only guide. It was very dense so I couldn't see more than a few feet. I could hear movement from the enemy less than 100 feet in front of me. But there were no lights to distinguish their exact location. I wondered how they could see to move, and I couldn't.

I was scared! I thought, are they massing their forces to attack our position? What if they attack while I'm out in front of our squad's foxholes? I could be caught in crossfire between our guys and the enemy. I knew I was doing the right thing to better fortify our position. I just wanted to get back to my foxhole unnoticed and prepare for the impending ground attack.

I located my first claymore and stuck the second one in the ground a few feet from it. I felt a little better knowing our position had another massive enemy repellant. Then I quickly and quietly retraced the clacker wire back to our foxhole.

When I reached our foxhole Jerry and Ted had finished digging and expanding our dirt fortress. We then dropped down into it and began to prepare ourselves as best we could.

We checked our M-16's and 20-round magazines to insure they were ready to fire. Then we each laid out two stacks of three additional magazines precisely close for rapid ejection of the used one and reloading of the replacement. We placed three hand grenades next to the claymore clackers in front of us. We were armed and ready!

A half hour after the mortar bomb barrage lifted, we heard a helicopter coming in the distance. About 75 feet behind me a white phosphorus illumination flare popped. The Medevac Helicopter located the bright light and hovered over the jungle canopy. Their search beam light shone directly down into the extraction area and illuminated the space as a long rectangular basket, attached to a retractable cable, was lowered to collect our dead and wounded.

The Medevac Helicopter hovered as the basket was raised and lowered several times. When the first Medevac left another one came and took its place. We could see the baskets of our dead and wounded buddies being lifted through the bright penetrating flood light. The medevacs returned and left again. And again! It was gut-wrenching, heartbreaking, and a most eerie sight!

In the reality of the moment, we felt the enemy would strike at any time. With the medevacs gone they could now attack us using total darkness as their background. We were all on alert. Claymore clackers in one hand and M-16 in the other, there would be no guard shifts tonight. We were all on 100% alert!

We nervously waited and waited. The tense night minutes ticked into hours. Maybe the enemy was going to wait until dawn and attack us? We discussed every situation we could think of, just to be prepared and to stay ready.

As the morning sun started penetrating the jungle canopy, we nervously watched every stalk of bamboo, every inch of the brush in front of us for the first sign of enemy movement. Staring into the jungle foliage strained our eyes hoping we would see the first sign of their attack before they advanced on our position. We thought our eyes might be playing tricks on us as we looked for movement but saw none.

The late morning sun shone bright on our night defensive position. There had been no attack by the superior forces of the enemy. We didn't understand their inaction. Maybe they got a late message that Ho Chi Minh had died and there was a three day ceasefire!

After we finished an unimaginably quiet breakfast, we rucked up to move a few meters. Around noon our point man discovered a fresh trail, so our C.O. ordered our squad to set up an ambush on it.

We were supposed to be recognizing a three day ceasefire. We didn't understand this aggressive offensive order, but we did as we were told.

Two hours later we heard the pop of a trip flare. Then there was at least a five second delay before the claymore was blown. That was way too long of an interval before the 'pop and blow'. Any enemy would be 25 yards away in that amount of time. They would be out of the dense jungle kill zone.

Our machine gunner began strafing the area to see if there was contact with the enemy. No enemy fire was returned.

Jerry and I were closest to the ambush site, so we quickly but quietly worked our way to it. We found Ted, for whatever reason, by himself. Huge Leadership mistake, Huge! No ambush should ever have just one soldier. The chance of being outflanked or overrun was way too risky. We were appalled by this tactical mistake.

I told Jerry we should inspect the area where the trip flare and claymore had been detonated to see if there was a body, blood trail or any sign of the enemy. We slowly moved our way up to the claymore steel ball Swiss cheese looking site to find no sign an enemy soldier had tripped the flare wire.

Then, in the silence of the jungle we heard the low muffled moan, "Help me, Help!" Thinking a lone NVA soldier had been wounded, I told Jerry we should move very slowly and cautiously toward the moaning "Help me" sound. We inched our way off the trail and into the dense jungle. We couldn't see more than 10 feet in front of us.

After searching step by step moving about 20 feet, the "Help me" cry sounded again. But this time it seemed to have moved a little further away from us. We went another 15 feet deeper into the jungle, away from our ambush site to hear the weakened pleading sound again. And again, the moan seemed to move just a little bit further away from us.

Sensing a possible luring ambush by the NVA, Jerry and I decided to give up our humanitarian mission and return to our unit. We reported to our squad and platoon leaders the failed ambush and the clear "Help me" cry of a possible wounded NVA soldier at the ambush site.

Our Squad and platoon leaders then forwarded our report to the C.O. He responded with his interpretation of the incident that it must've been a wild pig on the trail that popped the trip flare. Wild pigs don't cry for help! Our C.O. was totally incompetent and a total jerk!

After the three day ceasefire ended our squad and platoon action reports were submitted to our company headquarters. Their review recommended me to be awarded accommodation for Valor. The Distinguished Service Award stated, "I distinguished myself by heroism in sustained combat operations against hostile enemy forces......" It was ironic, a mere three days earlier I was chided for my actions and now I was applauded as a hero. This was not the first nor would it be the last combat medal I would receive.

Our next mission was going to be another month long; no one geographically would know where we were type again. We were flown into a heavy canopy that couldn't see anything below in the jungle area, with barely enough space to land a lone helicopter.

After being deployed for nine days we were informed, for whatever reason, our regular three-day resupply helicopter would not be able to meet us for an additional three days. This meant we were going to have to survive on what food and water we already had for six days instead of three. Ammo was not a problem as we hadn't yet engaged the elusive enemy!

On a previous occasion we had used a helicopter-based ruse to ferret out the slippery unsuspecting enemy. When they thought we had flown out of their active high traffic area, they emerged from hiding and our concealed ghosted troops sprang a successful ambush.

I was beginning to think; not bringing a helicopter to our remote inactive location might be a different type of ploy to get the enemy to relax into making a strategic maneuvering mistake. However, we were to discover this was not the purpose of our delayed resupply this time.

On our fifth night, anxiously anticipating our resupply the next day, everyone was out of food and water, except me. On every mission I had always planned for the best but prepared for the worst. I had actually allocated my food and water to last at least four extra days.

As we were setting up our NDP I took my final canteen cup of water, heated it, and added powdered chocolate to make a refreshing serving of rare jungle hot chocolate. Jerry and I were sitting next to our freshly dug foxhole passing my piping hot chocolate filled canteen cup back and forth when Ted walked up to join us.

He asked us what we were drinking. I told him it was jungle hot chocolate. Ted was eager to have some, so we handed him the canteen cup. He took a quick sip savoring the hot aroma filled rare treat. Ted asked, since everyone was out of water, how did we find enough to make hot chocolate.

I said, "Ted, I have always conserved my food and water rations. We're always told we're going to be resupplied every three days, but what if for some reason our resupply source was interrupted. So, to be on the safe side, I have always prepared myself to ration all my supplies to last longer and be prepared just in case I ran into a situation just like this one."

I continued the what if's with," What if we became separated from our other fighting men and had to forage, find a way back to them or search for a friendly 1st Calvary Fire Base, which would surely be several jungle infested miles away." He nodded his head in affirmation and took another sip of the rare jungle hot chocolate. Smiling toward me, Ted said he appreciated my frugal rationing efforts. The sharing moment, the jungle hot chocolate and the camaraderie was an uncommon small pleasure in a very scary place.

In November, our platoon was preparing to set up our night defensive position when a disagreement erupted between our new unseasoned platoon leader, 1st Lt. Gereke and the four combat proven Sergeant Squad leaders. Our point man had discovered an enemy footpath trail and Lt. Gereke wanted to set up a night ambush on it.

The squad leaders agreed with the night ambush, but they disagreed with Lt. Gereke's method of troop deployment on the trail. Lt. Gereke wanted to set up our platoon parallel along the side of the trail, with the ambush directly in front of the extended platoon's position. The experienced squad leaders wanted to set an ambush at each end, perpendicular to the trail, with our platoon in the middle. Their method was our usual recommended night defensive position.

Not happy with their opposition, Lt. Gereke asked me what I thought of his NDP concept. I was amazed he would ask my opinion! All four squad leaders outranked me, so I was confused why he had asked my advice.

Encouraged by Lt. Gereke, I looked at the trail and walked up and down it at least twenty feet each way. I noticed the trail had not been used in about two weeks. This meant the enemy traffic had been interrupted by another army unit, air force bombing raid or some other reason for its likely recent abandonment. Overriding our squad leader's sound judgement, I told Lt. Gereke his NDP concept would work at this site.

After an uninterrupted night with no enemy contact, Lt. Gereke asked me, the next morning, what I now thought of his NDP set up. I explained my observation of the likely abandoned trail. I also told him we were okay last night, but the squad leader's NDP concept was actually the correct one to use. He appreciated my insight and honesty.

Two weeks later Lt. Gereke sent for me. He told me he had watched me in our combat operations, recognized my team leadership and had reviewed my file. He said based on my performance and credentials he selected me as his platoon's Soldier of the Month. He further stated that in the evening each platoon's Soldier of the Month representative would be interviewed by all Charlie Company Officers.

The soldiers, based on their military knowledge, field experience, education, and poise, selected by the officers would be sent to the battalion headquarters. There each of the battalion's five company's selections would compete for the "Battalion Soldier of the Month."

At the meeting I was selected to represent Charlie Company at the battalion challenge. The next day when the resupply helicopter left to return to headquarters, I was on it.

Later that day I reported to the Tactical Operation Command, aka 1st Calvary 5th Battalion Headquarters, for my interview. I was told I was too late. The contest between the four company Soldiers of the Month representatives had been held earlier in the day.

Disappointed, I started to leave the TOC when the battalion's top sergeant stopped me. He told me since I missed the formal proceedings, he would give me my choice of three unbelievable in country noncombat opportunities. They were 1] attend Bob Hope's show, an American entertainer at Christmas, 2] go to Vung Tau for a three day in country R & R, 3] become the battalion commander's, Lt. Colonel Sanders Cortner, aide. Without missing a single beat, I told TOP, as he was called, I wanted to be the Colonel's aide.

There would be no return to the jungle fighting for me! I was ecstatic! I would now have a roof over my head, bed to sleep in, clean uniform; shower every day and no one shooting at me. The balance of my deployment in South Vietnam would be a total contrast to the previous six months.

LTC Cortner and I hit it off immediately. He had profound respect for me and my service as a combat vet and treated me with much kindness. He always called me Burnie, my adopted Vietnam name, and occasionally asked my opinion of the online soldier's view of certain situations. He made sure everyone in the TOC knew who I was. I was given the full battalion's respect due to him, me as his agent.

In return, I knew and respected LTC Cortner as the competent leader of our battalion. In spite of the opinion of my former C.O., I knew our battalion received the best field support available to a remote air mobile fighting unit. I never doubted the LTC's command and commitment to his troops.

However, LTC Cortner was a career man, a lifer as we, the on-line troops, called them, and I was a draftee. We never discussed our opinions or the politics of the Vietnam War.

One morning, shortly after receiving my new position, the LTC left to monitor the movement of a supply convoy through some active enemy territory. Hovering over the convoy in his helicopter he witnessed the single file column come to an abrupt stop, with the exception of one large, armored M-48 Patton Tank. The 45-ton behemoth's track treads continued rolling over a small leading jeep until it stopped, resting with the crushed vehicle under its enormous metal plated girth.

When the tank backed off the jeep two mangled soldier's bodies were discovered in the wreckage. The unsuspecting accident victims were placed on the LTC's helicopter and flown to the base camp for their final journey home.

On several occasions, I directly and indirectly was made aware of soldiers becoming accidental victims of the Vietnam War. I often wondered how their deaths were reported and what the parents were told of their honorable child's death.

In April 1970, LTC Courtner left our battalion as commander and was replaced by LTC Maurice Edmonds. With that transition occurring the opening of battalion correspondent became available. I elected to take that position so I could write combat action related articles and take photographs for the 1st Cavalair, our weekly 1st Calvary Division Newspaper.

On April 30, 1970, President Richard Nixon addressed the people of the United States of America stating an incursion into Cambodia was imminent. The NVA had been using the Cambodian area adjacent to South Vietnam as a crossing point for their fighters to escape and evade our troops while resupplying theirs.

The United States intelligence reports indicated the North Vietnamese had been stockpiling weapons, ammunition, medical supplies, and food to support the rebellion of the sympathetic Viet Cong against the South Vietnamese ARVN. It was the U.S. Government's and military's plan to extend the fight into this NVA safe haven, resupply and storage area.

On May 4, 1970, several hundred NVA crossed the Cambodian Border into South Vietnam. They attempted a massive surprise attack on Fire Support Base Wood, our 5th Battalion 7th Calvary Headquarters. Earlier in the day LTC Edmonds had received intelligence reports of a planned night attack. In preparation he ordered a defensive "Mad Minute" firing strategy, the first scheduled at 10:45pm.

The enemy was indeed preparing to attack FSB Woods, lurking 100 meters outside the base camp's perimeter. The "Mad Minute" caught them by surprise and their attack quickly became disorganized. After twenty minutes of fierce fighting the enemy disengaged. The NVA left behind 77 dead and three wounded. They also abandoned 15–107-millimeter rockets aimed at FSB Wood, several unspent 60-millimeter mortar bomb projectiles, and many discarded AK-47 rifles. Our losses were six wounded soldiers.

My two-person Quonset hut sleeping quarters took a direct hit from an enemy mortar projectile. Every inch of the small space was perforated with penetrating shrapnel. My sleeping area was totally destroyed. Fortunately, I was not in it.

The next day, May 5, 1970, 18 Huey helicopters appeared on the horizon, landing, loading, and deploying the fighting men of 5th Battalion 7th Calvary, a short distance from FSB Wood into Cambodia. There these gallant soldiers would encounter an enemy fiercer, more engaged, and more protective of the caches they'd spent years accumulating.

The Cambodian Incursion would become an epic battle between two committed major forces. The NVA did not want to lose its enormous, stored cache of revolutionary supporting food, weapons, ammunition, and medical supplies. The invading 5th of 7th Calvary was charged to take them and deny their use in the destruction of South Vietnam.

Every foot of ground gained in Cambodia was contested. The battles were continuous and unrelenting. The persistence of the 1st Cav paid off with their first big find on what was to become known as Shakey's Hill.

After three days of intense fighting up a large foliage covered almost impenetrable hill, Chris Keffalos, aka Shakey discovered a small, camouflaged opening in the dense jungle floor. He immediately realized it was the entrance to a cavernous storage area. When he excitedly stood up, openly exposing his position and loudly announced the find to his camouflaged buddies, Shakey was instantly killed by the cache protecting enemy.

Within three weeks many of the stored NVA caches were discovered in dense jungle hollowed out hills. Among them were thousands of still uncrated rifles, millions of rounds of ammunition, tons of food and rice and medical supplies, enough to supply several hospitals. The caches became so cumbersome and overwhelmingly many were destroyed in place. There was no timely way to get it all out of the mountainous jungle area.

A day before our initial Cambodian invasion, May 4, 1970, university students and many others, mostly youth-oriented groups, across the United States were protesting President Nixon's announcement to send ground troops into Cambodia. They wanted the Vietnam War to end, not be escalated.

At Kent State University in Kent, Ohio, the student protestors were marching and chanting in the common area of the university grounds. The Ohio National Guard had been called out to maintain order during the student protest on the KSU campus. The two groups, students, and National Guard didn't physically clash, but the vocal students did taunt the guardsmen.

At 12:24 pm the soldiers of the Ohio National Guard formed up, knelt on one knee into a firing position and were ordered to shoot the student protestors. During the next 13 seconds 67 rounds from the guardsmen were fired from their rifles, killing four unarmed and unsuspecting innocent students and wounding nine others.

I first heard and then read about the murder of the four student protestors by the Ohio National Guard at Kent State, a day later on May 5. I was incensed! I was pissed! I couldn't believe the military guardsmen sworn to protect our homeland had intentionally and maliciously killed four young U.S. citizens.

Here I was in South Vietnam patriotically serving to protect my country, The United States of America, from the supposed spread of communism and the Ohio National Guard is murdering our innocent citizens. My mind became numb to the incongruity of it all.

I tuned out the war around me and began to plan my exit from South Vietnam.

I checked with the battalion information director and discovered I could get out of the army up to five months early to attend school. So, I wrote a letter to Ball State University inquiring about readmission and found out the second session of summer school classes began around mid-July.

The one glitch in this early out education plan was I would have to extend my 52-week tour in South Vietnam two extra weeks. This was not actually a big deal to me since, in my present capacity as battalion correspondent, I could go anywhere, at any time without reporting to anyone in our battalion area of operations. I was a free floater within the 5th Bn. 7th Cav. My war was over! I just had to serve my time.

On July 8, 1970, I boarded a jet airplane in Bein Hoa, with approximately 200 totally unfamiliar soldiers and unceremoniously left South Vietnam.

The next day, July 9, 1970, one year seven months and five days after my conscripted induction into the U.S. Army, I, Sergeant Charles J. Burnworth was honorably discharged.

Not So Homecoming-- Meeting Linda

On March 16, 1968, in a military mission against a supposed Viet Cong controlled area, Son My Village, Charlie Company of the American Division's 11th Infantry Brigade attacked and brutally killed approximately 500 unarmed villagers.

In the My Lai Hamlet, of the Son My Village, the platoon led my 2nd Lieutenant William Calley, raped, tortured, and massacred over 128 women, children, infants, and old men.

Ironically, of the 500 people murdered, not a single male of military age was found or killed!

The U.S. Army Officers, who ordered the attack, covered up their atrocity, even awarding accommodations to many of their contemporaries for a job well done.

For over a year the massacre was concealed from the public's eye, then in November 1969 the story, "The most shocking episode of the Vietnam War" was exposed. There was an international outrage against the U.S. Military's actions and the attempted cover-up of the mass killings of the 500 unarmed villagers.

After this atrocity was exposed the already inflamed Vietnam War protestors began to refer to Vietnam soldiers as rapists and baby killers. The media released many horrific photos of the defenseless civilian bodies with captions explicitly and vividly describing their ultimate fate.

It was an indelible stain painted on all military veterans!

Media stories and photos were shown of returning Vietnam soldiers being confronted in airports by protesters calling them baby killers, spitting on them and their uniforms.

This was this hostile environment I was coming home to.

I was on full alert for adversarial actions against me as I entered the San Francisco airport wearing my formal U.S. Army dress green uniform. The 1st Calvary Division signet patch, Sergeant Stripes, combat infantry badge with multiple medal decorations, which distinctly displayed my military status.

Without incident the sea of people parted as I approached and was given a wide berth as I navigated my way through the airport. Avoiding eye contact, every person I saw blankly staring in my direction never greeted or spoke to me. I did not receive a single nod of recognition, smile or attempted supportive handshake. My return home to the United States of America was frigid, sterile, and thankless!

When I arrived at my parent's home in Muncie, I took off my uniform, put on benign civilian clothes and hoped to find a way to fit back into the society I left behind a year and a half earlier. It was not to be!

My attitude toward authority figures, big business establishments and the government had fully evolved from admiration, honor and recognition to motive questioning, skepticism, and varying degrees of disrespect.

I didn't trust anyone! My only belief was in myself, and that seemed, at times, in constant fluxion. Feeling confused, disconnected, and disorientated I began a pity party road of self-medication with beer and bourbon as my primary sources.

I returned to Ball State University to finish my degree and sleep walked through my last two classes. Within six weeks of leaving the hostile environment of Vietnam I was a college graduate, still unsettled and confused. Now, what next?

On the pretense of looking for a job, I moved to Indianapolis and took the spare bedroom in JT's apartment. Having shared many of the same post-war experiences, he was the one person I felt reasonably comfortable with.

We didn't talk about the war. We didn't want to relive the bad memories. But on one occasion, after a few beers, I asked JT about the business books I had loaned him, sources for the classes he needed to finish his degree at BSU.

JT looked me straight in the eye, with his quick wit and amazing sense of humor he said, "Joe, I was almost killed over there and looking at your skinny little ass I didn't think you had a chance. So, one Friday afternoon, short of cash, thirsty and needing beer money, I sold your books." We both burst out laughing! It was a great bonding moment, noting mutual respect between two great friends, who could appreciate each other's war experiences.

My actual interest in getting a job was far different than my level of commitment to physically getting one. Early on I developed a philosophy and schedule for seeking employment.

It was perfectly clear to anyone seeking a job that Monday was the recovery day from the weekend, a day for planning the week ahead and certainly not one for interviewing job candidates. Tuesday was dollar matinee day at the movie theater, when the best shows of the season were played at a bargain price. Thursday was a, 'let's get ready for a great weekend day' so the hiring mindset of an employer's representative would be benign. Friday, a great day for mind wandering, envisioning the fun and excitement awaiting the weekend was the last block in the hiring obstacle course.

Wednesday was the perfect day to find a job. So, I scanned the newspaper, found a few prospective job openings and, during the period of three months, had two interviews. One company was interested in me, and I was not interested in them. The other was where JT worked, and they probably felt they had their hands full of Vietnam Vets and passed on hiring me.

After four lame over-self-medicated months, I ended the charade of seeking employment. My pity party had come to an end.

I decided I could either let the Vietnam War ruin my life or I could take charge and begin to command my own destiny.

During a day of clarity, I formulated a plan to attend BSU Graduate School and study toward attaining a master's degree in finance. I submitted my application, which was accepted and soon was a full-time student attending three-night classes a week.

With my savings from Vietnam, very hard to spend money in the jungle, I purchased a Datsun 1600 convertible sports car. A crazy funny guy named Mark, who had played a year of pro football, asked me to live with him in his funky eclectically decorated house. I was in graduate school driving a cool sports car, and substitute teaching at the local high schools. All of a sudden, my life was good again.

Meeting Linda

In March 1971, I went to a friend's apartment to hang out and enjoy some fun communal time. Among the dozen people sitting around yakking about the latest trends, fads, movies, etc. was a standout, show stopping, fabulous looking young woman.

She was physically a beautiful young lady! With jet black shoulder length hair, a radiantly engaging pearl white smile, highlighted with ruby red lips and pleasing dark brown eyes, she was dressed like a New York Model.

She was poised, composed, and had a quiet self-assured dignity in her soft mannerisms. In this small gathering I was captivated by her presence and demeanor. But shortly after I arrived, she and her friend, who I knew as Dee, left. I didn't even know this dazzling showstopper's name.

A few days later I saw Dee and asked her the name of the girl who had been with her. She told me her new roommate's name was Linda Anderson. I asked for and received Linda's phone number. Step one, a success.

The next day I was driving through the BSU campus and saw Linda walking. I offered her a ride and she told me she was going a short distance to her class and declined my offer. Step two, a setback.

A couple of days later I called Linda, asked her for a date this coming Saturday. She declined me again stating she had a date for Saturday. Step three, disappointment. I had a standing date for Friday but decided, before disconnecting our phone conversation and accepting total rejection, to break it and ask Linda to go out Friday. She accepted. Step four, elation.

We mutually decided to go to a movie theater. It featured two great full-length Academy Award winning shows, "Mash" and "Patton". After sitting in the theater for five hours we went to my house for pizza.

Linda, I discovered, was from Elkhart, Indiana. She was an accomplished violinist, had received a full ride music scholarship offer from Miami of Ohio but declined it to attend BSU as a History major.

She had an amazing comprehensive mind and a natural relaxed mystifying sense of humor. With her intellect and wit, she was the funniest person I had ever spent time with. Being such a serious guy, she immediately opened me up, relaxed my inhibitions, and unknowingly was playing me like her fiddle.

She told me she had noticed me at the party by the shoes I was wearing. They were distinctly different and probably none other like them on campus. But to be attracted to me by a pair of shoes. Oh well, whatever the allure, we were together, and we were coordinated.

I did not want this magical night to end. We talked and laughed our way into the wee morning hours falling comfortably asleep on my sofa.

When we woke up in the morning I made breakfast. Not skipping a beat, we continued our humorously connecting, probing conversation where we had left off the night before. During this mutual exchange, our eyes totally affixed, we were intensely cramming to learn about each other in a most consuming way.

I learned her full name was Linda Lou Anderson. She was born On October 5, 1950, in Elkhart, Indiana the daughter of Robert and Gloria Mercer Anderson. Her parents were divorced when she was two years old and her father took off for parts unknown, rarely to be heard from again.

Abandoned and without any resources, Linda, her mother and older brother Bob moved into their Grandparents, Morrell, and Jessie Mercer's home. Linda adored her grandparents and lived happily growing up in their comfortable supportive environment.

After a few hours Linda told me she needed to go to her apartment to get a shower and change clothes. I told her I would wait, and we could have lunch together. While at her apartment I told Linda, once again, how much fun I had had and how much I enjoyed our time together. With her radiant smile beaming, it was obvious she felt the same way.

The strong unbreakable bonded magnetism between us had taken over. She did not want our, now 16-hour, date to end either. So, she called the boy she was supposed to go out with that night and cancelled their date. We left her apartment and went to lunch.

Our mutual unspoken agreement had been made. We were now committed to each other and immediately became an inseparable couple.

For two months we covered almost every detail of each other's lives and our separate desires for our futures. We had even jokingly talked about marriage and what it would be like to be wed, a humorous little lunge and parry conversation.

One night Linda and I were sitting, facing each other, talking when, out of the blue, she said, "Would you rather get married October 16th, The Sweetest Day, or December 25th?"

I was amusingly caught off guard by her alternative proposal dates and with a knee jerk reply I said, "Nobody gets married on Christmas." Then, without hesitation, she said, "October the 16th it is."

Wow, I did not see that coming! However, I did not offer any resistance to her October 16th date of getting married either. There was no reason to hesitate when we were in agreement, and both really wanted the same thing.

After a few weeks of getting used to the "we're getting married" idea we decided one of us was going to have to get a job. I was in graduate school taking night classes and Linda was an undergraduate, attending school during the day. So, it was mutually decided, I would seek employment.

With my degree in finance and management, I found a management training position at Mutual Federal Bank. There, among other things, I learned to review personal financial and business statements as well as small business proposals. All of these areas would serve me well in the future.

On July 3, 1971, leaving Elkhart for a holiday weekend at my parents' lake house in Celina, Ohio, I pulled over to the side of the road and gave Linda an engagement ring. Not very romantic, I must admit, but I wanted my waiting family to know we were formally committed to each other.

We began preparing for our wedding with heightened enthusiasm, but very little money. Riverside, my parent's church, would provide the setting and officiating service for $15.00. Holiday Inn, a local hotel, provided a nice reception room for $25.00. We were fortunate to have a few friends, who chipped in to take photographs, prepare our wedding reception, and provide music with plenty of frivolity for all.

Of all the things I remember on our wedding day, my single most illuminating memory was looking at my future wife, perfectly poised to walk down the aisle to me. Linda was absolutely gorgeous! She had fashionably curled her hair, so the long dark dancing coils floated to her shoulders meeting her superbly grand white wedding dress. Her eyes glistened through her white lace wedding veil. When our eyes met her red lips parted and her brilliant smile melted me in place. I knew looking at her, briefly pausing before taking her first step toward me, I would never see anything more beautiful than Linda the rest of my life. I had been truly blessed!

Looking into Linda's affixed eyes I cited my personal commitment vows to her. I had practiced the words I would be saying to Linda, but at the actual moment of speaking to them; I had a problem getting them from my brain to my mouth. The words were shaky and halting as my emotions were creating a minor interruption in their delivery. A few small tears trickled down my cheek as I finished the grandest personal statement I would ever make. My vows to Linda were accepted and we became husband and wife.

After our wedding and reception Linda and I drove an hour to my parents' lake house in Celina, Ohio, for our brief honeymoon. A few days later we resumed our joint responsibilities of Linda getting back to her classes and me to the bank.

Early Family Years

On our first anniversary, October 16, 1972, Linda & I purchased a four-bedroom, two-bathroom house on Neely Avenue. It was located halfway between where I was born and where Linda and I were married. Our, new to us, home was originally a two-bedroom one bath house, but the previous owners had added the extra rooms to the back of the original structure. The added space was accessible through the main and side door entrances.

It was our intention, when we bought our new home, to live in the front two-bedroom area and rent the two bedrooms and bath in the rear. All we needed to do was add a door separating the two spaces. The only drawback to our plan was we would have to share the kitchen.

Our Neely Avenue home was located a short distance from the rapidly growing BSU campus, which was suffering from a shortage of student housing. We felt we could create a situation where our residents would pay enough rent to cover our house payment, thus allowing us to live rent free and save for future investments.

Linda contacted her former dormitory roommates about moving into our rental space and they agreed to do so. It worked well sharing the kitchen space with someone we knew for the first school year. However, in preparation for future new residents we built a kitchen and living room area in the basement. With this addition our communal living came to an end.

I developed a philosophy of purchasing a house a year. My thought was when it came time to leave the everyday work environment; I would have 40 houses to support Linda and me during our retirement years.

Working with the underserved BSU students, I realized their prepaid rent would assist me in financing the new home purchases. My business model was simple. The students were on the academic quarter system, so I required them to pay the three month's rent in advance. Additionally, with the shortage of housing as my leverage, another condition I imposed was, the students needed to pay the three month's rent one month prior to the first month's due date.

This business model, in practice, allowed me to use the unneeded but prepaid rent as a down payment for another house. This allowed me to move faster than anticipated in my investment acquisition plan.

Within a year of purchasing our first home we found a three-bedroom house, again close to campus, and purchased it. Prior to closing the loan on the house, we found three students looking for a place to live, collected their deposit and signed a lease with them.

In our third year, a person contacted me wanting me to buy three homes with nine apartments in them. The next year a person I had assisted at the bank sold me two properties with 11 apartments in them. Within five years we had accumulated 25 houses and apartments. We were earning more from our rental properties than I was working at the bank.

Financial leveraging and preleasing, I found, would become the key to our future business success.

The Chairman of the Board of Directors of Mutual Bank, along with the President of the bank, were grooming me to become the President's successor. They courted me, inviting Linda and me into their homes, encouraging me to join the right local organizations and promoting me over longer tenured management personnel. I was their "Golden Boy."

But I was bored with the bank. Maybe it was me realizing what the "end game" was and not seeing a major challenge ahead of me. Also, I was still having authoritarian issues from my time in the military and just didn't care for "the system".

Outside of the bank I was able to move at my pace, be creative, and grow faster with fewer deadwoods, inept personnel, around me. I had too much energy and talent. The bank environment, where I was advancing at a rapid tortoise pace, was smothering me.

Linda and I found a small printing company, PDQ [Pretty Darn Quick] and purchased it. Linda managed the three-employee business and I continued to labor at the bank. We found a very desirable ranch style home on Muncie's soon to become busiest street, purchased and remodeled it. Once completed, we moved PDQ into a better high traffic location. Gaining more exposure, we planned to grow then sell the business for a profit.

However, Linda became pregnant. We delivered our first child, and she decided to become a stay-at-home Mother.

Our PDQ business plan had worked in a circuitous fashion. We lost around $12,000.00 tax deductible dollars on the PDQ printing business operation. However, we purchased the converted home for $25,000.00 and sold it two years later to a person opening a jewelry store for $75,000.00. We had lost money on the printing business but made it back, and more, on the sale of the real estate. Another good lesson we learned in our enterprising real estate investment program.

The down payment for our former PDQ building included one of the jeweler's favorite stones, a Watermelon Tourmaline. As a courtesy to us, he crafted the stone into a custom fashionable one of a kind pendant for Linda. While wearing her new pendant in public, she was stopped several times by admiring people, including jewelers, astonished by its unique color clarity and quality. It was a good deal for all!

During our third year of marriage, we decided to start our family and become parents. However, for over a year and a half we had no success. Then frustrated over some testing and attempting several recommended approaches, Linda found an old-fashioned method and became pregnant. Great news! We were going to become parents.

Now we had to refinish the 2nd bedroom into a nursery. There were many decisions to make; what color to paint the walls, furniture to buy, carpet versus hardwood floors, etc. With each decorating decision to be made Linda would come up with an idea and we would discuss it. Finally, she made her decision and asked me if I could live with it. That became the way we would make most of our future household decisions, "Can you live with this"?

We took our becoming new parents' role very seriously. We read books, attended new parenting classes, learned, and practiced what would be happening in the hospital delivery room. We would be a team, working together during the delivery. I would be calming, holding her hand, and focusing on my partner and Linda, well we knew her job.

On April 19th, 1976, Linda and I had some friends at our house visiting and discussing our dinner arrangements for the evening. She was having intermittent pain and contractions but still thought it would be okay to go out to eat. Her friend's husband told Linda; instead of going out to eat we should go to the hospital.

Taking his advice, we immediately changed our plans and went to Ball Memorial Hospital. At about 1:20am, April 20th Linda was in the delivery room, me by her side, when the doctor and nurses urged her to begin pushing. Our child was ready to come into this wonderful world. First the little head with dark hair appeared then a few seconds later the rest of the body was exposed to the attending personnel. Then someone said, "It's a boy!"

Linda and I looked at each other and gleefully smiled. He was here. Our waiting was over. Hallelujah, Amen! Immediately our son was whisked 10 feet away to have the birthing residue cleaned off of him. He was then wrapped in a white blanket and handed to Linda for his first informal introduction to our family.

We didn't know whether we were going to have a son or daughter, so we had chosen a name for both. Now knowing our new child was a boy, we immediately announced his name to all, "Neil Gregory Burnworth."

After a few moments Linda offered Neil to me, and I lifted our new Son into my arms. I carried Neil to the other side of the hospital room looking at him into his dark eyes. I began my first conversation with him. As his father, in the hospital room, I made several promises to him.

I told Neil how happy I was that he had come into our lives, and I would never leave him. I would always be there for him, and I would create a safe and happy home for him. Our confirmed private conversation lasted a few minutes and we proudly rejoined Linda in her bed.

The next day we took Neil home to our house on Neely Avenue. Within an hour I realized he needed his diaper changed. As I removed his soiled diaper and prepared to put on a clean one, Neil peed on my shoulder and the right side of my head. This was my first formal lesson in real life parenting.

In 1977 I was doing research into any business I could start in Muncie where I would have a good chance of success. I traveled to Indianapolis and Fort Wayne, two cities much larger than Muncie, to look around, assess the changes occurring in their towns and what, if anything, would transfer benefits to my town.

I came across the rapidly growing roller-skating industry. I was intrigued by the industry's concept and its balanced level of success. My research indicated the operators of the roller-skating rinks rarely suffered business failures and enjoyed a consistent annual level of attendance. Additionally, the industry involved real estate investment and a large amount of capital. These were two criteria I liked because it had a limited entry component, i.e., the business couldn't be opened on every street corner by someone not knowing what they were doing.

I contacted the owner of three roller skating facilities in Fort Wayne. Jim Wall and his wife Marge had been in the business for twenty years. In addition to owning his facilities, Jim was an industry consultant and equipment supplier.

I hired Jim to do a feasibility study for me to gauge the potential success of a new roller-skating facility in Muncie. Presently a skating facility is operating in town, two blocks from my childhood home on Mock Avenue. I wanted to ensure there would be enough business for two operations in Delaware County.

Jim prepared a detailed projected report breaking down the population by age group, income and expected attendance for a new roller-skating facility. He also provided a line-item analysis, by the month, of anticipated income and expenses I could expect. His final summarization was that the business would succeed, and he projected a net income of $15,000.00 per year.

This was the amount of money I was earning at the bank plus our real estate investments. We imagined we would need to sell some of our investments for 'seed money' to start the roller-skating business but would still be in a better financial position than we were presently. So, we committed to 'go all in' and I quit working at the bank.

While visiting several existing roller-skating facilities, I went to a recently remodeled operation in Dayton, Ohio and discovered a new concept called "Disco Skating." Similar to disco dancing night clubs, the roller-skating rink had a state-of-the-art sound system, with the resonating deep bass beat of Disco music.

The disco program also incorporated the pulsating multicolored, red, yellow, blue, and green lights synchronized with the music and a mirror ball for glancing light beam effects. Together, and with a few other enhancing amenities, the place was totally mind-body movement energized. My eyes and ears were excited, and my heartbeat was engagingly electrified with the sights and sounds of this new roller-skating concept.

The environment at this business was night and day different from the standard roller-skating operations I had previously visited. At this roller rink the skaters were engaged. They were skating to the heavy bass beat of the music, twirling, spinning, shuffling their feet to the disco sounds. There were singles doing 'their thing' and couples synchronically dancing on wheels.

At this new concept disco arena, there were also at least twice as many people in attendance as any other place I had previously visited. It was noticeably apparent they were interacting together having huge fun showing off their new skate/dance moves. These disco skaters were having a way better time than the other facilities, which were running the same old tired programs they had boringly done for years.

I was sold! Although the new disco installation was very pricey, I liked the fun-loving environment of the new disco roller skating rink. And since I was going to be working there, I felt it would be good for me as well.

Linda and I made an official announcement of our intentions to open the new skating business with an article in the newspaper. We also placed a large sign on the properties location prior to beginning construction.

Two weeks later another company made a public announcement, they were going to open a new skating facility in Muncie as well. What the Hell! Linda and I were in shock. We were immediately tied up in mental and physical knots. We knew there was not enough population for two new roller-skating businesses and if both opened, one for sure would fail.

Not knowing the opposition's true intentions, we agonized over the dilemma of going forward or dropping our business plan. Two weeks later a real estate representative for the opposition called to meet with me. He said perhaps it would be a good idea if we combined our efforts and opened the business at their site.

He made a minor slip of the tongue when he said they had an option on the ground at their location. This error, on their part, let me know they had not formally purchased the site and thus could back out of their deal.

For the first time in my budding business career, I was induced into playing a game of bluff poker. I knew the first person to blink would lose and I didn't want that to be me. After a few more agonizing sleepless nights I made the decision to proceed with our business plan. The opposition, realizing they had run into a person not afraid of the unknown, dropped their option and was never heard from again.

I had learned my first lesson about the toughness needed in the game of business. I also knew, as I advanced my entrepreneurial career, this would not be the only difficult decision I would need to make.

In November 1977, our new roller-skating business, Skateaway, opened to a nice large crowd. The first attendees were amazed and in awe of the disco skating concept. They spread the word, and like a wildfire, our business positively erupted. We had to wait in lines to get in to see this new sensation, disco roller skating.

The old-style skaters accustomed to organ music and scratchy records quickly adapted and developed their exciting individual interpretation of skate dancing. New to the scene skaters watched, first mimicked, and then evolved into new creative routines as well. People came from surrounding towns to enjoy this eclectic, electric, exciting, and revolutionary environment.

With this new added skating concept, our business model went off the income charts. We ended our first year earning five times our projected net profit.

With our new business going well, Linda and I decided to sell our present shared home and custom build a very nice two-story cathedral ceiling single family home. We were now in a financial position to make a normal standard house payment.

We sold our home on Neely Avenue for twice the amount we had paid for it seven years earlier. Our shared home had been a very good investment.

As we began planning to build our new home Linda discovered, six months earlier than we had planned, she was pregnant with our second child. Our architect, construction supervisor and crew stepped up the pace to have the house completed before our second child was born.

Three weeks before the construction on our home was completed Linda told me it was time to go to the hospital. Our new child would not wait. It was ready to come into this wonderful world.

Arriving at the hospital I dropped Linda off at the emergency room entrance, parked our car and went to join her. A nurse met me at the entrance and told me to go directly to the delivery room. Linda was going to give birth to our new child sooner than expected.

In a matter of an hour our new son was born. We named him Reid Morrell Burnworth. Reid's middle name was his great grandfather's first name, Morrell Mercer. Linda's grandfather had given her childhood through college support and provided a home and safe sanctuary to Linda, her mother, and her brother. He was a very special person in their lives.

Like Neil before him, I whisked Reid away to have a private conversation with him. Making Reid the same commitment, I had 2 ½ years earlier to Neil. Gently telling Reid I would always be there for him. Guide and support him and attempt to be the best Father ever.

Three weeks later we moved our family into our new home. It was beautiful! We had given our architect and construction supervisor some latitude with the design and finish details, which really made our new home a very unique and special place to live. With a few modifications it would serve us well for 25 years.

Linda and I were both progressive people and wanted more than one roller skating business location. I visited several surrounding cities and decided Lafayette, Indiana, a town approximately the size of Muncie, would be a good location for our next operation.

In 1978 I found a great location in a strip shopping center in West Lafayette on the edge of Purdue University. It was across the town from the existing roller-skating rink, which was 20-25 years old and using the aged skating program of most outdated facilities.

When we opened for business, it was like Muncie but even better. Locating our 2nd Skateaway close to Purdue paid major dividends. We hadn't counted on the university students as skaters, but so many came that we had to run a special late-night session just for them. It was a tremendous success!

The following year we purchased an existing roller-skating business in Dayton, Ohio. It was twice the size of our other facilities with half of the building utilized as a teenage dance club.

It was great! Business couldn't have been better. Through hard work and dedication, we were realizing the "rags to riches" lifestyle dreams are made of. However, the reality of it all wouldn't last.

On July 29, 1979, at Comisky Park in Chicago, Illinois between baseball games an ill-fated promotion, "Disco Demolition Night", was staged. The on-field promotion entailed blowing up a crate filled with disco records. The highly publicized promotion was dubbed, "the day disco died." It was mimicked across the country. The general public bought into the concept. It was time for a change!

Simultaneously the video game craze hit the personal household market. Games like Space Invaders and Missile Command, formerly played on large heavy commercial consoles, could now be played at home.

The hand-held control of the portable new concept video game was connected, by a small cable, to a television-like video screen. It was the same game with action, characters, and drama our young customers paid us to play. Now, several versions of the games could be played for hours in the uninterrupted privacy of their own bedroom.

Young people went wild over the ability to play games at home.

International companies like Atari were annually making up to 800 million of the play at home games. The portable game playing phenomena created a frenzy of new concepts and companies, which gobbled up our young excited former patrons.

Our roller-skating business had begun its rapid downturn spiral into oblivion. In three short years we went from people having to wait in lines to get into our facilities to barely being able to pay our utility bill. We sold at a loss, our businesses in Dayton and Muncie. Lafayette would stay open a few more years.

It was time to figure out my next entrepreneurial business move. There was no going back to the bank.

Entrepreneurial Housing

During my entrepreneurial dilemma time period the economic climate, nationally and internationally, was in dire straits. The countries of Saudi Arabia, Kuwait, Iran, Iraq, and Venezuela were the main oil production countries. In the 1960's they formed a coalition, referred to as OPEC, to control the international flow of oil.

During the next three decades, while the international need for their product was increasing, OPEC would systematically reduce oil production. This move would create an economic tsunami sending interest rates skyrocketing.

In reasonably normal times, the prime interest rate would be between 3-6% and mortgage rates hovering around the 6-8 % rate range. In 1979-1986 they were now in the 15-21% and 11-13% ranges, respectively.

In 1981 I was looking into the horizon to get an idea of what business I could start to offset the losses we were incurring from our, now declining disco roller-skating business. Many industries were struggling from the economic recession our country had slipped into.

One of the hardest hit was the housing industry. With the exorbitantly high mortgage interest rates the market was stalled, at a standstill. Nothing was happening. No one was building homes. Muncie's local builders were either out of business or so badly financially wounded they were not functioning.

I was very familiar with the housing market as it had been one of my main areas of focus at the bank. In my position as a bank loan officer, I reviewed builder's home design plans, construction costs, and financial projections. After all of these components were reviewed, I approved their building loans.

The multiple aspects of the home building business were familiar territory for me. From this vast collection of accumulated knowledge, I was able to formulate a working business model.

My plan was to build a new affordable model home, with some custom design enticing upgrade features. From that I would presell various similar plans to people wanting to own a new home.

The only caveat to my plan was most people desiring a new home had to first sell their present home. Thus, I developed a safety net plan to guarantee they ultimately wouldn't own two homes when their new one was finished. If their house wasn't sold, within 90 days from its original listing for sale, my company would buy it at a discounted price.

My plan worked perfectly! There was a pent-up demand for people who had wanted to build a new home. But due to the frozen housing market, they were frustrated and unable to do so. They jumped at the idea of my guaranteed purchase plan.

In my first year of business, I pre-sold and built 16 new homes. The next year I pre-sold and built 20 new homes. My guaranteed purchase plan was working to perfection.

My success brought me some much-desired attention. In the fall of 1983, two long-time local commercial developers, Joe Allardt and Bob Dailey owned a two-acre piece of vacant land close to the Ball State campus. The economy was bad. The land just sitting there was costing them money. They couldn't figure out what to do with it and needed someone with a new idea to help them develop it.

They called me and asked me to meet with them to discuss an idea for developing the land. I told them, with their financial backing, I would have my architect design a plan to build apartments on the ground.

In recent years, the enrollment at Ball State University has grown from approximately 8,000 students to well over 11,000 enrollees. The freshmen and sophomore students were required to live in on campus dormitories, while the upperclassmen were relegated to older homes and apartments scattered in the community.

I knew there was a shortage of good housing for the underserved BSU students. I was confident; with my previous pre leasing experience, I could convince enough young students to sign contracts for, yet to be built, new apartments.

With the help of my architect, we designed a scale model of the buildings to be built. The model showed the exterior of the three-level building and, with a removable roof, displayed the interior floor plan as well.

In January 1984, when the BSU students arrived back on campus after the winter holiday break, I initiated my preleasing program. The leases guaranteed delivery of their new apartment by the beginning of the fall academic session.

The students were excited with the opportunity of living in a new modern clean apartment. Within 60 days, I was able to lease all 36 proposed apartments. The show and tell, yet to be built project were an overwhelming success.

Now, I needed to hire a superintendent for construction, set a budget and timeline and build the 36 apartments. These project supportive efforts were fulfilled and construction began in March.

In August, prior to fall semester beginning, Sunreach Apartments were finished. The student residents happily and excitedly moved into the first new student apartments built at BSU.

We, Allardt, Dailey and I, were ecstatic over our successful venture. It had been their intent to lease, build and sell the Sunreach Apartments to a company packaging projects for major investors.

An added bonus was their real estate company represented the BSU Foundation, which owned 80-100 acres a mile from the BSU campus. With Sunreach on the selling block, we optioned 18 acres of the BSU Foundation ground.

On the site we planned to build 120 Silvertree Apartment and a recreation center for BSU students.

In January and February 1985, I pre-leased 24 Silvertree Apartments, built and finished them for August occupancy. Allardt and Dailey were happy with my production but the sale of the Sunreach and now Silvertree was not happening. The investor market was leery of student housing and backed away from our package proposal.

Allardt and Dailey had originally told me, with a handshake, I would be 80% owner of Sunreach Apartments. Then, when we started Silvertree, Allardt told me we were 70%-30%.

A year later he said we were 60%-40%. At that time, I told him we were 70%-30%. He said, "Can you prove that?" and I said yes! Nothing further about the percentage agreement of our partnership was mentioned.

With the first change in partnership percentage my, "I'm not sure I can trust you antenna had gone up." During that year and a half expanse in time from the inception of Sunreach to the completion of **phase** one of Silvertree, two IRS partnership tax returns had been filed. This was the proof I needed if they ever challenged our partnership split.

With the loss of investor interest Allardt and Dailey had withdrawn their support in the completion of the Silvertree project. I knew my personal financial status would not be strong enough to finance another phase of Silvertree buildings so I would need a new partner.

My accountant, watching my performance with the projects, recommended one of his clients, Jan Etchison, as a good new partner for me. I explained the planned pre-leasing and financial aspects to him, which required no money out of his pocket [with the higher rents the students were paying, along with my sweat equity, the bank loan covered 100% of the construction costs].

Jan was all in and we began phase 2 of Silvertree. This included an additional 24 apartments along with the planned club house and swimming pool. When construction was completed, for reasons known only to him, he stated he wanted out of the project.

I paid him a negotiated amount for his equity in phase 2. I then began to plan the competition of the balance of the Silvertree project.

By this time, I had accumulated enough credibility; net worth and income that Tom Fiedler, CEO of Merchants Bank in Carmel, Indiana agreed to finance my future pre-leased buildings. In 1989, with his financial support, all 120 Silvertree Apartments were completed.

During the final phase of building the Silvertree Apartments, I discovered a common interest with another university student oriented developing team, Ron Rubeck, and his nephew Keith Rubeck. They, the Rubecks, were developing, preselling, to parents of students, and building condominiums on university campuses.

Their base of operations was in Bloomington, Indiana, where Ron lived. Keith, originally from Bloomington, now owned a small horse farm close to Dallas, Texas.

They had recently developed, presold, and built approximately 100 student condominiums in Bloomington. When we met, they were developing a 24-unit condominium project in West Lafayette, Indiana, home of Purdue University.

We realized a mutual interest in collaborating to build condominiums on more university campuses across the country. Our collective synergy, we agreed, would assist us in seeking out new markets, discovering quality locations and developing successful projects.

The collective effort initially worked well as we developed three new condominium communities at Ball State University [Muncie, In], Southern Illinois University [Carbondale, Il] and Ohio University [Athens, Oh].

The next year, 1991, we had plans to do a 48-unit project at Ball State and 36 condominiums at Florida State University in Tallahassee, Fl. The sales of the two projects stalled. When I investigated the reason, they had not moved forward as planned, I discovered Ron Rubeck had not fulfilled his responsibilities to timely hire staff to pre-sell the units.

Ron, I discovered, had not properly set up his sales teams. The tardy placement of qualified personnel at these sites led to confusion regarding their marketing and sales responsibilities. Thus, no presales had been made.

I was livid! We had purchased the ground, started building the 48 condominiums in Muncie and had no sales. Upset with the ever-shifting projected timetable, I bought Ron and Keith out of the project and converted it into an apartment project, Windsong Apartments.

Our project in Tallahassee, overlooking the amazing FSU Football Stadium, a guaranteed slam dunk, had to be abandoned. We were forced to set back our development timetable a full year.

This would be a very costly oversight. I had counted on these projects to continue our expanding base into other states and more projects.

When my disgust at this expensive failure and delay of two projects was brought to the group's attention, a finger pointing eruption ensued. After the smoke cleared Keith and I agreed to drop Ron from the malfunctioning team.

Additionally, we agreed, the two of us would proceed ahead researching and developing new projects.

My responsibility was researching new locations and securing financing. Keiths were getting the projects properly zoned, hiring our sales team, and managing construction.

Simultaneously, I continued construction of additional apartments in Muncie, geared to BSU students. One project, Linden Place, had a low-lying spot in the neighborhood and thus became a swampy water catch basin. I had the 40' X 100' pond drained; years of natural decomposition sludge removed and drove steel pylons 25 feet deep to secure the soon to be built four level building.

The project was going along smoothly, with all of the apartments pre-leased and our tight construction schedule being met. Three days prior to the resident's move-in date, my construction manager called and said we had a problem.

The local building inspector told him the basically completed apartments had small construction issues which needed to be completed before he would give us a building occupancy permit. Without the permit our new residents would not be allowed to move into Linden Place.

The inspector would not put the issues in writing so we guessed what they might be and went about completing them. The next day the building inspector looked through the building and gave the project manager the same verbal report.

We had a day to go before our residents would be moving into their new apartments and we were stressed about the lack of cooperation we were receiving from the inspector.

I knew the Mayor of Muncie, Jim Carey. I called him and set up a meeting where I could tell him of our problem with the building inspector. A few hours later we had a written report of what we needed to complete to receive our occupancy permit.

The next day, move in day, our crew went about completing the small number of items on the inspectors to do list. At three o'clock in the afternoon, I received an urgent phone call from my construction manager requesting me to come to Linden Place immediately.

When I arrived the building inspector was in Linden Place finalizing his permit inspection. Cars, vans, and trailers filled with the new resident's furniture and clothing circled the perimeter streets waiting for the starter's flag to be dropped so they could offload into their new apartments.

My construction manager pulled me aside, holding a white nondescript five-gallon bucket. With a surrounding group of our crew, he held it up for me to peer inside. As he was revealing its contents, he said they were doing some final excavation when they discovered this potential impediment to receiving our occupancy permit.

The bucket contained a dirty fleshless white skull with matted long brown hair. I looked at it with amazement barely containing my emotions. For two to three minutes, I just stood there analyzing this potentially disruptive situation. My gaze went from the bucket to Linden Place and back again.

Then I looked up into my construction manager's eyes where I saw a hint of a smile across his face. I knew I had been duped. The skull in the bucket was a fake.

These guys had been pressed to the limit the past few days by a building inspector, possibly looking for a handout. They needed some stress relief and I had just provided it for them. Laughter erupted and we all enjoyed their prank.

A few minutes later the building inspector emerged from Linden Place and gave his formal approval. The loaded waiting cars, vans and trailers converged on the site like a Wild West Land Rush.

In our first year together Keith and I located and successfully began developing and selling condos at the University of Kansas in Lawrence, Kansas, University of Idaho, in Moscow, Idaho and Washington State University in Pullman, Washington.

Our only joint developing hiccup came in Pullman when an archaeological review group challenged our proposed development. The great Palouse Prairie thick grassy region of Southern Washington and Idaho, for centuries, had been home to the indigenous nomadic Nez Perce Indians. The semi-sedentary hunter/gatherer Nez Perce roamed the asymmetrical rolling hills and winding rivers of the "Great Palouse." The area served as one of their many seasonal village sites.

The archaeologists claimed our site was a potential Nez Perce Indian burial ground. Their inquiry delayed our building permit while a complete historical review of the area was studied. When the formally commissioned report was released, no signs of Nez Perce activity were found. With respect, we employed many Nez Perce tradesmen and proceeded with our project.

At the end of October 1992, Keith and I had successfully developed, built, and sold 72 condominiums. We equally divided our, after expense, profit from the year's efforts and began planning for more success in 1993. During the year we acquired adjacent land at all three locations. There was no reason for us not to expect to have another good year.

In 1992 Steve Lowry came to me with a business idea. He wanted to develop a community of quadraplexes for Empty Nesters, aka Active Adults. The prospective client base was generally people whose children had grown up and left home.

I was very interested in this Active Adult Market, which personally I was soon to become a part of. This classification of people was referred to as the post-World War II, "Baby Boomers." The "Baby Boomers" were the largest market shifting group of people in the country. In this massive shift many opportunities, for the prepared, would emerge.

The housing industry recently has begun recognizing and focusing on this special group of people. Some of the major national builders were experimenting in developing housing products to serve their evolving wants and needs. I wanted to become one of the active participants in this new fresh industry.

Steve had the idea but no experience in developing products in the housing industry. I had the building and developing experience, along with the financial strength to be the catalyst for this new venture.

With the same nurturing attitude I was given by Joe and Bob, I set Steve up as the majority head of our new operation.

We found a great 15-acre location in Muncie. With the normal amount of neighborhood protest, we got it zoned correctly and began our new joint venture. The project was designed to consist of 80 total one level two-bedroom brick condominiums and a community center. With a projected 20 sales a year, the new concept, Applewood Park Villas would be a four-year project.

Our 1993 preselling season at all three university locations went well with almost all units sold before we broke ground in April. However, the spring rains set in, and all our projects were slipping behind schedule.

If our projects weren't completed on time as promised, the committed family's children and their roommates would be housed, rent free, in a local hotel. It became very expensive for us when we weren't in sync with Mother Nature.

One such delay resulted in the students living in a Hyatt Regency, one of the most upscale hotels in the country. With complimentary breakfast, room service, happy hour bar and the prestige of living in the Hyatt, the freeloading students were, "living the dream." When their weather delayed condominiums were finished, they groaned and moaned as they reluctantly carried their bags from these luxurious surroundings. Now they would have to make their own beds.

In mid-July 1993, Keith called me and said he was going to make a motorcycle trip across the country. His trekking plan was to ride from Texas to Bloomington, spend a couple of days with his family, Mother and Brother. Then he was going to spend day and night with Linda and me. When he left us, in Muncie, his plan was to stop at his Brother Brad's in Chicago for a day then ride through to our projects in Lawrence, Moscow and Pullman.

When Keith arrived at my office, we discussed our project delays and how they were being mitigated. By now we knew we were going to need to provide temporary housing in Lawrence and Pullman. Our contractor in Moscow had pulled a rabbit out of his hat and was on schedule.

In spite of our weather-related construction slowdowns, we were pleased. All 72 units at our three locations were sold. One of the buyers in Moscow was Baseball Hall of Fame player Harmon Killebrew. We thought selling a condo to someone of his stature was pretty cool.

Keith and I also discussed two new proposed projects at Northern Colorado University in Greeley and University of Kentucky in Lexington. We finished debating the pros and cons of evolving into the Active Adult condominium market.

After our meeting we went to our house where we met Linda, had a wonderful meal, and sat outside on our deck enjoying the warm evening breezes. We laughed and talked well into the late-night hours. While he was 13 years younger than me, with biking, running and sports in common, Keith and I had built a close personal relationship.

During the evening, Keith revealed one of the reasons for his visit. He said he and his wife were going to get a divorce. During the divorce legal proceedings, he was going to be forced to file personal bankruptcy.

Without hesitation, I told him I had his back! He had my full support.

I assured Keith our business plans would go forward while he handled his personal issues. Further, I told him, as he well knew, our relationship went beyond our business agreement. I finished by telling him I would do everything I could to help him come out of this situation intact.

Early the next morning he swung his right leg over his motorcycle, started its engine and rode off to complete his cathartic cross-country journey.

On Friday August 6, 1993, at 3:25 pm Keith called my office from South Dakota to check in and let us know where he was. Just three days and five minutes later Keith was in Kooskia, Idaho where his motorcycle collided with a semi-truck. He was killed instantly!

I was shaken! My personal loss was immense. My business loss was incalculable.

I personally had felt several dimensions of death, natural and unnatural, but the breadth and scope of Keith's death was different. It affected me in so many ways. It was going to take a while for me to adjust to this horrific loss.

Fortunately, my staff in Muncie and his in Texas, feeling much the same as I did about Keith, came together. We stabilized our projects under construction and kept our business moving forward. Most of our joint team were very helpful in making sure nothing was being overlooked.

Only Steve Lowry, after Keith's funeral pledging to take his place as my committed business partner, turned on me. I had exhibited the same confidence and extended courtesy to Steve that Joe and Bob had given to me. I had given him a managing interest in the Applewood Park Villa project. Now, somehow fearful I would lose control of our weather delayed potential financially embarrassed projects; he took advantage of my perceived weakened position.

A month after Keith's death, Steve moved out of my office. He took all the Applewood records with him and severed communication ties with me. He continued to build the estimated four-year Applewood project without my seasoned input. His foolishness ultimately led him to total business failure.

While admittedly, with all the negative situations affecting my business there was some cause for concern. But, always optimistic, I saw it as a short-term bump in the road. Any who doubted my tenacity would soon realize how resilient I could be. My focus quickly switched to my business' long-term opportunities.

The year after Keith's death my reorganized company, including his former staff, built additional phases of student condominiums, 24 units each, in Lawrence, Moscow and Pullman. We added new developments, 24 units, each in Greely,

Colorado and Lexington, Kentucky. In addition, we met with our architects and engineers to formulate plans for two new Active Adult Communities, 80 units each, in Fort Wayne and Evansville, Indiana.

People either rise or fall in the face of adversity. I was determined to push my company forward to a higher level of success.

With a slow and methodical movement, my business evolved from the long travels building university student condominiums on faraway campuses to the more regionalized focus on the Active Adult Communities.

Each year I, along with some of my staff, visited active adult projects in various phases of development, learning and borrowing the best ideas the other developers had to offer. Some of the more progressive projects were in the warmer climate states, Florida, Arizona, Texas, and California, where older retired people were migrating.

We attended national seminars, which focused on the burgeoning future growth of the largest population demographic housing swing in modern history. I wanted not only to be a part of this major national housing movement, but I also wanted to be one of its leaders.

The housing product we offered our customers evolved and changed to match their specific needs and desires. Listening to our customers was the key to our business success. We weren't always the least expensive housing option for our customers, but we were the best. Our company motto was "Quality lasts long after price is forgotten." We were selling a good quality product at a reasonably affordable price.

Our new active adult housing concept was accepted well in Evansville and Fort Wayne. We added two new projects in Indianapolis and another in Fishers, Indiana, all were 80-100 condominium projects with a sell and buildout timetable of 20 units per year. All of our active adult projects were meeting our projections both in the sell-out time periods as well as profit projections.

Our new business model was working perfectly. We were the leading active adult condominium developer in the state of Indiana.

Front-Joe, Jonetta, Rick-Back-Dale, Phyllis, Mother [Francis] and Father [John]

50ᵗʰ Anniversary- Mom and Dad-Rick, Phyllis, Joe, Jonetta and Dale

Five Generations-Front-Phyllis, Great Great Grandmother Hunt, Dale-Back-
Great Grandmother Evans-Collins Dad, Grandmother Burnworth holding me

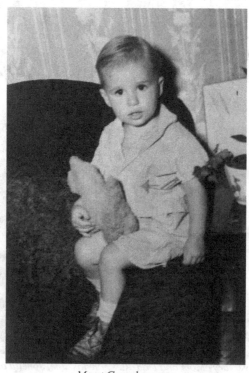

Me at Grandparents

Me with Lady, Grandpa Bickner's farm dog

Milk cows coming to Grandpa Bickner's barn for evening milking

*Rick, Cousin Sarah, Jonetta with Grandpa Bickner,
riding in back, Cousin David and myself*

Catch of the day with Grandma Evans-Collins, Rick, Me, Phyllis and Dale

Delivering newspapers, 1958

My first car, 1956 Ford

Beginning 30-day mission Vietnam

Refreshing shower after 30-day mission

Large Anti-personnel weapon

Linda with her Mother, Gloria and my Mother

Linda, The Most Beautiful Bride Ever

After our vows

Linda with her Grandparents, Morrell and Jessie Mercer

Linda and me at West Point for the BSU versus Army football game

Ready for my 7th Mini-Marathon

A little summit in Phoenix

Bop to the Top in 2012-36 Floors, 780 Steps, 500 Vertical Feet

Exploring Kittiwake Shipwreck in grand Cayman

Neil created his own daredevil bicycle jump

Neil and me in Idaho

Neil and Reid in Reid's Star Wars Themed Bedroom

Walleye Fishing in Lake Erie

Reid and me going to a formal lunch

Linda and Me on a live-aboard dive boat in Palau

Linda and Me at a high school reunion

Linda, Neil and Me, SCUBA Diving in Grand Cayman

Neil getting some Cuban smooches

Outside a gorgeous but declining cathedral in Havana

Fabulous setting sun on the 20th Century in Australia

Linda and Me celebrating the beginning of a new century

Celebrating the New Century at the Sydney Opera House

Enjoying our time in Sydney

Arriving in Fiji

Prepared for falling coconuts in Fiji

Mother and Me

Me at Wave Dancer book signing event in Richmond, Va.

Neil's graduation, Ball State University

Neil and Taryn, Married-10-01-2023

Neil with Alexandra Morgan and Tristan Matthew

Linda and Me celebrating our 50th Wedding Anniversary

Linda and Me at Grand Canyon

Our Wonderful Family

Our Wonderful Family on my 80ᵗʰ Birthday

Reid, Mindy, Ethan and Evee

Linda and Me with our Wonderful Grandchildren, Alex, Evee, Tristan and Ethan

My Two Wonderful Sons and Me toasting My 80th Birthday

Gary Schliessman, Ramon Avila and myself out for our daily six mile run.

Our New Century Adventures

In the early 1990's I began thinking and even openly discussing, with some close friends and associates, the approaching change from 1999 to the new century 2000. It appeared to me there could be a seismic shift in marketing, product shift, attitudes and a multitude of changes that may come with the advent of a new century.

The number one concern with progressive people worldwide was, what would or could happen if our personal, business national, international, etc., computers would not numerically correctly advance from 1999 to 2000? For years, the most brilliant computer programming minds were put to task to ensure a catastrophic paralytic failure affecting our interactive worldwide cultures was correctly synchronized to avoid such an occurrence.

The synchronized 1999 to 2000 computer adjustment was referred to as the "Y2K problem", the millennium bug formatting and storage of calendar dates. There was the possibility of program errors such as the incorrect display of dates, the inaccurate ordering of automated data records or incorrect reporting of real-time events.

People in all walks of life were in fear that their computer systems would malfunction when the new century calendar year changed. If so their personal and financial lives would be disrupted to a confusing stressful mess for who knows how long.

In 1997, Linda came to me with her interest in what we, as a family, would do to commemorate the introduction of the "New Century". She wanted us, as a family, to do something with special significance to mark this once in a lifetime historic event. Linda felt both of our sons, Neil & Reid, would likely be in college as the century changed. She cringed at the thought of them celebrating such a memorable occasion hanging out with college buddies involved in some forgettable inane party-based activity.

Linda's idea of a monumental family celebration distinguishing the historic changing of the centuries was to visit one of the places where it would first occur, Australia.

She proposed the idea of us reserving four of the twenty-eight accommodations on the Mike Ball Spoilsport SCUBA Diving Yacht. The 105-foot luxury live-aboard yacht's promotional advertisement was based on their maxim of "eat, sleep and dive", where a diver could do as many as five dives a day.

The Spoilsport dive expedition cruise was a six-day seven-night diving extravaganza on the "Great Barrier Reef," the world's largest natural reef system in the Coral Sea.

Linda said the cost of the trip would be expensive, but one none of us would ever forget. I was immediately onboard with her proposal. I did, however, add one condition of my own. I felt if we were going to travel halfway around the world we should extend our trip another two weeks. This would make our unforgettable new century celebration an incredible three weeks.

My single biggest single concern of the millennium, the changing of centuries, was now solved. I felt if we were on a yacht in the middle of the ocean, we would be safe from any "Y2K Problem." As long as the yacht's compass pointed in the correct direction, we were good! There would be no messed up computer drama issues for me.

Within a couple of months Linda, along with a travel agent, had set up our full travel itinerary, purchased the airplane tickets to Australia and reserved space for us on the Spoilsport. She also had made plans for us to spend five days touring and shopping in Sydney and a week at the Cousteau SCUBA Diving Resort in Fiji.

Both Neil and Reid were certified as SCUBA Divers when they were 12 years old, which was the youngest age they could officially dive. Neil and I were certified together, while Linda and Reid followed 2 ½ years later. As a family we had been SCUBA diving for years in the closer-to-home Caribbean Islands. Now, with the new millennium as our excuse, this was our chance to venture into a whole new diving experience.

It was a normal winter day, cloudy and cold, when we flew out of Indianapolis, the day after Christmas, December 26, 1999. Our plane stopped at Los Angeles then went direct and nonstop to Sydney. At Sydney we changed airlines, flew to Brisbane then on to our final destination, Townsville. From start to finish our travel time, with no hotel sleepovers, was 36 hours.

When we arrived at Townsville, we were sleep deprived and travel weary. Halfway around the world the seasons had changed to our delight. When we stepped out of the airplane terminal the sun was shining. It was a "Welcome to Australia" 80-degree summer day. The great weather brought new life to our tired bodies.

Three members of the Spoilsport crew were waiting outside the Townsville airport terminal to greet us. After their brief introductions, they grabbed our heavy dive equipment bags and the accompanying three-week clothing luggage. They loaded us into their vehicle for a short ride to the waiting Spoilsport.

The gleaming yacht singly moored at the end of a short pier was a great sight for our tired eyes. Two smiling crew members, wearing their Mike Ball Spoilsport t-shirts, shorts and no shoes welcomed us aboard. They led us to our cabins where our personal items had been deposited. As they left us their last comment was, "you can leave your shoes with your luggage. At the Spoilsport there will be no shoes, no worries, just diving and fun in the sun. This is a new century special week. You're going to have a great time"!

We had seen the advertising photographs of the Spoilsport, which was similar to a live-aboard we had previously been on in the Bahamas.

This beautiful luxury yacht had a twin hull design for stability and motion reduction when at sea. The three tier Spoilsport offered a sky deck on top where, between dives, guests could meet for some rays or to read a book in the shade of a canvas canopy. The deck below contained the wheelhouse and captain's quarters, the large salon for meetings, guest entertainment and dining.

The main deck contained the guest cabins and camera tables for underwater photographers. The lower level was the action dive deck where we suited into our dive gear and executed a giant stride into the welcoming Coral Sea.

We had arrived at the Spoilsport a few hours early so we were able to take a refreshing four-hour nap. We requested a wakeup call at 5:00 pm. We were told the ship's captain and recreation director were to address their new guests at 6:00 pm.

We arrived in the salon at 6:00 and were greeted by the Spoilsport's captain, recreational director and 12 young adventurous crew members. The captain made formal introductions of all his crew, including their individual skills, such as Dive Instructor, Dive Master, and Chef.

Additionally, he acquainted us with the layout of his boat, the daily routines we could expect and the many diving sites we would be visiting during the week. He informed us we would be able to make up to five dives a day, with or without a dive guide. But he told us, we must check in and out on the dive deck so they could account for all their guests at any one time, adding, we must have a dive buddy. No solo dives were allowed.

The only exception to diving without a Certified Dive Master or Dive Instructor, the captain explained, would be the day we feed the sharks. On shark feeding day, he emphasized, we would all dive as a group to ensure our mutual safety.

He went on to state that after each night dive, while we were sleeping, the Spoilsport would be moving to a new location. This meant we would wake up to a new dive site each day. He added we could eat breakfast, go for a dive, and come back for fresh chocolate chip or oatmeal raisin cookies, then go for a second morning dive. After lunch we could dive again, take a break to enjoy salsa and chips then do a second afternoon dive.

In the evening, after dinner, we could elect to do our fifth and final dive of the day. This would be a night dive where, in total darkness, our waterproof flashlights would be our only way to observe the nocturnal sea life. However, if anyone had any alcoholic beverage with dinner, there would be no night diving for them.

When the captain ended his orientation, everyone was smiling. We were all looking forward to a great diving experience, with the added historic, "Changing of the Century" significance attached to it.

At the conclusion of his orientation spiel, we, the crew and guests, lingered for a while meeting each other to develop a comfort level and establish some early sense of comradery. It was going to be a memorable seven days together. The good times started now!

Always an early riser, at 6:00 am I emerged from our cabin. I immediately realized we were in the open waters of the Coral Sea. There was no docking pier, land, or other boats in sight.

I walked up the stairs to the top deck to soak in the beautiful pristine turquoise water surrounding the Spoilsport. The sun was rising to a warm clear cloudless day. The air was slightly moist from the gentle ocean breeze. There was a small ripple in the calm water. Alone, I stood motionless as this holistic scene engulfed my body.

I felt a most calming effect radiate through my system. It was great to feel so intimate with my environment. I paused for several inhaling breaths before reengaging my senses.

Off the bow of the yacht, I noticed the line was tied up to a white mooring ball. The mooring ball, securely attached to the beautiful reef below, meant we were at our first dive sight.

I went down to the main deck and smelled breakfast being prepared, grabbed a cup of coffee, and followed the stairs down to inspect the dive platform. All of our diving gear had been stowed in individual lockers and tagged appropriately with our names. Close to the giant stride step-off platform was a dry erase board with a line-item list of all the guests' names. Next to each name there was a small square open box where an on and off board designation could be noted.

After breakfast, the diving crew and guests met in the salon for our first dive briefing. All the guests were Advanced Divers, but the fundamentals of safe diving off the Spoilsport were a required discussion.

We were given a colorful description of the dive site, what types and variety of sea life we will encounter, layout of the coral reef and strength of current we may have to navigate. We were told we would be doing our two morning dives at this site. During lunch, our boat would move to another distant mooring ball where we would do our afternoon and night dives. This, we were told, would be the general diving routine for the week. With their final instructions being said, we were told, "The pools open. Let's go diving".

We all headed for the dive platform, suited up, double checked our gear, and did our first giant stride off the Spoilsport.

Entering the pristine water of the beautiful Coral Sea was absolutely breathtaking. The water was very clear making the visibility seem like looking into 'coral reef infinity'. Close to the surface the reef was vibrant with color diminishing with each finning into the depth. The sea fans and anemones, waving in the mild current, beckoned us to explore every inch of their underwater paradise.

As I was making my buoyancy adjustments, the sea around me began to come to life with a variety of small colorful fish. Different and much more plentiful than those I encountered in the Caribbean; they kept curiously darting in and out of the reef. Comfortable with me in their environment, the larger fish began to appear as well.

I gave the OK sign to my dive buddy; Linda and we began to navigate this lovely new adventure. The water temperature was 82 degrees, perfect for warm water diving.

Starting against the mild current, I checked my compass to chart our general direction. We planned our first dive to last approximately 40 minutes at a maximum depth of 50 feet. I knew, based on the current, we would want to go against it for approximately 22 minutes, returning to the boat in 18 minutes. Getting comfortable with our new environment was our goal before diving deeper and staying down longer.

When we returned to the boat, we climbed the short ladder to the dive deck, removed our gear, showered off in fresh warm water and checked the 'back on board' box next to our name.

The between morning dive snack was oatmeal raisin cookies, my favorite. So, I slid a few on a plate, grabbed a soft drink, to wash away the saltwater taste in my mouth. Then I went to the top deck to exchange, "guess what we saw?" stories with the other divers.

We did all five dives on the first day. Two were at our morning dive site, with the afternoon and night dives on our second mooring. Since we had done the night dive sight during daylight, our dark nocturnal experience was enhanced. Night dives on a familiar reef, with a cloudless sky and a bright full moon are my favorite.

Our first day on the Spoilsport was exceptional. The weather was tropical-like, and the diving was great. The staff was over the top courteous and helpful. In addition to assisting us with our dive gear, they served us three great meals along with two post dive snacks.

The bonus of our liveaboard diving trip was meeting new exciting fun-loving people from several countries around the world. Exchanging stories about both family and culture was making this a once in a lifetime experience. I went to bed tired but with a head full of pleasant memories. I couldn't wait for day two.

The next day, as before, I woke up at 6:00 am, grabbed a cup of coffee and ascended to the top deck for a moment of solitude. Day two was a mirror image of day one. The surrounding environment was warm and quiet, welcoming a new gentle peaceful day.

After the dive briefing Linda and I decided to dive three times instead of the offered five. We wanted to enjoy the relaxing hospitality the Spoilsport and the Coral Sea was offering. We loved our diving opportunities, but we didn't want this to become an exhausting experience. Relaxing on the top deck, reading a book, and talking with the other guests was an important part of our itinerary as well.

On December 31, 1999, I awoke as usual, made my routine trip to get a cup of coffee but more excitedly climbed the stairs to the top deck. On this special day, the end of the 20th Century, I wanted to reflect on the past year and all life's many blessings I had received.

I lingered a few extra minutes on the top deck. At 56 years of age, I knew I would not live to see the changing of another century. I wanted to enjoy each and every minute of this day, saying goodbye to the old century while welcoming the new 21st Century. My spirit was full of joy!

When I came down for breakfast there was an electric feeling in the air. Passengers and staff were excitedly engaging each other, more so than any other day. The contagious joyful feeling of this special day was being shared by all on board the Spoilsport.

Before the second afternoon dive, the boat's recreation director announced a little side activity he had planned. He, some of the staff and any guests who wanted to would take a small boat to an uninhabited island a half mile from the Spoilsport to watch the sunset.

Neil, Reid, and I, along with six fun loving staff, boarded the dinghy to set off for our afternoon adventure. When we stepped onto the small island, we realized how tiny it was, a mile long and a half mile wide, at most. It was barren but served as a white sand oasis for many nautical birds, including Sea gulls, Terns, and Blue-footed boobies.

We found the island had a good-sized population of hermit crabs. So, to enhance our afternoon adventure, we decided to have hermit crab races. It was great fun watching our chosen shelled crab slowly moving in the direction we intended. There were very few victories but a lot of laughs!

As the sun began to set, from our island vantage point, we could see just how amazing it was going to be. It was a beautiful clear cloudless sunny day.

The Spoilsport was between us and the setting sun. It was on the same horizontal plane with the boat's bow, slightly protruding into our vision of the setting sun, making it part of this breathtaking scene.

Through its extension the setting sun created a golden path across the blue ocean reaching out to us. I have faith, but taking a step on that golden path, well, it was meant to be enjoyed not taken.

The sun had disappeared! We walked toward our little dinghy to leave the island. We were about ten feet from the water's edge when we saw several sea turtles preparing to make their way out of the water onto the beach. When they saw us, they cautiously delayed their movement and curiously waited to see what we were doing in their migratory space.

We soon realized they were endangered female sea turtles coming to lay their eggs. We hurriedly got in the dingy and pushed off the shore. We went out about 20 feet, dropped anchor and watched as the large turtles emerged from the surf. They were using their flippers to pull their majestic shelled bodies up on the small island.

Preparing for the next generation of hatchlings, the female turtles were looking for the perfect place to dig a nest and lay their eggs. In a few hours, their parental duties would be finished. They would return roaming the Coral Sea.

It was an amazing sight! This was one of the most spectacular experiences Mother Nature has to offer. 'My eyes and brain were filled with magical moments from that afternoon, December 31, 1999'.

Back on board the Spoilsport we began our preparations for the festivities of New Year's Eve. The guests and staff were all dressed in costumes. To heighten our excitement, the recreation director had a few contests we could engage in.

At 11:59 we began our countdown to the new century. When the clock struck 12:00, we all jubilantly celebrated this joyous occasion. The boat's cook, a former Australian Special Army Ranger, went to the bow of the Spoilsport and began shooting, the only form of fireworks we had, emergency flares. After shooting off a few the captain ordered him to stop and save a few, just in case we actually had an emergency. By land standards it was a benign muted celebration, but special, nonetheless. The new century had formally arrived!

Our Sons, Neil, and Reid, always up for extended periods of merriment, stayed up most nights to play card games and have a few drinks with the crew. They were a joy to travel with and always found ways to extend themselves, enhancing our vacations together. This New Year's celebration was another opportunity for them to do just that.

The next morning Neil proudly showed us a photograph of his younger brother, Reid, wearing a tall white chef's hat with faux dog poop on top of it. After the New Year's guest celebration subsided, they and the crew decided to gather, as they had several previous nights, in the now vacated salon. They had a few additional drinks and played several rounds of a card game called, "shit head." It was a spirited contest where the loser had to wear the ghastly adorned chef's hat for the night. The supposedly embarrassing photograph actually showed Reid smiling, quite proud of his accomplishment.

Not to be the only star of the day, Reid brought his brother's notoriety to our attention as well. Neil, he stated, was always sleeping in from their late-night frivolity. He was never out of bed until way late in the morning. The yacht's early rising crew, making sport of Neil, placed a saucer of milk at his cabin door.

It was all another fun way to bring in the new century.

Our daily dive briefing included the much-anticipated afternoon shark feeding event. Two years earlier, we as a family, had been involved in a shark feed in the Bahamas. Additionally, we had been diving in the Caribbean with sharks on several occasions, mostly with 6-foot reef sharks and 8-to-10-foot nurse sharks. So, we were comfortable being in the water with sharks. But we realized in each situation, diving with the major predators could be dangerous.

The description of this briefing seemed very similar to our previous shark feed diving experience, with one major difference. In the Bahamas we entered the water together and formed a large circle approximately 40 feet in diameter, at a depth of 30 feet and knelt in the sand. A large 10-gallon sized bucket of frozen fish and chum was lowered from the boat to attract the sharks. The shark feeding experienced dive masters and instructors monitored the attracted frenzy feeding sharks. They held 3-foot-long cattle prod like steel bars, just in case the sharks ventured too close to us.

On the Spoilsport we were told all divers would enter the water together, navigate our way to steel bar cages, much like a jail cell, situated in the white sand below. When in the cages, like in the Bahamas, a 10-gallon sized bucket of frozen fish and chum would be lowered from the boat to attract the area sharks.

The idea of being in steel bar cages made us seem a little leerier about what type and size of predators we may be encountering on this shark feeding dive.

The shark feeding plan, which the Spoilsport crew had carried out on several occasions worked perfectly. As soon as the frozen bait ball was lowered it began melting. The sharks were attracted to the scent of an easy meal. Immediately, much like in the Bahamas, 10-15 of the 4 feet to 6-foot reef sharks began a feeding frenzy. The hungry predators circled the rapidly defrosting fish, ripping and tearing at the now exposed aquatic buffet. The shark's movements were rapid, precise, and vicious in their attacks on their dangling dinner.

Similarly, even though we were in cages, the dive masters and instructors held 3-foot-long cattle prod like steel bars, just in case a big Tiger Shark was attracted to the buffet, or the others became overly aggressive. Sharks feeding on the bait ball was accepted, even encouraged, attempting to attack the guests was not. Many miles from any emergency medical facility, we were adequately protected as the feeding frenzy took place.

In 15 minutes, the shark feeding frenzy was over. The once large fish ball was all gone and so were the sharks. We sifted around the sand under where all the action took place, collecting sharks' teeth that had fallen in their eagerness to attack the frozen fish.

When we were back on board the Spoilsport, the recreation director told us there was another part of the shark feed attraction yet to be displayed. As we gathered on the rear of the main deck, we looked down at our 'special ops' cook as he prepared to put on a show for us.

He secured a previously frozen Tuna on a sturdy extended metal pole and held it approximately four feet above the water. Dangling and dripping with now thawing chum, the Tuna began attracting sharks to the surface. One of the half dozen circling sharks breeched the water and chomped on the Tuna. He didn't get much of the fish but enough to pique its interest.

The next shark followed suit, but this time bit so hard into the Tuna it hung on the dangling fish. With its full body out of the water the shark thrashed about trying to chew the Tuna off the pole. The sturdy cook held fast. But ultimately the shark got what it came after and the bait was gone. Another Tuna was attached to the pole and the show of man versus wild animal continued for another round.

That night Linda and I decided to do the night dive. The water was clear, the moon was out and the lights from the boat drifted down 20 feet below the surface. After approximately 40 minutes of a comfortable enjoyable dive, I guided Linda back to the boat to begin our safety stop. Our usual decompression stop was at 15 feet for three minutes.

As I ascended to 15 feet, I looked up into the lighted area at the back of the dive platform. I saw four to six reef sharks, probably from our earlier feeding frenzy group circling around it. I watched, wondering what they were doing at our dive platform and, more importantly, how were we going to get past them to get back on board the boat.

I had plenty of air left in my tank so there wasn't a sense of urgency, rather one of safety. I waited and watched closely as the sharks seemed to be calm and controlled as they maintained their circular swimming motion.

Then I saw some small wavy rings in the water spreading out from a point of impact. One shark casually swam to the place where the circular wavy rings originated. It appeared to open its mouth, grab whatever was in the water and fin a few feet away.

I watched as a few more splashing surface impacts occurred. The rings spread and other sharks leisurely swam up and swallowed the plopped item. After watching this eerie scene one more time I realized someone on the boat was feeding the sharks.

It wasn't a semi-controlled feeding frenzy scene as we had witnessed earlier, it was more like feeding fish in an aquarium. However, I was in this very large aquarium with several really big predatory fish.

Cautious and wary, between timed plops in the water, I finned toward the surface. Avoiding the circling sharks, I reached the dive ladder. Then quickly slipping off my fins I climbed to the dive deck. When I removed my dive mask, I saw the culprits of this shark feeding prank, mischievously smiling at me.

Neil, Reid, our recreation director, and our army ranger cook were each holding a platter of leftover steak from the evening meal. They obviously had decided to add some unexpected adventure to our night dive.

With Linda now by my side we laughed at the misadventure of our sons and their supporting cast. Something told us this is not the first time the recreation director and cook had pulled this prank.

The next day, our last on the Spoilsport, was a great adventure. At our afternoon briefing the dive instructor told us we would be making two afternoons and one night dive on the wreck of the SS Yongala. He told us about the Yongala, a 350-foot-long luxury passenger steamship, carrying 49 passengers and 73 crewmembers sunk during a Cyclone in 1911. It went undiscovered for forty years.

He said due to Yongala's long isolation on the Great Barrier Reef and its location 48 miles from land, it had become a magnet for marine life. He said we would discover every inch is teeming with life, from soft corals covering the hull and swarms of tropical fish to giant trevally and schools of barracuda, sea turtles, sharks, sea snakes, manta rays and eagle rays. All are common, he said in this undersea mecca.

He told us the Yongala is sitting upright with its top deck at 50 feet and the wreck descending to100 feet, resting in the sand. Our visibility, he stated, would be between 30 to 50 feet and we should stay on the starboard side of the Yongala. He cautioned us saying they have been spotting tiger sharks feeding in the portside sand area and he didn't want an unfriendly encounter with them. Our instructor finalized his briefing by telling us; this is a national historic site and as such we weren't allowed to touch or penetrate the wreck.

The current was strong as we moved hand over hand to the mooring ball, descending down its anchored line. This was definitely an advanced diver's playground.

I was in awe as the swarms of fish appeared surrounding the Yongala. There were more schools of tropical fish than I had ever seen at any previous dive site. The trevally and six bar angelfish were twice the size of any others we had encountered. There were turtles and spotted eagle rays in abundance. Menace looking large barracuda patrolled the wreck like silver soldiers on patrol. My eyes were filled with the plethora of extravagant nautical offerings this amazing historic dive site shared with us.

A few feet from the Yongala I spotted a black and pearl banded sea snake. It was beautifully undulating around the wreck. The poisonous snake was about three feet long with a flat tail for streamlined movement. I had seen them on special sea life television shows and was enamored by their grace underwater.

Another one came into view, and I followed its slow carefree motion. I finned close to the venomous snake, aware of its docile nature. The sea snake's small fangs were situated in the back of its mouth, used more for feeding than attacking.

Curious, I gently put my bare hand under the passing snake and let it roll over my palm. I finned alongside the snake and let it glide over my hand one more time. Knowing it's, "Not nice to mess with Mother Nature", I moved on exploring more of the Yongala.

When we emerged to the deck all the divers were oohing and awing over the beautiful variety and amazing size of the fish life on the Yongala. Many were saying it's by far the best dive site they've ever been on. We were euphoric with our superlatives passing them around like large candy bars to small hungry children.

Everyone, dive masters, instructors as well suited up for the second afternoon dive. No one wanted to miss a moment in this magical underwater aquatic arena.

Again, after emerging, the stories of did you see that, or wasn't that the greatest thing you've ever seen, resonated through the divers and crew.

However, during the second dive the current had picked up dramatically. The degree of difficulty getting hand over hand to the Yongala and back had increased. But that was barely discussed between us.

At dinner we all were excitedly planning our night dive. We wanted to hurry up, eat, skip the desert, wait an hour for sunset and then finish our final dive of our trip at the Yongala.

We were acutely aware the early morning calm water had evolved into white capped waves getting larger by the hour. The bow of the Spoilsport was rising higher and falling deeper seemingly with each wave. But we were optimistic that the rough sea was surface prevalent, and the water below was still calm enough to dive.

Anticipating the night dive briefing in the salon, the captain of the Spoilsport greeted us instead. He told us there was a cyclone heading our way and we must take safety measures, abandon the night dive on the Yongala and head 48 miles to Townsville.

As he spoke, the large solid coffee table, weighing at least 40 pounds slid from one occupied sofa in the salon to the other. With the next wave it moved back to its original position. The captain's point was being reinforced.

We were all very disappointed! However, we did not want to end up next to the Yongala as an added attraction to one of the world's best SCUBA diving sites.

The next morning, we awoke safely at our port in Townsville. A member of the crew told us two smaller boats, along with all passengers and crew aboard, had been lost during the cyclone. Our captain had made a really good decision!

Later that day Linda, Neil, Reid, and I flew to Sydney, where we would continue our New Century Holiday Vacation for the next five days. Our travel agent had reserved accommodation for us at the Hyatt Regency Hotel in the Sydney harbor area known as "The Rocks."

From our boutique hotel we could see, less than a mile from us, the famous Sydney Harbor Bridge and the world's most recognized building, the Sydney Opera House. They were two of the 'must visit' places in Sydney.

The weather was sunny, warm, and very pleasant. Everyone we encountered seemed bright and cherry. We were "Yanks," and the locals were happy to have us visit their country.

We first inquired about taking a guided tour of the Sydney Harbor Bridge. We had read about climbing the 463-foot bridge tethered to a safe walkway, while gathering a breathtaking 360-degree panoramic view of Sydney. It sounded like a great safe adventure ascending the bridge over the largest natural harbor in the world, but it was not to be. We were told there was a waiting list for the climb. Reservations, this time of the year, needed to be made at least two weeks in advance. Out of luck, but not out of spirit.

We were able to secure tickets for a guided tour of the Sydney Opera House. This magnificent structure was considered one of the 20th Century's most famous and distinctive buildings. It was designed by Danish Architect John Utzon to specifically fit in the Sydney Harbor. The massive structure resembled an extraordinarily large multi-tiered ship with several triangular shaped sails, bent bracing to catch the sea winds.

We were over the top excited to tour a few of the 1,000 rooms, walk down some of the 300 corridors and visit one of the great performing venues in the Sydney Opera House. Our tour guide described, in great detail, the design, construction and performances in the acoustically perfect opera palace.

After the tour inside the Sydney Opera House, we went outside and walked around the massive structure. It was breathtakingly beautiful situated in the harbor shadowing the Sydney Harbor Bridge.

During the next few days, we walked around the downtown area referred to as "The Rocks" shopping and dining. The weather was perfect and the people, staff, and locals were very polite and courteous.

When it was time to leave Australia for Fiji, the last leg of our century changing holiday, we packed up and headed for the airport. We arrived at our departure gate to find we were an hour late and our plane had left. We had overlooked a time change in our itinerary.

This oversight meant we would have to spend another night in Australia and wait a day for the next day's flight to Fiji. We were disappointed that we would be losing a day of adventure in Fiji.

We booked a room in a hotel close to the airport, enjoyed an evening dinner and went to our rooms. At least Linda and I did.

The next morning, I awoke and walked toward the bathroom to prepare for the day. I stopped when I noticed something slid under our hotel room door. At first, I thought it was our bill for our overnight stay. But when I bent over to pick it up, I fanned out seven $100.00 bills. I looked in amazement at this large financial discovery. I tried to piece together a scenario as to how that much money would be secretly placed under our room's door.

At breakfast Neil and Reid looked tired but they had a mischievous demeanor about them. When I told them I had discovered seven crisp $100.00 dollar bills slid under our hotel room door, they erupted in laughter.

They filled our breakfast conversation with their adventure from the night before, when they discovered our hotel had a casino in it. They said after dinner, and a little restless, they roamed around the hotel and found the casino.

They related that the casino had a variety of gaming tables, including Blackjack, which was their preferred card game. There were only two blackjack tables with more people wanting to play than spaces available. Neil and Reid were able to secure two seats and began to play the best odds against the house game. They made some good plays, which garnered attention from some of the people looking on. Bored with standing and watching, a few of the spectators became engaged. They began to place bets on Neil's and Reid's cards.

As Neil and Reid won, so did they. Our boys were not only winning money with their best cards, but they were receiving gratuities from their participating wannabes.

They told us when their lucky streak began to run out, they decided to cash their chips into real green folding money. With much fanfare from the people betting on their cards, they left their seats at the blackjack table.

We all had a great laugh and cataloged another treasured memory.

Getting to the airport on time, we arrived in Fiji later that day. Like Australia, we were met by representatives from our vacation destination, Jean Michel Cousteau's Resort and Spa on Savusavu Bay.

We had chosen this resort for a variety of reasons. First and foremost, the recommendations from former guests were very good. The second was its proximity to the world famous colorful soft corals and big critter dive sites of Fiji. The third and very interesting reason is the owner, Jean Michel Cousteau, was the son of Jacques Cousteau, the inventor of the aqualung, our most important SCUBA diving device. Jacques also recorded many underwater exploration adventures, which were presented in a television series. The exciting diving episodes piqued our initial interest in SCUBA Diving.

We were also very interested to embrace and interact with the culture of the Fijian people. We had read quite a bit about their Polynesian customs, language, and their natural gracious hospitality. The transition from the bustling Sydney lifestyle to the laid back "no worries" Fijian's was greatly anticipated.

Our accommodations at the eco focused resort were ocean front bures, situated less than 100 white sandy yards from the beckoning turquoise water. The open-air plantation shutter windows covered over 50% of the bure, providing shade from the sun while capturing the gentle ocean breezes.

The bures were spaced gently into this natural environment allowing us to feel one with nature. birds, geckos, iguanas appeared oblivious of our presence, as we seamlessly blended in with theirs. It was a very ethereal holistic feeling.

One palm tree, outside our bure, sported a sign reading, "watch out for falling coconuts." In jest, I gathered Linda, Neil, Reid, and myself under a large blue and white umbrella to take a playful family memory photo.

Our second night, after dinner, Neil and Reid joined three local Fijians in a ceremony involving Kava. We were not familiar with the South Pacific Islands tradition of sharing Kava, but soon discovered it was a great way to embrace the culture of the Fijian people.

We noted Neil's and Reid's group was seated on the ground in a relaxed yoga style. In the middle of them was a large shallow bowl of what appeared to be cloudy water. They were enjoying the serenity of the evening talking and humming along with a softly played guitar.

Occasionally one of them would clap their hands and a small hollowed out coconut cup with Kava was passed to the clapper. We soon realized, one clap meant "low tide" or a small portion of Kava in the cup, while two claps noted "high tide", with a larger pour in the cup.

Soon Linda and I joined the group, which welcomingly spread out and replenished the Kava bowl. Two claps were the main request of this evening. We realized the mood elevating and relaxing effect of the Kava was clearly one of the reasons the Fijians were a laid-back people.

After we returned from our New Millennium Vacation, Linda and I sat down and recounted our many adventures with Neil and Reid. We knew this was probably our last family trip together.

During the previous ten years we had visited 18 countries, mostly SCUBA diving related vacations. In each of these countries we studied the various cultures and interacted with many of their local citizens.

We had increased our knowledge of the many ways other cultures lived, worked, played, and were educated. In each country we tried to share some of our culture with them as well. It added up to many great experiences and, most of all, a plethora of wonderful fun filled life lasting memories.

The Terrorist Attack on The World Trade Center

The World Trade Center's large complex consisting of seven buildings, totaling a combined 13,400,000 square feet, was located in lower Manhattan, New York City. It was the focal point in New York's financial district, featuring the landmark Twin Towers, which officially opened on April 4, 1973.

The Original 1 World Trade Center [the North Tower] 1,368 feet high and 2 World Trade Center [the South Tower] standing at 1,362 feet, both containing 110 levels, were the tallest buildings in the world. The South Tower contained the tourist's favorite, "Top of the World Observation Deck," where visitors were at the highest man made point in the world.

About Noon on February 26, 1993, Ramzi Yousef and Eyad Ismail drove a yellow box truck, filled with 1,331 pounds of a urea nitrate-hydrogen gas enhanced device, into the underground parking garage below the North Tower of the World Trade Center. They parked the rented truck, lit a 20-foot fuse, and fled. Twelve minutes later their bomb exploded generating enough pressure to open a 98-foot hole through four levels of sub concrete.

The bomb sent smoke billowing all the way up to the 93rd floor, filling stairwells with the thick black haze. The bomb, originally thought to be an electrical transformer explosion, cut off all power in the North Tower, making evacuation of the building difficult, and to some impossible. Hundreds of people were trapped in the building's elevators for several hours.

When the North Tower was finally evacuated the police reported, six people had been killed and another 1,042 were injured in the massive explosion. The perpetrators of this horrendous crime fled the United States before the facts of their murderous atrocity was discovered.

During the formal investigation by the ATF, FBI, and NYPD the extensive details of the bombing plot were discovered. As the authorities pieced together the elaborate scheme, they discovered the WTC Bombing was an "Act of Terrorism."

The motive for the WTC Bombing, cited in a letter from Yousef to the New

York newspapers, mailed just before the attack, was: "Islamic Fundamentalism." His letter cited "American foreign policy in the Middle East and U.S. support for Israel as the justification for their Act of Terrorism." Yousef identified himself as a freedom fighter for the Liberation Army Fifth Battalion.

The demands Yousef released to the media included, "End U.S. interference with any Middle East countries' interior affairs…End aid to Israel and end diplomatic relations with Israel."

In 1994, after scouring the international community, four of the six active WTC bombing participants, all from mid-East countries, including Jordan, Pakistan, and Iraq, "the bombing squad" had been convicted. The investigating authorities discovered many of the terrorists had been prepped at an Al-Qaeda training camp in Afghanistan.

In 1995 the mastermind of the WTC bombing, Yousef, from Kuwait, was captured in Islamabad, Pakistan. He was caught while in the process of making a baby carriage bomb. Yousef was immediately deported to the United States to serve his two life prison sentences.

During his incarcerated interrogation, Yousef's intent was to place the bomb in a location to topple Tower 1 over onto Tower 2, collapsing them both and killing 250,000 people. According to a structural engineer's released study; Yousef's bomb was approximately 150 feet from achieving his desired results. Yousef also revealed the financial support for the terrorist attack came from his uncle, Kahled Sheikh Mohammed.

On the morning of September 11, 2001, I drove to my office, CJB Enterprises, located at 3417 Bethel Avenue, Muncie, Indiana. My normal workday began at 8:00am and wrapped up around 6:00pm.

At Noon I would take my lunch break, go to the Ball State University men's locker room, and change into my running gear. Then, joining my running buddies, Gary Schliessman, an insurance sales executive, Ramon Avila, a Distinguished Professor in Marketing, would go for a 10K run.

Gary would regale us with his favorite previous night's half hour television show, which he would stretch to cover our entire 48-minute run. Or Ramon would discuss his favorite sporting events and activities. I was a good listener!

On this day, however, our pleasant, healthy invigorating, stress relieving, interactive routine would be interrupted.

Shortly after 9:00 am one of my staff came into my office and said there had been a plane flying into a building in New York City. I didn't think too much of it as a couple of other incidents with planes flying into buildings had previously occurred.

I had a television in my personal office, so I turned it on. A few of my staff gathered around it as well. We watched a stream of black smoke about three fourths of the way up the tall building pouring out of a side of one of the World Trade Center Towers. It appeared that a small plane, perhaps full of tourists, had accidentally flown into the building. The WTC building was so massive the smoldering smoke, while significant, seemed to be contained to a small area on one floor.

As we continued to watch the TV commentator, confused as we were, became more animated describing the flames and smoke were actually spreading into another level of the building.

Watching in absolute astonishing amazement we observed a second airplane appearing on the TV screen and instantaneously, with purpose, flew directly into the second WTC Tower. Within a few seconds there were two highly visible streams of black smoke coming from the two buildings.

The commentator, barely able to keep up with the news being passed to her, became even more verbally animated as she conveyed both planes had been hijacked and intentionally flown into the WTC Twin Towers. From our televised vantage point, at present, the smoke and flames appeared contained to just two floors on one side of the buildings.

More of my staff, growing curious with the in-office conversations, came in to watch the in-time TV coverage. The confusing tragedy was occurring before our very own eyes. We were all in absolute disbelief watching the aftermath of the damage being created by the two intentional self-guided missile-like airplanes.

As the TV coverage of the thickening black smoke continued to billow out, the commentator revealed that at least two additional similar commercial passenger airplanes had been hijacked as well.

Within a half hour a third hijacked airplane, a piloted guided missile crashed into the west side of the Pentagon building in Arlington County Virginia. We did not have any TV coverage of that attack, but I began to fully comprehend the synchronized orchestrated planning, which was taking place in front of me. The massive destruction being created by these yet unknown hijackers was overwhelming.

The fourth and we discovered the final, hijacked airplane now identified as United Airlines Flight 93, with a crew of seven carrying 33 passengers, left Newark New Jersey airport approximately 30 minutes later than the other hijacked planes. The now fully understood suicide missions of the three other planes being reported was picked up by some of the very concerned families of passengers on Flight 93. This extremely dire information was telephoned to them, now being held hostage, by their loved ones.

Some of Flight 93's passengers, knowing full well of their imminent death, rushed their captors in an attempt to regain control of their airplane. Somehow their heroic attempt forced the hijackers, heading for their target in Washington D.C., to crash the plane in a field near Shanksville, Pennsylvania.

Many lives were lost in the crash of Flight 93, but more were saved by the passenger's heroics!

But the worst on 9/11/2001 was yet to come.

As we watched live news feeds from the WTC, ash, smoke, and dust residue permeated the surrounding area. An adjacent building's downstairs lobby was being used as the command center for rescue efforts.

The once black smoke billowing out of the buildings had now turned into full jutting out flames. The Twin Towers were on fire!

Firetrucks and police cars, with sirens blaring and lights flashing were rushing to the flaming disaster. "Duty First!" was their call to action.

Since the elevators were not working, we witnessed brave firemen in full rescue gear go into the buildings. They entered the WTC fully aware of the danger they were facing. Heroically, without regard for their own personal safety, they started climbing up the stairs to the stranded, fearful, and certainly some hysterical occupants.

Most of the fortunate people on the lower floors escaped down the stairs as the fireman trudged upward passing by them.

Periodically we would hear a thud on the lobby canopy. The commentator sadly would report the sound of someone jumping to avoid the flames.

It was horrible watching this tragedy unfolding but we are Americans. This is our country! We are under attack! We don't know why, and we don't know by whom. But we owe our support to those suffering during this most difficult time. I would not leave them. Still confused, I was going to stay tuned in to the live television coverage until the who's and why's were disclosed.

At 9:59 a.m. the South Tower collapsed! It came crashing down, a little slowly, then in a rush to hit the ground. Debris dust exploded from the collapse clouding the air and simultaneously covering the surrounding area. I inhaled the fright of it! I closed my eyes and then reopened them trying to unsee what had just happened.

At 10:28 a.m. the North Tower collapsed! Much the same as the South Tower had, leaving this unimaginably huge void in the sky where the Towers had been majestically standing just an hour and a half earlier.

It was eerie! It was scary! It was traumatic! It was hurtful! It was sad! The surprise brutal attack was deadly!

After quelling some of my emotions and getting some solid thinking back, I told my staff to put a closed sign on the front door and go home. "Comfort and be with your families," I said. Then, I too left, locked the door behind me and went home to be with my family.

Five minutes later I was at home with Linda, who had the news coverage of the WTC terrorist attack on our television. We were in shock by the destruction caused by this horrendous attack.

Before our eyes we saw dark gray ash dust covering everything in sight. Cars, streets, signs, all of it appeared soot covered. The live news feed scene before us looked like a spooky movie set waiting for some sign of movement.

Standing alone just a few city blocks from Ground Zero facing the camera, the solemn, yet strong, female news person, Ashleigh Banfield, began describing the situation in graphic detail. As she spoke a solitary individual emerged from the gray cloudy backdrop behind her. The figure looked ghoulish, covered from head to toe with dark gray ash dust. There was a total lack of color in his appearance. All we could distinguish were his eyes jutting out from his grit covered face. He moved hurriedly walking, with a getaway purpose, down the middle of the vacated street.

Then others began to appear from the cloudy mayhem. Sensing a rebirth, they walked toward the light without dust.

Ashleigh continued by telling us the Port Authority, who managed the WTC turnstiles; reported as many as 16,000 people visited the buildings daily. This statistic did not bring us any comfort.

She did confirm the news, President George W. Bush was safe, but his location, for security purposes, was unknown. The same statement applied to Vice President Dick Chaney, who had earlier ordered US F-15 Fighter Jets to shoot down any unidentified or hijacked aircraft.

Since approximately 9:30 a.m. all airplanes in the United States had been ordered grounded. The commercial air space in the U.S. and Canada had become a no-fly zone. Unbeknownst to us, the fatal heroic Flight 93 had been flying directly into the F-15's crosshairs.

She continued to report updates from the FBI and CIA, findings about the hijackers. Although all of their identities were not yet known, they were confirmed to be affiliated with al-Qaeda. This is the same radical Islamic terrorist organization that, in 1993 had attempted to bring down the World Trade Center Towers. This time they had been successful!

A short time later, we were told an estimated 6,000 people, in and around the WTC had been killed. The number of estimated dead was staggering, but far less than the potential 16,000 possible deaths reported earlier.

As the sorrow filled day dredged on a flicker of good news would be reported. A person known to have been working in the WTC, would find a phone and call a family member to assure them, to their joyous relief, they had escaped the tragedy. Then another call and another was made, and all were ecstatically received. At the end of the day over 2,000 families, thought earlier to have been directly affected by this massive attack, were saved from its devastation.

The, now realized, tragic scene of the brave firefighters with their firetrucks and emergency vehicles racing to the WTC, along with the many heroic police officers, was repeated several times during the day. In my mind I tried to imagine the courage it took for those brave people to have attempted to fulfill their mission. Vacantly, I could not!

Being in a war knowing I could fight back, protect myself, was entirely different than these, now deceased, brave rescuers climbing up those WTC stairs totally defenseless.

The breathtaking videos of the hijacked airplanes, guided by the radical al Qaeda terrorists were repeatedly shown impacting the Twin Towers.

The redundancy and the repetition of the on-scene newscast drove home the full effect of the Hero versus the villain and coward concept. I wondered if this was the way my parents had felt when the Japanese had cowardly and secretly executed a surprise attack on Pearl Harbor on December 7, 1941, two years before my birth.

The day after Pearl Harbor was attacked, President Franklin Roosevelt and the Congress of the United States of America declared War on Japan. I began to wonder what retaliatory action was going to be taken against the multinational al Qaeda terrorists.

Much like the aftermath of the assassinations of President John F. Kennedy in 1963, Black Civil Rights Leader, Martin Luther King Jr. in 1968 and presidential hopeful Robert F. [Bobby] Kennedy, a few months later in 1968, we would be continuously watching our televisions mourning this tragic loss for several days.

The deeply personal disastrous stories of families with lost loved ones, persons thought dead emerging from the building's cloudy rubble, updated police reports of who was involved in the terrorist attack were streamed live to us as we closely watched the updates.

To ensure future safe air travel, the civilian air space of the United States and Canada was closed, with all airplanes and thousands of waiting passengers, grounded until September 13. This two-day period gave the government time to ensure there were no other terrorists waiting to hijack more planes. It also allowed the authorities' time to institute new air travel screening procedures. In order to avoid financial panic, the global business structure of Wall Street was closed until September 17. Out of both respect and concern, many businesses across the country closed as well.

It soon became obvious; the world as we knew it yesterday would never be the same!

The next day, September 12, the public learned Osama bin Laden, founder of al-Qaeda, was the person who had orchestrated the WTC terrorist attack. It was also revealed Khalid Sheikh Mohammed; the financial backer of the 1993 attack on the WTC had funded the previous day's disaster as well.

Osama bin Laden had long been an active threatening figure to the United States. A member of a wealthy family in Saudi Arabia, he implored his countrymen to rise up against its "criminal tyrant", the United States of America. For his overt militant actions, he was expelled from Saudi Arabia. In open defiance and the growth and influence of his radical followers, bin Laden set up a terrorist training rebel base In Afghanistan, where he was protected by the militant Taliban controlled government.

From his rebel base camp, Osama Bin Laden, in 1998, declared a holy war on the United States, citing the oppression of Muslims, support of Israel, presence of

U.S. Troops in Saudi Arabia, sanctions against Iraq and a litany of other radical Islamic causes. In the next two years he was involved in a series of terrorist bombings including a U.S. Embassy. For these and many other terrorist focused criminal actions Osama Bin Laden was on the FBI's Most Wanted List.

In early June and July of 2001 several of bin Laden's known radicalized terrorist followers, using false passports, entered the United States. Some began attending airplane flight schools in Florida and Minnesota. Their odd questions about flying an airplane with no interest in landing it raised red flags with their instructors. Their concerns were sent to the FBI.

The CIA was watching several of the falsely documented terrorists as well. They took surveillance photos and passed them along, without significant emphasis or details, to the FBI.

This lack of coordinated effort between the FBI and CIA allowed the known terrorists unhindered movement and training in preparation for their attack on the WTC. The significant hints of an imminent terrorist strike on the soil of the United States were overlooked.

We soon learned the oversight and uncoordinated efforts by our government agencies, CIA, and FBI, resulted in the deaths of 2,977 innocent lives. Of that number 343 were heroic firefighters and 72 were sacrificing law enforcement officers. Additionally, more than 6,000 people were injured with many more suffering from the cloudy air contaminating residue.

Most of the countries of the world condemned, including predominantly Muslim, the terrorist attack on the WTC and many wondered if their country could be the next target. Their support and alliance were much needed during our country's most difficult time.

While we were mourning our losses in the United States, thousands of Palestinians were dancing in the streets of Iraq. They were celebrating the rebel militant terrorist action against the Israel protectorate, the United States.

Afraid of retaliatory action against their religion and its peaceful followers, Muslim leaders in the United States were quick to react, condemning the terrorist actions of the radical Islamic group. To show their support for their fellow American citizens, the devoutly religious Muslims, organized blood drives and developed many fundraising programs. Their belief was that when one suffers, we all suffer, was paramount in these efforts.

On September 14, not being able to place this terrorist attack on one country, the U.S. Congress passed the "Authorization for Use of Military Forces Against Terrorists". This congressional act allowed the President the authority to use "all necessary and appropriate force" against those who determined, planned, authorized, committed, or ordered" the September 11 attacks or who harbored said persons or groups.

On October 7, approximately one month after the WTC attack, the U.S. led a coalition of international forces in a campaign against the Taliban and al Qaeda in

Afghanistan. The coalition initiated pinpointed aerial bombing attacks on Taliban and al Qaeda camps then later invaded Afghanistan with ground troops. This led to the overthrow of the Taliban's rule in Afghanistan on December 7, 2001.

Osama bin Laden eluded the international community's combined efforts for his capture and remained secretly in hiding, suspected to be in Pakistan.

In 2007 one of bin Laden's most trusted couriers was spotted traveling in a remote area of Pakistan. In 2009 the location where the courier and his brother lived was discovered. Later in 2010 the CIA informed President Obama they were 90% sure the compound where the courier and his brother were living was the home of Osama bin Laden as well.

The private residential compound custom built in 2004 was surrounded by 12' to 18' concrete walls topped with barbed wire. Inside the fortified walls were a few small buildings and a large three-story mansion. Arial surveillance revealed very little coming and going activity but concluded, among a few other residents, one man approximately 6'4", large for most Arabs but the height of bin Laden had been spotted moving about inside the compound.

In April 2011 President Obama ordered a covert operation, "Operation Neptune Spear", to kill or capture bin Laden. After meeting with the National Security Council, planning a secret mission, Obama gave his order to carry out the raid on the suspected hiding place of bin Laden.

On May 2, 2011, the CIA led operation secretly launched two Blackhawk quiet helicopters, with low radar visibility, into Pakistan territory. Each helicopter carried a squad of highly trained and well-rehearsed Navy Seals. The helicopters landed inside the walls of the compound and began their search for bin Laden.

While securing the area the Seals engaged in a brief firefight with the compound's protectorates, killing three while losing none of their own. Advancing inside the mansion, Navy Seal Robert O'Neill entered a third-floor bedroom. There he encountered Osama bin Laden, unarmed, standing behind his wife. Revealing to his superiors, including President Obama, the encounter on his body camera. O'Neill shot and killed him.

Within 24 hours of his death Osama bin Laden, in Islamic tradition, was buried at sea.

Hurricane Iris and The Wave Dancer

Less than two weeks after the World Trade center terrorist attack, my son Reid and I were scheduled to attend a Multifamily Building Convention in Las Vegas. We felt confident the U.S. Government had developed a better passenger screening program, making it safe for us to fly to our annual builder-developer convention.

When we arrived at Indianapolis' Weir Cook Airport, we immediately noticed an intensified effort in the security and screening of all passengers. Additionally, we realized there were probably more security personnel than potential passengers.

As we boarded our 160-passenger airplane we looked around and counted less than ten other passengers on our flight. The ultimate signal was that people were very reluctant to put their lives in an uncontrollable situation soon after the World Trade Center attack. There was most definitely fear in the air.

When we arrived in Las Vegas, we expected to see fewer people than normal, but not the level of vacancy we encountered. The gambling, entertainment, and fun-loving town of Las Vegas, one of the largest vacation destinations in the United States, hosting 39 million guests each year, appeared almost a ghost town.

The gaming tables in the casinos had a mere scattering of gamblers. The normal bustling pedestrian filled sidewalks now were home mainly to a few pamphlet passing promoters. And the retail stores were occupied by a lonely skeleton sales staff. Very few people had ventured on airplanes to get to the glitz, glitter, and frolicking capital of our country.

At our national multifamily builder's convention, the conference projected to have several thousand attendees may have had a couple of hundred. Reid and I gained an advantage being able to engage some of the knowledgeable leaders in the multifamily marketplace. The multifamily convention was a successful venture for us.

During the last few days of September, a poorly defined tropical wave moved across the tropical Atlantic. An extremely hostile upper-level wind environment caused by a large, upper-level trough with an "embedded low" centered just to the northeast of the Lesser Antilles, prevailed over the Atlantic. As the tropical wave reached 50W on the third of October, the upper-low became detached from the trough and began to move toward the southwest over the eastern Caribbean Sea.

Linda and I had planned to celebrate her birthday, October 5th and our 30th wedding anniversary, October 16th, going on a SCUBA diving liveaboard yacht with its dive location, Belize. Known for the second largest barrier reef in the world, famous for SCUBA diving and affectionately known as "Mother Nature's Best Kept Secret," Belize had beckoned our presence.

Linda made reservations for us on the Belize Aggressor, a 110-foot liveaboard SCUBA diving yacht, October 6th through the 12th. On two previous occasions we had visited Belize, SCUBA diving from land-based operations. This floating, moving live aboard operation would allow us to dive a large variety of highly published notable dive sites, including "The Blue Hole."

A week before we were to leave for Belize a representative from the Aggressor Fleet Company called Linda. She told her 30 people from the Richmond Virginia Dive Club were going to be on the dive trip as well. She said 20 of the 30 members were going to be on the Wave Dancer, 120 foot live-aboard and the other ten would be on the Aggressor. She told us they were a fun-loving group, as guests, may not be what we were used to, but they were all good, certified divers. Linda and I wished we had a dive club in our community, so we were looking forward to meeting them.

In Richmond, Virginia, the Richmond Dive Club held a meeting with the 30 Belize traveling members to assure them their travel plans, post 9/11, were still pretty much unchanged. Two of the original members signed up for the trip, frightened by the thought of flying so soon after the WTC attack, cancelled their reservations. The "trip of a lifetime" was so popular that two people on the standby list took their place. Two of the RDC members, originally booked on the Aggressor, were given priority status, and moved from the Aggressor to the more club dominant, Wave Dancer.

At 4:00 pm on Saturday October 6, Linda and I were sitting by the swimming pool at the Radisson Hotel in Belize City, relaxing and enjoying some quiet time together, when the 30 RDC members arrived. We introduced ourselves to a few of the weary looking but smiling travelers. They told us they were exhausted, had a late change in their flight schedule and had been traveling since 4:00 a.m. They said, however, they were ready for sun, fun and great SCUBA diving.

At approximately 5:00 p.m. two crew members from the Belize Aggressor and Wave Dancer walked through the pool gates. They directed us toward the two waiting yachts docked at the Radisson's pier. Both stylish modern yachts gently swaying on the green tropical Caribbean struck a welcoming sight.

Looking down at the 200-foot-long sturdy wooden pier, Linda paused a step. An ominous eerie feeling struck her as she looked to her right at the blue, white and chrome trimmed yacht. Hoping it was not the Aggressor, she sighed in relief when she scanned to her left to see "Belize Aggressor" embossed on the hull of the black and white yacht.

We carried, rolled, and struggled with our heavy dive gear down the long pier. Reaching our destination, an Aggressor crew member told us to drop our heavy luggage and follow him to our top deck cabin.

For our anniversary, Linda had secured the spacious top deck cabin for a little added luxury. When we arrived the crew member told us: "leave your shoes and worries behind. We'll do all the work while you enjoy great fun, sun and diving".

Before Linda and I left our home in the U.S. we knew a small storm was brewing in the ocean hundreds of miles away in the Atlantic. It was hurricane season, and we were on high alert as we continued with our vacation plans.

Unknown to us, at 5:00 p.m., the National Hurricane Center announced that Tropical Storm Iris had now become Hurricane Iris and was a level one storm.

At 6:00 p.m., as planned, The Aggressor and Wave Dancer left the Radisson pier.

After dinner, our Captain, Jerry Schnabel, and his staff met with all the guests in the salon for our initial briefing, orientation of the Aggressor and diving program for the week. Each of the staff made a brief introductory statement as to their jobs on the boat, work experience and place they referred to as home. We were told of their five dives a day program, in between snacks, dining, and freedom to move about the boat, with the exception of the engine room and staff quarters.

Captain Schnabel told us the Aggressor would be moving to two new dive sites each day, one while we were sleeping and the other while we were eating lunch. He further told us there would be a dive site briefing before diving at each new location. Further, he stated we were required to have a 'buddy' to dive with, must check in and out with the dive deck manager, could request a dive master as a personal guide, but otherwise we were on our own.

When he seemed finished talking Schnabel stood up, paused, and said, "Some of you may be aware Tropical Storm Iris has been upgraded to Hurricane category one status. My latest report showed Iris is headed north and west of Belize making landfall in the Yucatan. We are monitoring the progress and path of the storm and will give you updates as we receive them. Have a good night! See you at tomorrow's dive briefing."

Linda and I were relieved with his informative and candid approach to Hurricane Iris. We had been in the path of hurricanes and cyclones before and knew the more information we had the more comfortable we would be. We also knew hurricanes' most common trajectory was a north and west movement. A good sign for our 30th anniversary diving trip.

We each got something to drink and went to the top tier of the Aggressor. Looking out over the calm Caribbean water into a cloudless sky, the stars were gleaming brightly, and the air was fresh and clean, I thought, life just doesn't get any better than this!

With the gentle rocking of our boat, in the calm Caribbean breeze, an insomniac, I slept motionless. At 6:00 a.m. Sunday I awoke, slipped on a fresh shirt and pair of shorts, got a cup of coffee in the galley, and went up to the top deck.

Alone, I inhaled the full beauty of the environment around me. The gorgeous slightly rippling turquoise Caribbean water, gentle refreshing breeze, cloudless sun filled sky and a small palm tree filled island in the distance. Greeting card picturesque, I thought, this is great, just great!

As I walked from the bow to the stern of the Aggressor, I saw we were tied up to a large white mooring ball. This would be our first dive site on the world's 2nd largest barrier reef of the day. I was really excited about diving in Belize and enjoying this natural wonderful underwater environment.

After breakfast, the dive staff and guests met on the dive deck for our first briefing. Using the white dry erase board, with colored markers, the dive master had laid out the dive area we would be exploring. Each color he had used depicted coral reefs, swim troughs, variety of fish, and a few arrows showing the direction of the current.

As we were eagerly listening to his colorful description of the coral reefs, large and small fish, I looked around the dive deck and noticed someone was missing. Captain Schnabel, promising to be at our first dive briefing, was not there.

Still, eagerly Linda and I suited up for our first dive of the day. We did our giant stride into the clear Belizean water and descended to 40 feet. It was our goal to cruise around the shallow reef, acclimating our body and refreshing our diving minds to this new environment.

Always careful not to push our limits on our first dive, we emerged 45 minutes later. We removed our dive gear and enjoyed a warm open air rinse shower. Toweling off we went to the galley, grabbed a couple of fresh baked chocolate chip cookies, a mouth cleansing soft drink and went to the top deck.

Interacting with other divers, getting to know our fellow dive boat buddies, we exchanged a few diving stories. We discussed what we had seen on the first dive, our accommodations on the Aggressor and some of the places we had dived on prior trips. After our required dive interval, we went back to the dive deck and prepared for our second dive of the morning.

When our second dive was completed Linda, and I went to our cabin to freshen up for lunch. At our dining table we all again exchanged stories of our morning dives and more, getting to know your stories, which included where we called home, family, all good stuff.

Toward the end of our lunch Schnabel came into the dining area with his promised updated hurricane announcement. A professional, with a mannerism befitting his position, he appeared not quite as confident as the night before.

Schnabel told us Hurricane Iris had shifted a little south of its originally projected path and was now moving more toward the northern part of Belize and south of the Yucatan. He said, according to the reports he had received, Hurricane Iris may be increasing in force. Schnabel further stated he had been through two previous hurricanes and assured us he would error on the side of caution when it came to the safety of his guests, crew, and the Aggressor.

Finally, he said, "As you have noticed the Aggressor is moving to our next dive site. We will do our afternoon and night dives at this location. Our dive master's will have a briefing for you shortly after lunch. I will have an update on Hurricane Iris for you at dinner. Enjoy your day!"

Immediately the conversation in the dining area turned from great weather and memorable diving to Hurricane Iris.

During our first afternoon dive, I saw a rare Pigmy Seahorse clinging to a waving coral whip. It was a great find! However, after three successive dives, Linda and I decided to skip the next one, grab a book and lounge on the top deck.

There was a little more anticipation at dinner as we were all waiting for our Hurricane Iris update. When Captain Schnabel entered the dining area an immediate hush fell over the room.

He told us Hurricane Iris was now a stronger, more threatening storm, heading directly for Belize. He said, after the night dive the Aggressor was heading for Belize City to top off fuel, get a better bearing of the storm and make plans to avoid it. He said he expected, with the storm making landfall somewhere in Belize, we would likely miss diving on Monday.

At approximately 2:00 a.m. Monday October 8, I looked out our cabin window to see we were tied up to the Radisson Pier. I saw Captain Schnabel on the pier talking with a couple of other men. Knowing he was in charge of the situation I went back to sleep.

At 6:00 a.m. I awoke, went to the galley to get a cup of coffee, and saw Schnabel there as well. We had spoken a couple of times before about Hurricane Iris. He knew I knew my stuff, wouldn't ask him a bunch of asinine questions, and so he was open with me about what his plans for the day were.

He told me we were going to a safe haven in southern Belize called Big Creek. He said it was approximately 90 miles south of Belize City, a place where the Aggressor had successfully tied up in 1998 during the devastating Hurricane Mitch.

Later at breakfast, Captain Schnabel told all of us Hurricane Iris was now a powerful Category Three Hurricane and could increase in force as it makes landfall later in the day. The present direction of Hurricane Iris has it hitting Belize between Belize City and Placencia, a small tourist town less than a mile from Big Creek. Further he said, the Aggressor would be at Big Creek in about an hour.

When asked by one of the RDC members where the Wave Dancer was located, Schnabel said he didn't know. He told us they had tried to make radio contact with the Wave Dancer but did not receive a response.

At 9:00 a.m. Captain Schnabel navigated the Aggressor into the narrow fifty-yard-wide channel of Big Creek. As the Aggressor emerged through an opening in the surrounding mangroves, safety appeared in the form of a large, well-built concrete dock with an adjoining pre-engineered metal warehouse building.

The six-hundred-foot-long concrete dock, two-trucks wide, with six equally spaced Samson Posts were the main tie up points to secure stationary boats. Rubber bumpers spaced ten to fourteen feet apart ran the face of the dock. The dock itself sat six feet above water level and included a concrete apron connecting it to the warehouse. The massive metal structure, large enough to house four boats the size of the Aggressor, was substantially affixed to a five-foot block wall, which was then anchored to its foundation. The two structures were the largest of their kind south of Belize City.

Schnabel maneuvered the Aggressor's bow twenty-five feet from the stern of Miss Gayle, a previously secured small tugboat. He ordered his first mate to prepare the ropes to secure his boat. There were ample ropes to affix the bow and stern lines to the Samson Posts, with enough slack to allow the boat to rise during the anticipated surge of the storm. He also set up spring lines to keep the boat from moving fore and aft and avoid hitting Miss Gayle.

When completed there were four boats secured at the Big Creek Dock with sixty feet available for another, who may scurry in later.

Schnabel made several phone calls inquiring about potential more hurricane proof accommodations in the general area. None were found.

After lunch Captain Schnabel told us Hurricane Iris had changed its path south and was headed directly for the Big Creek-Placencia area. Further he stated, Hurricane Iris was now listed as a category four hurricane, which meant we were going to get the full blast and major surge from this now monstrous storm.

We began preparing the Aggressor, storing all loose equipment, dive gear, anything that could become a misguided projectile during the now advancing hurricane.

At 2:00 p.m. the Wave Dancer appeared through the Big Creek mangroves seeking refuge from Iris.

Captain Martin, clearly surprised at his predicament, navigated the 120-foot Wave Dancer to the sixty-foot available space on the concrete pier.

Captain Schnabel and some of Captain Martian's Belizean crew suggested Martin run the Wave Dancer into the mangroves for protection from the imminent storm and its predicted ten-fourteen-foot surge. But he refused stating he didn't want to get his boat scratched up from the brush and limbs in the dense marshy area.

Instead, Martin secured the bow of the Wave dancer to the same Samson Post as the stern of the Aggressor. Approximately fifty-foot inland, close to the warehouse, was another Samson Post, where Martin attached two less sturdy spring line ropes.

When completed the fifty to sixty feet of Wave Dancer's stern floated in Big Creek, exposed to the elements of Mother Nature.

Glenn Prillaman, President of the Richmond Dive Club, was a warm, friendly, fun loving prankster type of a guy. His business card read.

Used cars-Land-Whiskey

Manure-Nails-Computers Verified

Wars Fought-Governments Run-Counterfeiting

Horse Trading-Ballot Boxes Stuffed-Revolutions Arranged

Wheels-up Landings-Parties

GLENN PRILLAMAN

804-320-2989

Wenches-Wrenches-Banquets-Military Secrets

Dancing Girls-Bootlegging-Artificial Insemination

Seductions-One-way Rides Arranged-Wiretaps-Balls

Black Market Surplus-Suicides Committed-Orgies Organized

Also, an Assortment of Nuts and Bolts-Mostly Nuts!

Prillaman and the RDC members had all planned to have a fun filled week with, as they envisioned, the two Yachts, Aggressor and Wave dancer, tied up to the same mooring ball, or at least within visual contact. Their collective idea was to play pranks on each other, which involved participants from both boats.

When the Wave Dancer Was moored, Prillaman hollered to his friends on the Aggressor "Don't come over here without a beer and a blonde." He had staged a few bragging rights pranks, one of which included changing their evening menu to dry erase board to display an elaborate five-star dining experience.

Another Prillaman clowning caper involved the Wave Dancer's lack of amenities. It didn't have a hot tub like the Aggressor, so while one of their co-conspirators videotaped them, Prillaman and one of his buddies jumped in a large freshwater rinse tank. Sporting sunglasses, cigars, and a beer, they frolicked in the tank while another participant turned the valve on a SCUBA tank, inserting it in the rinse tank creating the needed bubbles to simulate their hillbilly hot tub.

In the warm afternoon sun filled sky the members of the RDC drifted from boat to boat sharing stories and bragging about their accommodations. After a couple enjoyable hours, the reunion came to an end. The gravity of our impending situation began to set in, and everyone returned to their respective boats. The threat of Hurricane Iris was real!

After dinner we relaxed, as best we could, watching a slideshow of cave diving narrated by one of our dive masters. Then the calm before the storm, Hurricane Iris, came to an abrupt end.

At approximately 8:00 p.m., Hurricane Iris came out of the Caribbean Sea with its full force, directly focused on the land at Placencia and Big Creek. The small but powerful Hurricane Iris hit us with its full 145 mile per hour Category Four blunt force winds. All the passengers, except Linda and I, went below the main deck into their cabin hallway and sleeping quarters.

Thinking of the disastrous Titanic sinking in 1912 and knowing things usually didn't turn out well for people trapped below deck, I didn't want to go down those stairs. The marine glass windows in the salon were designed to withstand winds up to 150 mph. I liked my chances where I was.

Captain Schnabel joined us crouching low in the Salon.

The heightened roaring wind was so loud we could barely hear each other's calming reassurances. Hurricane Iris was a massive force pulling, pushing, and tearing at our boat. The ropes were straining against the 145 mile per hour winds. Then, Iris' storm surge lifted the Aggressor, almost above the concrete dock.

The shear brutality of Hurricane Iris had struck so fast and with so much savage fury there was no time to think. It was perfectly obvious we had no control over our situation or outcome. We could only hope our initial decisions of time and place would carry us through safely.

Approximately 15 minutes after Iris slammed the Aggressor, an unexpected wind forced projectile crashed through one of the salon's marine glass windows shattering shards across the carpeted floor. Not daunted, we looked at each other, took a deep breath but stayed in our semi protected position. A few minutes later another unidentifiable projectile blew out a second window. Then a third window exploded, spewing glass all around our crouching area.

The risk of staying in the shattered glass-filled salon seemed to be growing by the second. So, we started crawling, hands and knees, through the shards of broken marine glass. Leading the way, I had covered about 20 of the 30 feet needed to reach the stairs when I looked over my left shoulder and saw the lights of the Wave Dancer. Thinking the Wave Dancer's captain was moving his boat to a more secure area in the mangroves, I told Schnabel what I had just seen.

When we descended the stairs into the cabin sleeping area, our fellow passengers all stood clustered in fixed positions with horrified looks on their faces. One person was stirred up in a panic mode, commanding us to stay calm and swearing about our situation. The rest were scared, tense but avoiding the lone panicked outbursts.

Captain Schnabel left Linda and I at the top of the stairs and opened the salon's adjoining door to the dive deck. Despite the reality of flying debris, he had to ensure his boat was still secure and Iris' surge had not broken his spring and stabilizing lines.

The fierce winds from Hurricane Iris, still strong enough Schnabel had to grip on a fixed object, were seemingly beginning to wane a bit. After checking his anchored lines, he peered into the darkness looking for the lights of the Wave Dancer. There were none!

Schnabel secured a search light and panned it along the edge of the mangroves. His light stopped suddenly as it reflected the white hull of the partially submerged bottom of a large boat. As he traversed the searchlight over the boat Schnabel saw a glint of blue, identifying the Wave Dancer's main deck. The Wave Dancer had capsized!

The winds from Hurricane Iris were still raging and the environment was dangerous, but Schnabel ordered his first mate to put the Aggressors six passenger dinghy in the water and go to the Wave Dancer on a rescue mission.

The news of the Wave Dancer capsizing was passed down to us. We were struck by the reality that some of our diving buddies from the RDC and crew from the Wave Dancer were in danger.

I climbed the stairs following two of our more skilled diving passengers, Dave Mower, and Rob Salvatori, offering our assistance where needed. Hurricane Iris' winds, while weaker, were still strong enough to create white caps on Big Creek's water.

The dingy returned to the dive deck with three survivors from the Wave Dancer. The first mate reported the situation on board the Wave Dancer was dire. He said the area was very dark, no lights were coming from the Wave Dancer and more dangerously, the water around the boat was covered with oil slick diesel fuel.

A few moments later, Captain Martin swam up to the Aggressor's dive deck dragging a motionless Glenn Prillaman. Rob's wife Jennifer, and Mary Lou Hayden, one of the three dingy passengers, both registered nurses, began life saving resuscitating procedures on Prillaman. We were standing close by, slightly traumatized by the situation, trying to make ourselves useful in any possible way we could.

After ten fruitless exhaustive minutes, Jennifer pronounced Glenn Prillaman, President of the Richmond Dive Club, dead. We were in a state of disbelief. If Prillaman was dead, what was the fate of all the other members of the RDC and staff on the Wave Dancer?

I, along with another member of the RDC moved Prillaman's body from the dive deck to the concrete dock and covered him with, the only thing we had available, remnants of a cardboard box.

The powerful merciless wind from Hurricane Iris had subsided, but the damage at Big Creek had been done.

Schanabel and Martin conferred on what had happened, what needed and could be done to rescue those remaining on the Wave Dancer. They began to develop a more in-depth rescue, and now more probably recovery mission.

I was an advanced diver, with more than 500 dives, but not a rescue diver so I gave my dive gear to the fortunate surviving first mate of the Wave Dancer. My immediate task had been decided. I would be on the dive deck to assist lifting survivors, or dead bodies from the dingy. In the next hour I was able to assist three more survivors of the dingy.

The rescue divers, masks blinded with oily diesel fuel and tethered to ropes, penetrated the Wave Dancer. Hoping to find survivors in air pockets, only recovering bodies.

The dingy returned with three bodies, then three more on the next trip. At 2:00 a.m., exhausted and impeded by darkness and diesel fuel, the rescue and recovery efforts were called off. The team all agreed to get some rest and resume their efforts at dawn.

At 6:00 a.m. the rescue and recovery team met on the dive deck. They decided to split their efforts, with one team of three people searching the marshy mangroves and two people in the Wave Dancer. At this point, the biggest hope for survivors was in the mangrove area.

At 9:00 a.m. a Special Rescue Team from the British Army arrived at Big Creek to take over the rescue and recovery mission. By then a total of 12 bodies had been recovered, both from the mangroves and the Wave Dancer. Eight people from the Wave Dancer were still missing.

It was a bright warm sunny Caribbean day. Hurricane Iris with all its fury had long since passed. Linda and I decided to go for a short walk, get away from the horrific scene surrounding the tragedy of the Wave Dancer.

We had walked approximately a quarter of a mile when we rounded a corner and saw a local Belizean woman, maybe 50 years old sitting on a small box next to a large basket with clothing and personal items in it. She looked disheveled, tired, and weary.

We asked her if she was okay, did she need any help? She told us Hurricane Iris had blown her house down, her furniture was ruined, and all her worldly possessions were in that large basket. As we attempted to show some sympathy toward her situation, she stopped us. She said how bad she felt for us having lost so many friends.

Wow! Linda and I were totally taken aback by her sincere caring comments.

At noon Captain Schnabel called us all together into the salon. He told us the U.S. Embassy is making arrangements to get us back home to our families. He said after lunch we would be leaving Big Creek and heading for Belize City.

Before we departed the rescue team had recovered six additional bodies and laid them, with the other victims on the large concrete dock. The last two victims of Hurricane Iris and the capsizing of the Wave Dancer will be discovered two days later.

With Robert Robinson's recorded voice singing "The Lord's Prayer" over the Aggressor's sound system, at 1:30 p.m. Tuesday October 9, 2001, The Belize Aggressor III slowly pulled away from the Big Creek dock. The tearful passengers stood in quiet reverence as they took one last glance at the partially covered bodies on the dock. They saw their bare feet sticking out; knowing 72 hours earlier their friends had been told to leave their shoes and worries behind for the vacation trip of a lifetime. For all, in one way or another, it was.

The next day the passengers from the Aggressor and survivors from the Wave Dancer all gathered at the airport to depart Belize. We were a solemn group, suffering from the shock of the tragedy at Big Creek. There was very little interaction between our clustered departing group and the other passengers around us.

One of the Wave Dancer survivors, Dave DeBarger, mentioned to us he heard people talking about the loss of life aboard his boat. The conversation he had overheard was people saying the victims aboard the Wave Dancer were drinking, mostly drunk and having a wild hurricane party. These comments severely bothered him! Not only was his best friend and several other members of the RDC dead, but they were being defamed by uninformed insensitive gossiping people.

Linda and I heard similar impersonal degrading comments about the deceased members of the RDC in the airport as well. We also heard similar general negative comments about the tragedy at Big Creek on our plane ride home.

Some of the sensationalist media both print and television, covering the tragedy of the Wave Dancer focused on the supposed RDC's party-like atmosphere. They alluded to their lack of preparation for Hurricane Iris. The fictitious and maligning rumors about these fine people, who were part of our SCUBA Diving brotherhood, bothered Linda and I a lot.

We discussed the tragedy at Big Creek on several occasions, read several, mostly negative, they should have done this or why did they do that? printed articles. We were unable to let the comments about the defenseless deceased victims from Hurricane Iris languish.

A year after the Wave Dancer tragedy Linda and I decided to right the wrong that was still lingering in our minds about all the innocent victims at Big Creek. We began to collaborate, to write a book about The Richmond Dive Club's great planned "trip of a lifetime" to Belize.

In order to be objective and write a credible book, I visited Belize twice and Richmond, Virginia four times. On those visits I interviewed survivors of the Wave Dancer as well as several other people with direct knowledge of the many tragedies inflicted by Hurricane Iris.

After three long years of writing, editing, and searching for a publisher, in 2005 "No Safe Harbor, The Tragedy of the Dive Ship Wave Dancer "by Joe Burnworth was released in several bookstores across the United States.

The reviews of "No Safe Harbor" were good. The book was applauded by the members of the Richmond Dive Club and SCUBA Divers around the world.

"No Safe Harbor" had its intended effect of making the public aware, the victims on board the Wave Dancer during Hurricane Iris were just that, innocent victims. The responsibility for the loss of their lives rested solely and entirely on the Wave Dancer's owner, Peter Hughes, and its captain, Philip Martin.

The real-life tragedy described in "No Safe Harbor," the loss of life of unsuspecting victims served to heighten the awareness of active SCUBA Divers. Many divers around the world responded by writing reviews highlighting that they now knew they were ultimately responsible for their own individual personal safety.

The book," No Safe Harbor," also changed the way the live aboard dive industry operated, addressing their passenger safety. They were particularly attentive to becoming proactive when there was a storm threatening their dive destinations. While the live aboard dive industries change in their safety protocol was less than Linda and I had hoped for, the passenger safety changes were significant.

No Safe Harbor; Library of Congress Cataloging-in-Publication Data
Burnworth, Joe
No safe harbor: the tragedy of the dive ship Wave
Dancer/ by Joe Burnworth.p.cm.
ISBN 10: 157860219X, ISBN 13:9781578602193, 1. Wave
Dancer (Yacht) 2. Hurricane Iris, 2001. 3. Shipwrecks-
Belize. 4. Scuba divers—United States. I. Title
GV822.W36B87 2005 910.9163'65—dc22 2005008479

Almost exactly a year after Hurricane Iris and the tragedy at Big Creek, compliments of The Aggressor Fleet, Linda and I returned to Belize. It was eerie looking down the long wooden Radisson Hotel Dock with the Belize Aggressor moored at its end. With much trepidation we took our first steps toward the Belize Aggressor, haunting visions and anxiety came, but diminished with each stride.

We stepped aboard the yacht, slipped off our shoes and handed our luggage to our waiting host. We went to our cabin, unpacked our clothes then on to the salon to mingle with the other guests. Linda and I had decided, in advance, we would say nothing of our previous experience aboard the Aggressor.

After dinner we met in the salon with the captain and crew for our welcome aboard briefing. We began to settle ourselves into the familiar yet infamously memorable surroundings of the Aggressor.

At 6:00 am the next morning I went to the galley, got a cup of coffee, and walked up to the sky deck. Alone I inhaled the beautiful morning sun glistening off the calm turquoise Caribbean water. I observed the white mooring ball connected to the Aggressor. It was going to be a great day for diving!

The Fall of CJB Enterprises

On September 11, 2001, when the World Trade Center collapsed normal daily business trade came to a screeching halt. The New York Stock Exchange, scheduled to open Tuesday morning, delayed opening for several days. The government encouraged banks to stay open to avoid panic in the streets. Most other businesses continued operating as best they could.

The tragedy of the terrorist attack on the WTC petrified the general population in the United States. Frightened, they came to a collective long extended pause as they needed to take time to assess their individual present situation.

Overnight they began changing their priorities as they reevaluated the importance of their needs versus wants. Conservatively, only necessary day-to-day items were being purchased as the panicked populace worried about their insecure future.

When 9/11 occurred, my sole owner business, CJB Enterprises, was going and growing incredibly rapidly and strong!

From 1986 to 1992 we had, developed, presold, and built approximately 460 university student condominiums in 11 states across the U.S. Additionally, we had preleased then built 356 apartments and townhomes for Ball State students in Muncie.

In 1993 CJB transitioned to developing condominium housing communities for active adults and retired people. This segment of the market, "Baby Boomers" was projected to be the fastest growing and most underserved in the country.

To better facilitate our growth and become a leader in this new active adult market, my staff and I attended informational seminars, sponsored by the National Home Builders and National Multifamily Housing, focused on these burgeoning Baby Boomers. At these seminars, many classes were offered teaching developers; what floor plans designs attracted/ turned off potential purchasers, how to market our product, community amenities, etc.

We visited new condominium projects in Florida, Arizona, and Las Vegas to compare what we were developing to what major national companies were offering their new residents. We gleaned many ideas, concepts, enhancement offerings, etc. from our now semi-annual trips to these new projects around the country.

From 1993-1996 we went from one 80-unit active adult condominium project in Muncie, to three projects in Evansville, Fort Wayne, and Indianapolis. My idea, with this new concept was to stay in Indiana, reducing my travel, away from home and family time.

All of our new active adult projects contained 80 condominiums, each including a clubhouse and swimming pool. We were selling 20 condominiums at most projects annually, which, excluding planning time, allowed us to enter and exit a project in approximately four years.

Our new active adult business model was working great. With each project new ideas were added, going from one car garage to two, two bedrooms to three, adding finished sunrooms, etc. Our customers loved the changes and enhanced their new condominium homes with many personal styles and upgrades.

We decided to focus on the faster growing communities in Indiana, Indianapolis, Fishers, Fort Wayne, and Lafayette. No longer wanting to travel the 2 ½ hour one way drive to Evansville, we sold a franchise to a local builder.

In 1998 CJB Enterprises, with four active adult projects under construction, sold 78 condominiums. In 1999 we added another project and sold 98 condominiums. We added two more projects in 2000 and sold 130 condominiums.

We had architecturally designed and professionally enhanced our condominiums so well we entered our new community, product and plans in the annual Indianapolis Builders Association of Greater Indianapolis, (BAGI), MAME Awards program. The MAME (Major Achievements in Merchandising Excellence) Awards recognized the "Best of the Best' in several home and condominium design, marketing, decorating, landscaping, etc. categories.

The style and appearance of the actual MAME Award was a mirror image of the Academy Award given annually at the 'Best of the Best' in the motion picture industry. During the MAME awards ceremony when the winner of a category's name was called the recipient walked to the podium to receive it.

In 1998 I walked to the podium three times as CJB Enterprises was recognized as the 'Best of the Best' in three of four entered categories. In 1999 CJB Enterprises entered our product in six categories, winning four MAME Awards.

In 2000, we hit our high-water mark winning eight MAME Awards. I was actually slightly embarrassed, but extremely proud, hearing CJB Enterprises name being called repeatedly. After walking to the podium and receiving two of the MAME Awards, I designated my marketing manager and other contributing staff members to collect the last six.

Sales were brisk and demand was on the rise for our highly recognized and well-regarded condominium homes. Presently there was a six-month waiting backlog in our seven active adult condominiums communities for new homes.

Flushed with confidence from our many successes, in the spring of 2001 we purchased ground for a new, what would be the eighth active project. We met with our architects and engineers to design our most progressive project to date in Fishers. We began some advanced advertising and had several people ready to sign purchase contracts.

Then, on September 11, 2001, when the World Trade Center was attacked our business, CJB Enterprises, hit the proverbial brick wall.

Our condominium home buyers, the active adults, mostly over 55 years old, preparing for their retirement and Golden Years, were highly sensitive to any negative news that may affect their life earnings nest egg. With the terrorist threat against our country, more than most, they, like a turtle, pulled in their arms and legs and refused to move.

No coaxing, no financial or time delay incentive worked. Our advertising program wasn't effective and walk-in community visits dropped to the non-existent category. Many of our committed buyers cancelled their contracts and demanded their deposits be refunded.

We had experienced a similar setback in our condominium sales in January 1991 when the United States and its coalition forces first bombed then invaded Iraq.

January was the beginning of the pre-sale season for our university student condominiums. When "Operation Desert Storm," as the invasion was named, occurred no one was interested in buying our student condos, so we were forced to shelve our Colorado, Idaho and Washington projects for a year.

Fortunately, we owned the land, there were no condos under construction and no buildings previously built, so our carrying cost overhead was low. In January 1992 we started our pre-sale campaign at these three stalled locations. By April, all 72 condominiums were pre-sold, then built, with our buyers paying for them in September. The delay was expensive, but we were actually able to raise our selling price, which helped mitigate our one year carrying costs. This crisis was averted.

In 2001 we had approximately 560 active adult condominiums at our seven, soon to be eight, locations in some phase of planning, construction, development, or waiting to be sold. At seven of the eight locations we had two professional decorator designed model homes and a community clubhouse, with an attached swimming pool.

Additionally, all of the infrastructure, streets, sidewalks, and water and sewer lines were installed, ready for new condominiums to be built. Finally, we had a salaried salesperson at each active location, which was necessary when someone wanted to tour one of our condos. The salesperson also acted as security to protect our decorated model homes and finished unsold buildings from theft or damage. An abandoned or seemingly deserted community would have been an open invitation to vandalism, theft and other types of sordid activity.

Our overhead and carrying costs were enormous! An eminent major financial crisis was looming!

With the cash flow from our apartments, we were able to cover all of our overhead expenses from September until May. Then CJB Enterprises missed its first payment in over 30 years in business.

I called the representatives of our banks to inform them I was going to miss our company's May payment. When I spoke to each one, there were questions about what was happening with the business, how long I thought this bad bubble in active adult condo sales would last, etc. I explained our normal condominium sales from September to April would have been 40 to 50 homes and to date we only had five. But I told them our salespeople indicated there were renewed signs of increasing interest and activity.

All my bankers had obvious concern for my business, but CJB Enterprises was not the only problem in their loan portfolio. Many other businesses were suffering from the aftereffects of the terrorist attacks as well.

However, in early June I was told to attend a meeting of my bankers to more fully understand CJB's present situation and projected plans for survival. In preparation we created financial spreadsheets showing our present monthly income and expenses. Additionally, we prepared a few model 'what if' financial spreadsheet projections.

These model projections described several date sensitive avenues we could follow to survive our present financial crisis and repay our missed payment to the banks. All of our projections were conservative based, and none had CJB Enterprises fully restored in one, at most two years.

While preparing for this meeting I recalled having read one of Donald Trump's, (major international real estate developer, later to become President of the United States) books. In it he described facing a similar financial crisis. When he met with his unhappy bankers, like I was being compelled to do, he took the keys to his property and dumped them in the middle of their meeting table. He told them if they want his property here are the keys, take them. His bankers walked away from the table leaving the keys behind, thus allowing Trump to solve his businesses financial problems.

I had not planned to be as bold as Trump! However, having previously been in the banking business I knew bankers are horrible, the worst, property managers. In most cases they would rather work with the property developer, especially highly specialized property like ours, to allow them to solve the problems at their level. This would save them the huge legal fees and carrying costs associated with repossessing the properties. It would also save the banks from managing the properties until they could find a buyer at a highly discounted price.

On June 21, 2002, Linda and I went to a downtown Indianapolis office location and walked through an open door. Inside the room was a large almost square table with 14 men comfortably seated around it. Some I knew but most I didn't.

I was optimistic as I began to make my CJB Enterprise survival and emergence presentation. I was prepared for a long-drawn-out question and answer session. It was not to be.

After about 15 minutes of my one hour planned presentation one bank representative asked me about our personal assets and liabilities. After I told him what they were, and realizing we were out of cash, the meeting was suddenly, without any questions or comments, over.

Stunned, Linda and I stood up, looked around the room at stoic dry ice faces, trying to get a read from someone about our future. Finally, one person, whom we didn't know, walked up to Linda and told her he was sorry this was happening to us.

As we had moved a few feet toward the door, a representative for one of our banks came up and stood directly in front of Linda and me. Before I knew what was happening, he said Bloomfield Bank, the one he represented, was going to create a "train wreck" with my company. "It wasn't personal," he said, "just business."

Maybe it wasn't personal to him, but it sure as Hell was personal to us! Stunned by his words, the milksop grabbed my dangling unsuspecting hand, shook it and left. The 'Metz Executioner' had spoken!

Bloomfield Bank's owner, Stan Barkley, and I had successfully worked together for years financing our presold student condominium projects in Colorado, Ohio, and Washington. But, in 2000 an underperforming active adult community he financed needed a one-year loan extension. The active adult project had been projected, using professional analytics, to be sold out in four years. However, at the end of four years we still had seven of eighty condominiums unsold.

When we met to discuss the needed loan extension Stan became very vocal, admonishing me for the request, belligerent and shouting at me. Caught totally off guard, I had never been bullied, condescended, with demeaning conversation, like that with any supposed professional person. However, after his unexpected hostile tirade, he did grant the extension and I was hoping to never have to interact with him again.

Now, Stan was planning, and the other banks were reluctantly forced to stand by while he attempted to ruin me and my company.

His underlying goal, I discovered, was to find a way, in my weakened financial condition, to buy, at a discounted value, our 324 apartments and townhouses in Muncie. Stan, in addition to his banking operation, was a property developer as well, owned several apartments and hoped, upon CJB's forced demise, to add my portfolio to his.

While Stan Barkley and his Bloomfield Bank removed the linchpin keeping

CJB Enterprises together, it was my fault for allowing my company to be placed in such a vulnerable position. Our business had been going and growing so well for over 30 years I had overestimated our ability to survive such a severe economic slowdown.

I didn't realize it, but I had unwittingly entered CJB Enterprises into a sort of business-like Texas Hold'em Poker Game. In this world-famous poker game entrants at a card table systematically, based on their percentages of winning, with both the cards in their hands and those on the table, bet their valued chips accordingly. The rotating player's position on the table is important to the outcome of any particular hand.

When the player feels he/she has the overwhelming best chance of winning, they place all their chips in the middle and say they are "all in"! In essence that is what I had done with CJB Enterprises, unknowingly I was out of position on the business table when 9/11 occurred.

After the meeting, still trying to collect ourselves, Linda and I drove back to Muncie. We stopped to get something to eat. Neither of us really had an appetite, but were simply going through the motions, not sure what to do next. We talked about just gathering a few things, getting in the car, and leaving the State of Indiana. Let the circling vultures and roaming predators fight over the carnage.

But that was not really our style. Fighters we were and fighters we would always be. Not knowing what uncertainties lay ahead of us, we touched our glasses together toasting our commitment to survive and move forward.

A few days later I met with an attorney specializing in business workouts. We discussed the business and my intention to save, if not all at least part of CJB Enterprises. My life's reputation was at stake. I wanted to protect the business and my family as well!

My attorney and I developed a plan of action. He would compile, with my accountant's assistance, a list of all CJB's named business assets and liabilities. Additionally, he was going to assess the level of urgency our creditors had and how much time they would give me to put a workable plan of action in place.

My business was, as he told me, a complex one and most creditors would not want to push too hard or too fast to force action against me. Rather they would move at a slow pace to see if I was trying to make good things happen or attempt to delay the process to conceal valuable assets. The latter, if felt, would be the detonator to fast track the explosion of my business.

As soon as the big banker meeting was over, all but one of the active adult condominium community banks stopped funding construction and sales activity, freezing me out of any forward movement. While they didn't move against me, they were not going to allow the projects to be active, rather stall them until a survival or turnaround plan was in place.

I moved quickly to establish open and honest communication with some private investors, who had assisted me in my rapid growth. I met with them, as a group, on three separate occasions, to explain my circumstances and give them a current updated business status report.

I asked them, in order to save their investment and even enhance their financial position, if they would assist me with any one of the eight condominium projects. At each meeting I received no support. It was obvious they would rather lose their small personal investment than further assist me to keep my business afloat.

Meanwhile our apartments and townhomes were leased and creating some revenue to pay our obligations, staff and keep that side of our operation functioning. Some of our long-time loyal staff continued to assist me in my attempt to keep our business going until, hopefully, an economic turnaround kicked in.

But it wasn't happening. Nothing was moving in my direction. Days tuned into weeks and weeks into months. I was working feverishly, almost around the clock, trying to piece, place and put together anything to save even a small part of my life's work.

In late 2002, I communicated with a former partner, Ron Rubeck and the brother of my deceased partner, Brad Rubeck, about becoming involved in our Fishers, Indiana project, Waterford Gardens. We had previously successfully worked together on a few condominium and apartment projects.

However, there was always some 'alpha male' friction between Brad and me. Additionally, Ron had proven to be inattentive in our failed Florida project, but I was running out of time and options.

It had been over a year since our big bank meeting, and everyone affiliated with my business was beginning to get more restless. Time to save my business was running out, now the question was could the Fishers project be saved.

Our attorney, preparing for the now inevitable explosion of our family's business life, crafted a construction, sales management, and minority ownership agreement for the Waterford Gardens project with the Rubecks.

The agreement placed our sons, Neil & Reid front, and center as the family's representatives of the newly formed Waterford Gardens condominium project. Both, in various positions, had been working in our condominium business and were very familiar with the development, building and selling process.

One and a half years after the 9/11 terrorist attack, on March 28, 2003, the Waterford Gardens agreement was completed and signed. The rest of our business assets, apartments, and condominiums, would be signed over to the patient but unsupportive banks. Stan Barkley would not get the apartments he coveted and schemed to possess!

After 32 long years of personal sacrifice by both Linda and me, all of our planned dreams for future family and continued business success had evaporated. Our hope for a generational business succession, passing it on to Neil and Reid, had been minimalized. Our personal and family future was going to be challenging.

Linda had, all of her adult life, worked with philanthropic organizations, making things better for people in need. She raised money for those many organizations and worked long hours in support of them. She was instrumental in raising the money needed, getting my contractors to donate their services, to renovate and open a home for battered women. The list of her many selfless acts and contributions would have filled all the pages in our biased speculative daily newspaper.

My contributions were more financial and generally anonymous. I donated money to supply food pantries, found needy families and assisted them in their efforts and always supported organizations, which helped others. On one occasion a small startup church burned to the ground. I had no personal relationship with it but found the pastor and gave him a substantial check to rebuild his church.

Both Linda and I were committed to making things better for others. We knew assisting and giving to others, through our business and personal commitment, would bring us a real sense of enrichment and fulfillment. It's Biblical!

With the closure of CJB Enterprises we had lost that ability to help others. Many families had lost their fathers, daughters, sisters, and brothers. We could and would rebuild!

Waterford Gardens and Marquee Homes

The Waterford Gardens 48-month build and sell contract, with the Rubecks, began April 1, 2003. It was based on an eight-month startup and closing process, with the projected, 1 ½ to 2 sales per month at the 80-unit Waterford Gardens project. We started with four valid pre-sold condominiums. This set the stage for the WG project to get off to a good start.

Marquee Homes, our new family business, was the marketer, builder, and seller of Waterford Gardens. As with most contracted projects, Marquee was to be paid a monthly fee, with additional production and achieved goal enhancements. These enhancements included net profit from sales of upgraded custom features, with a staged performance bonus when 20, 40, 60 and the final 80 units were completed, sold and deed transferred.

The new majority developer, Rubecks, would be rewarded for their involvement toward the end of the project, when 60 units had been sold and their construction loan was paid in full. At that time, their profit would be from 75% to 100% of the sale proceeds.

As soon as the ink was dry on the contract and construction resumed the problems with the Rubecks began. Personal greed was prevalent in every decision they made. They delayed payment of our monthly management fees and withheld some of our earned incentives. Each time a condominium was sold, and we were to receive our custom feature profits, there was a complaint about the amount of money going our direction versus theirs.

They became the intimidating bully creating financial and other obstacles in an effort to force us to renegotiate the contract, more to their individual benefit. We held our position strong as we moved forward in this growing and more contentious relationship. It seemed that each month something new would arise to create a wider gorge between our two groups.

Finally, after the 68th condominium was sold and deed transferred, with none of the past performance incentives paid, we contacted our attorney to institute collection procedures against them. Their attorney countered, recommending we meet with an arbitrator to settle our financial differences.

To keep the Waterford Gardens project moving forward, our attorney encouraged us to agree to arbitration.

This, I didn't like! The arbitration concept is engaged to find a middle of the road agreement, where both parties have to give a little to settle the dispute between them. It is frequently used as a much faster way to settle disputes than through the slow-moving judicial court system.

Since our family was owed the money, through an arbitration agreement there was nowhere for our debt recovery position to go but down. Ultimately an impartial arbitrator was agreed to by both parties, with the arbitration meeting set for 30 days in the future.

I was not happy knowing, through arbitration, the Rubecks would likely end up paying us a maximum of 75% of the amount they owed. I knew this tactic, requesting arbitration, had been their strategy all along.

I never liked the "Business is War" concept, where one person or one company dominated, beat down and crushed their competitors. Rather my philosophy had always been to create opportunities where people of all parties benefited from my efforts.

In the past few years, our family had been financially depleted and mentally stressed. We had been marginalized! With Waterford Gardens we were trying to bring ourselves back to a place of renewed success.

With this forced arbitration we were being placed in a position to lose much of what we had clawed our way back to achieve. I resolved that was not going to happen!

If the Rubecks wanted a war, they were going to get a war!

At the beginning of the Waterford Gardens project one of the stipulations from the bank was their requirement of ten pre-sold condominiums prior to the start of construction. In the transition from us to them, we had given the Rubecks four of our valid purchase contracts.

To meet the bank's requirements, they manufactured enough purchase contracts to satisfy the bank. I discovered one from Brad's mother and a couple from Ron's business associates, each signed, with attached personal checks. I made a copy of them, just in case.

These manufactured contracts were never serious purchasers and not one of them followed through with their agreement to buy a condo at Waterford Gardens. Having these manufactured contracts gave me some needed confidence and the proverbial, "Ace in the hole."

A week before our arbitration meeting, I mailed Ron and Brad a copy of three of their manufactured contracts. No note, no threat, nothing in the envelope, just the contracts. I did not say anything to anyone about what I had done, just waited for them to ferment.

On November 14, 2006, at the appointed time and place Neil Reid, our attorney, and I met and were assigned a comfortable private conference room. The arbitrator came in, discussed the goal of the meeting, the amount of the money involved and the rules he expected to be followed.

He said he had previously briefed the Rubecks and their attorney, who were being accommodated in another office. There would be no direct interaction with them.

He left our room and returned approximately a half hour later with an initial settlement amount from the Rubecks. This was, of course, a low-ball figure to start the negotiations. There was no real expectation of acceptance.

I looked at our group and discussed their offer. There was no intention of us considering it. I told the arbitrator we wanted the full amount due to our family and sent him out of the room. Our attorney was perplexed by the abruptness of my action.

There were only three people in the two-room arbitration meeting who knew what was actually happening between the adversaries. I was sure the cowardly Rubecks had never revealed their potentially fraudulent contracts to their attorney. Thus, they were sweating, squirming in their seats, waiting for me to act, to settle this contentious issue. They were now hoping to keep their reputations intact.

Linda and I had discussed these manufactured contracts before our arbitration meeting. We evaluated the position I was taking and agreed 'the most powerful person in a negotiation was the one with the least amount to lose.' We were that person!

The arbitrator returned again, with a higher settlement amount. Our attorney and the arbitrator encouraged me to be reasonable. To counteroffer with something to keep the negotiation moving forward. I lowered our demand by 1% and sent the arbitrator back to the Rubeck camp.

After another back and forth I lowered our demand by a total of 2%, which the Rubecks immediately accepted. They had been soundly defeated and they knew it.

Within an hour the formal arbitration agreement was signed by the Rubecks and our group. When we were handed our executed copy, the arbitrator looked at me and said, "In all my years of arbitration I have never seen such a one-sided agreement." I smiled and left the room.

As agreed at arbitration, on December 1, 2006, three months before our Waterford Gardens contract was to expire, we unceremoniously locked the sales room door of Waterford Gardens for the last time.

It would be approximately five years before the Rubecks would be finished with the final 12 condos of the Waterford Gardens project.

With the proceeds from the Waterford Gardens project, Reid went to Phoenix, Arizona to seek out new development opportunities. Neil segued into building single family homes for active adults in Fishers and we purchased 20 of our most productive townhomes in Muncie.

We were preparing to make major strides into returning to our more productive development days when the United States economy was hit with a devastating economic recession. It would become the largest such recession experienced since the Great Depression of the 1930's.

The recession formally began in 2007, when the average family household debt rose to an unprecedented level of 127% of their disposable income. The national data reflected the recession lasted 19 months until June 2009. However, for many businesses and individuals it began well before that in 2006 and was still, in many ways and by many families, being felt through 2012.

The precursor for this devastating recession occurred in 1992 when the federal government passed The Housing and Community Development Act. Then a new law required two of the major federally backed mortgage underwriters, Fannie Mae, and Freddie Mac to purchase 30% or more homes related to affordable housing.

They encouraged relaxed lending standards with borrowers, who purchased homes with adjustable-rate mortgages. Many of the borrowers, being hustled by commission profit-based bankers and brokers, didn't fully understand their future payments, along with property taxes, would be increased, at a later date.

This subprime lending practice increased to a historical high of 20% in newly originated home loans. This led to a 'housing bubble' waiting for the right moment to burst. When it did burst the housing market crashed, sending families scrambling from their once cherished, safely secured homes to parents and in-laws' basements.

While the banks and many housing lenders were bailed out by the federal government, median household wealth suffered mightily, losing an average of 35% of most family's net worth. Many of the former homeowners would never recover, facing personal bankruptcy, divorce, and societal displacement.

This is the difficult time period we chose to enter the single-family active adult housing market in rapidly growing Fishers, Indiana. We knew older people still wanted to move from their two and three level homes to a more comfortable single level home.

We built a lovely single level model home with many luxury custom features to entice these potential buyers to contract us to build their new home. We advertised and marketed these homes for the active adult buyers similar to our successful Waterford Gardens program.

Similar to 1981, when the home loan interest rates were 17% and the housing market was slow, we set up a guarantee purchase program. Our agreement was designed to buy our contracted purchaser's homes, if they didn't sell by the time their new custom home was completed.

To entice our prospective buyers to sign a contract with us, we offered discounted custom features and reduced building lot prices. We tried anything and everything and none of it worked.

Due to the increased inventory of abandoned and repossessed houses many of our potential buyer's homes had lost value, by as much as 10-20%. They were unwilling, even with our buyer's incentives, to take any loss.

With the housing market in such dire straits, it was like we were swimming upstream against the current. People were afraid of their future, which had been exacerbated by this national and global financial crisis.

We designed, built, and sold a few custom homes but our monthly operating cost far exceeded the income from them.

In 1981 I had catapulted my real estate and building development career to stratospheric heights by having the courage to build new homes when others feared. This time there would be no repeat performance.

After two years of waiting for the housing market to turn in our favor and having bled through much of our available investment money, we ceased our business operation.

Exercise the Y and My Mental Focus

All of my adult life, I have enjoyed some form of exercise in my daily and weekly routine. This exercise routine, focusing more on my lunch time hour, allowed me to break up my workday, relieve stress and renew my focus.

When we moved to Fishers in 2003, I resumed running short distances, normally around three miles twice a week, lifted a few free weights, and used my donated rowing machine at the Waterford Gardens Clubhouse.

With our family's exit from the Waterford Gardens development, I decided to join the Fishers Y to continue and possibly enhance my exercise regimen. As I was advancing in life, I knew the positive effects a good exercise program would have on my aging body.

The "Y" formerly the YMCA [Young Men's Christian Association] was started in 1844 in London, England. The aim of the start-up YMCA was to put Christian Principles into practice developing a healthy "body, mind and spirit." A similar organization, the YWCA [Young Women's Christian Association] was started a few years later, with the same philosophy relating to young women.

In the early 1960's the two organizations began to merge offering more benefits not only to young men and women but expanded their services into more family-oriented programs as well. Along with the mergers the name was changed more frequently to simply the "Y,"

I had been familiar with the YMCA since my early youth when my father, Mother, two brothers and both sisters attended a family learn-to-swim program at the YMCA outdoor pool. We, as a family, wearing swimsuits, were featured, photo with our instructor, along with an informative narrative, on the front page of The Muncie Star. The YMCA was promoting their annual summer family swim program and its many attributes using our family as a model.

In the fall I attended an additional learn-to-swim class at the YMCA downtown indoor swimming pool, where we, as eight- and nine-year-old prepubescent young boys, swam nude. Shy as I was, being naked in and around the swimming pool with other people I didn't know intimidated me. I attended one session and told my mother, "No more!"

A generation later when our oldest son Neil was about eight years old, the YMCA had a nice interactive program for Fathers and young sons called Indian Guides. As we joined the program, we were encouraged to adopt native Indian names; mine was "Big Deer" and Neil's, "Little Deer."

The interactive program brought together six to eight fathers and sons twice a month, once to go on a recreational outing together, such as camping, bowling or simply going out to eat. The second monthly meeting would be more formal. We would meet at one of the parent's homes; make a craft, share stories, have a snack, and plan future outings.

When Reid was old enough, he too joined our small tribe and became, "Littlest Deer." It was a great way for me, a busy parent, to interact with my children.

The Fishers Y, I was to discover, was resplendent with many family activities. While most didn't directly affect me, I enjoyed seeing the young parents and their children interacting, smiling, and commingling. Their enthusiasm, laughter and overall happiness energized me!

I began working out a little longer, no more than an hour, using the "Y's" new multiple muscle toning exercise machines, while still doing some free weights. My self-directed program was to work out a group of muscles one day, move to a different group the next day, take a day or two off, and then repeat the cycle. It was not my intention to gain a lot of muscle strength, my physical frame was too small for that. Rather my goal was to be complete, total body strong, while increasing my range of motion.

Between running and working out at the "Y" I was able to build some missing solid muscle mass while maintaining a reasonable physical weight. During the bad weather winter months, I ran inside on the treadmill to keep up my running regimen, which helped me control my body weight.

In the spring, summer and fall months I ran outside complimenting me inside the "Y" workouts. Just for fun I entered a few special interest fundraising races and found my 5K [3.1miles] times had not diminished too much over the years.

In the fall of 2011, I entered the Fishers Y Wishbone 5K race, which was held on Thanksgiving morning. When I completed the race, I visited with the son of one of my old running buddies and left shortly thereafter. A few hours later his father, my old running buddy, called me and said at the post-race awards ceremony, which I didn't attend, the race coordinator announced I had finished third, in my age group. I was ecstatic!

All the years I had actually run races more for the fun of it, was good but not great, not for recognition or awards rather to stay in good physical condition, I had never won anything. Now, I had won a prize but hadn't been there to receive it.

I called the "Y" and asked for the race coordinator, who I knew personally.

She answered the phone and confirmed I had come in third place and had won a Thanksgiving holiday pumpkin pie. I asked if it was too late to claim my much-anticipated prize. She said she had the special event pumpkin pie and would be happy to meet and give it to me.

I hurriedly jumped in my car and drove three miles to the "Y." When I arrived, she was waiting, laughing at my excitement and agreed to take a photo of me and my coveted new first in a lifetime prize. Wow, at age 68 I had won my first racing prize!

A year earlier during one of my prior winter treadmill runs I met a person, who while running next to me told me I should try her Pilates class. I didn't know anything about Pilates but told her some of my goals for increasing my body strength and range of motion. She recommended this form of exercise, Pilates, would help me achieve my goals.

The next week she invited me, as her guest, to the Pilates class, which I was to discover was the most advanced form of this, new to me, exercise program. The full title of the class was Power Pilates Tools and Toys. The tools and toys were such items as a bosu ball, 36" long weighted bars, weighted medicine balls, large yoga balls, etc. These were all items our instructor would incorporate into a regular Pilates full motion movement to make them more focused, balance challenging and each extremely difficult.

The Pilates exercise concept was created by Joseph Pilates, a German physical trainer, in the early 20th Century, emphasizing control, centering, fluidity, precision and breath. His main ideas focused on strengthening the core muscles, stretching the body while challenging the mind and breath control. He was also very conscious of supporting the spine, keeping its surrounding muscles strong while remaining flexible.

Joseph Pilates said," we retire too early and die too young, our prime of life should be in the 70's and old age should come much later...." He was actively teaching his Pilates principals until he died in 1967 at age 84.

Our Pilates instructor would verbally incorporate Joseph Pilates step by step philosophies along with her own advanced teaching methods in our classes. She would discuss our core and larger extensor and flexor muscles but emphasized the importance of our smaller connector muscles, which helped us with balance and stabilization. Breathing, balance, strength of focus, range of motion, support of spine, each week she would incorporate a different tool or toy and present us with a different format so we would constantly be challenged and not get lazy.

Our hour-long sessions were extended into seven-week segments. In the final week, our instructor would put us through a series of exhausting core exercises, with three repetitions of each, after which time we were totally wiped out. We coined this seventh session "Tap out Friday" as we all wanted to quit sometime during this extended exhaustive routine but refused to capitulate.

Our Pilates instructor's "Tap out Friday" session was so rigorous it would have made my army basic training drill sergeant envious.

A few months into my Friday Power Pilates classes I discovered our instructor was teaching another class on Tuesdays listed as Yo-Pi, a combination of Yoga and Pilates. I had tried a few introductory Yoga classes a year earlier, liked the stretching and positioning concept but the time it was offered didn't fit my work schedule. This Tuesday Yo-Pi class time, I decided, would be far better for me.

Yoga is a group of physical, mental, and spiritual practices or disciplines, which originated in India almost 5,000 years ago. The concept of Yoga is the raising and expansion of consciousness from oneself to coexist with everyone and everything, uniting mind and body, man, and nature. It's holistic harmony!

In the 1980's Yoga became popular in the United States as a system of physical exercises and postures called Asanas.

The Yoga practice of raising awareness of my physical being while preparing for the advanced stages of my life had a major impact on me. While the evolution of my understanding of Yoga practice took some time, the impact on my physical body was immediate.

With the two practices, Pilates, and Yoga, being offered together I was able to better experience the benefits of both. My total body, mental and physical, was experiencing something I had never felt before. Through these two forms of exercise my body was being restructured and transformed for better overall long-term performance.

While I was going through my personal physical metamorphosis, I began to see on television and read about several professional athletes who were incorporating many of the same Pilates and Yoga movements into their daily workout routines. The training methods being used by them gave me the additional impetus I needed to continue down this new path of physical fitness.

For years, my twice a week routine with Pilates and Yoga was the basis for my overall physical fitness program. With the emphasis on these focused movements, the Pilates and Yoga classes had transformed me mentally into being more fluid in my motions and alert when concentrating on balance and individual muscle control.

After a few years of this two-pronged physical fitness program my body was feeling almost perfect. I was agile, flexible, strong, and healthy.

I always wanted to be outdoors in the natural environment doing some sort of sporting activity but lacked the hand eye coordination most athletic ventures required. Then I discovered Disc Golf. It was a game involving throwing, flinging, flicking, or slinging a small 8 ¼" disc at a pole basket target. The game is measured in a few hundred feet as opposed to regular golf being a few hundred yards. It normally takes one or two fairly calculated throws from the tee to reach the target area where an accurate putt is required to get the disc in the basket.

I practiced disc golf frequently to learn to throw the disc and became pretty precise, keeping it in the projected target range of the basket. While I was strong, I lacked the physical elasticity the more skilled younger players possessed, so my distance was a little deficient. But, my short game of putting, enhanced by my breath and balance control, was far better than most.

Wind, rain, and poor weather were the only impediments keeping me off the many disc golf courses in our area. I visited them all, frequently. There were no fees to pay, starting times to reserve and no carts to rent so my game was always played on my schedule. In my geographic area disc golf was played on public courses, in the city parks. It was free!

Disc golf also came with the many joys and frustrations of all other competitive sports. It was challenging, fun!

I followed the routines of basketball players, baseball pitchers, practicing almost every day, throwing up to 100 times a day. I wanted to continue to improve my game, become a formidable player.

For three years I played disc golf as often as possible, occasionally in the snow and light rain, continuing to make incremental progress. To facilitate my knowledge and skill, I watched professional disc golf player's videos, both playing in tournaments and self-improvement programs.

However, my mind was dreaming, fantasizing, flinging discs further, and making unimaginable putts, playing games my older physically fit body couldn't deliver. My small infrequent ignored aches and pains became more frequent and intense. The adrenaline was flowing, the endorphins had kicked in, too much.

One fall night, after a long day of playing disc golf and riding my bike up 'don't quit hill,' I felt myself being thrown out of bed in unimaginable agonizing pain. I wasn't sure what was happening to me as I grabbed the bedpost for support and pulled myself partially up from the floor, hunched over unable to straighten to a standing position. I stopped clinging to the bedpost for a few minutes while the intense pain coursed through the left side of my body, from lower back to little toe.

I didn't realize it at the time, but later discovered I had a sciatica attack. The excruciating pain lasted for several minutes before it abated, and I was able to lie back down. As my body relaxed, I rested, without moving for a few hours.

As I was to discover, the sciatica nerve is the longest widest nerve in the human body. I must have done something very wrong to have created this massive very painful attack.

Not able to totally kick off some of the lingering side effects of the sciatica attack, a few days later I discussed the issue with one of my friends at the "Y". She recommended I visit her massage therapist to see if she could work out the kinks in my left side muscles.

When I met with the massage therapist, Jenny Owens, I explained my sciatica attack, playing disc golf and pushing myself on my bike. She assessed me vertically and then horizontally on her massage table. She told me there was visual evidence my left side hip area was not in line with my right-side hip.

After relieving the supporting muscle groups on both sides of my hips and completing my full body massage, Jenny recommended a physical therapist to me.

I met with the physical therapist and explained my disc golf and biking activity. After performing some focused area testing, he recommended a few interactive stretches to realign my left hip to my right. He told me the extremely sharp jerky throwing motion I used playing disc golf caused some displacement in my left hip.

After meeting with him a few times my right and left side hip alignment, although not perfect, was much improved. While feeling better, I knew there was some low-level permanent damage done to my left hip area. I particularly noticed this injury when I executed some left hip motions in my physical workouts, resulting in some sharp, but minor pain.

I continued to meet with Jenny to evaluate my full body muscle groups. She suggested some additional hip stretches. She also told me my lower back muscles were not strong enough to support my body frame, to keep it full vertically erect.

Jenny was a certified massage therapist for the Indianapolis Colts, a professional football team, so I had confidence she had in-depth knowledge of the physical body muscle groups and their interaction. I had grown to trust her physical analysis of the muscular and bone structure of my body and took her advice to strengthen my lower back muscles.

The Pilates and Yoga classes, along with Jenny's recommendations, physically increased my body strength giving me more correct muscle tone to stand vertical, spine straight, shoulders back, eyes forward and chest out. No more hunched over slumping for me. My stride was direct with purpose!

In the fall of 2017, "Y" changed their group fitness program so much that our Pilates and Yoga instructor resigned. I was not happy with the "Y"!

I maintained my membership at the "Y" to work out three to four times a week, but I needed to find a Pilates or Yoga program to enhance my personal fitness regimen. For six months I visited other exercise and physical fitness locations, tried other programs, but they just didn't feel right and weren't working for me.

The "Y"'s new Yoga instructor had filled in some substitute classes for my previous teacher; I knew her and liked her well-articulated Yoga teaching method. I finally wandered into her class and was happy to roll out my Yoga mat again.

My new Yoga instructor focused on the Vinyasa Flow style of Yoga, which I had previously sampled in her substitute role. I immediately embraced it! As I continued on with her class, I discovered the variable nature of Vinyasa Flow Yoga. It helped me develop a more balanced physical body and prevent potential repetitive motion injuries.

Vinyasa Flow Yoga was also a more complete type of Yoga class for me. It weaved various poses and postures together so I would move seamlessly from one to another, using my inhale exhale breath as my prompt. This Vinyasa breath-initiated practice; I discovered, connected every action with intention and offered me a variety of poses and postures, with no two classes alike. The Vinyasa Flow Yoga practice was the perfect blend of poses, postures and enhanced mental focus for my body at this stage of my life.

Incorporating my daily ever changing routines increased elasticity stretching motions, using the muscle toning, full range of motion equipment at the "Y," visiting Jenny, my massage therapist, every few weeks and taking my Vinyasa Flow classes, at age 79, my physical body was functioning at peak performance.

COVID-19 Pandemic Era

2020-2022

In October or November 2019, a new coronavirus SARS-CoV-2, an acute respiratory syndrome coronavirus, was identified in 'patient zero' in Wuhan, China. On December 31, 2019, the Wuhan Municipal Health Commission issued an alert that there was a cluster of cases of "viral pneumonia" in Wuhan.

The initial source of the virus was said to have been an unidentified infected animal from the Wuhan wet market, a market selling live animals for food or pets. This claim was later abandoned by China.

An alternative possibility was that the virus-whether natural, man-made, or otherwise modified leaked from a lab at the Wuhan Institute of Virology, nine miles from the wet market.

However it originated, the new virus, COVID-19, was transmitted in January 2020 by an infected individual traveling from China to the United States. Additionally global travelers going to and from China unwittingly began spreading the disease to many other countries, creating world-wide concern for its transmission.

With a few cases of COVID-19 confirmed, by January 31st, President Donald Trump in conjunction with the National Institute of Health [NIH] and the Center for Disease Control [CDC] began taking aggressive action to protect our country's population. By February 9th, all flights between the U.S. and China had been suspended. On March 11th, all air and maritime travel between the U.S. and other countries had been suspended as well. Finally on March 19th the U.S. sealed the borders between our country with Mexico and Canada. The United States was formally sealed off from the rest of the world.

The National Institute of Health is the primary agency responsible for biomedical and public health research. The NIH's medical research agency's commitment is to discover ways to improve the health of the American public and save lives.

One of the departments of the NIH is the National Institute of Allergy and Infectious Disease [NIAID]. The Director of NIAID, Dr. Anthony Fauci, soon to become the national authority on COVID-19, would daily stand side by side with President Trump as they cautioned, educated, and updated the American public of the medical and physical dangers involved in the aggressive and growing threat of the COVID virus.

The Center for Disease Control and Prevention [CDC] was organized to protect America from health, safety, and security threats, both foreign and domestic in the U.S. The purpose of the CDC is to conduct critical science and provide health information that protects our nation against dangerous threats and responds when they arise.

These two federal agencies, NIH, and CDC, working independently both analyzing the rapidly advancing COVID disease, began using real time data of deaths and hospitalizations to develop projection models to help guide health policy and mitigation planning. Then through media coverage, the American public was alerted to the preventative measures to be taken to avoid catching and spreading this new virus.

Finally, the World Health Organization, the United Nations agency, connects the nation's partners and people to promote health, keep the world safe and save the vulnerable so everyone everywhere can attain the highest level of health.

Together these three highly accredited health focused organizations [NIH, CDC, WHO] developed a uniform set of guidelines. They were designed to assist the individual and separate national federal governmental health leaders in guiding their citizens during this time of an advancing imminent crisis.

Their recommendations were as follows; 1] When in a public place keep physical distance of 6 feet apart. 2] Wear a properly fitted face mask, covering mouth and nose. 3] Clean hands frequently with alcohol-based hand rub or soap and water. 4] Cover your mouth and nose with a bent elbow when you cough or sneeze. 5] Avoid crowded indoor settings, where people talk loudly, breathe heavily or sing.

On March 11, 2020, the WHO declared the novel Coronavirus [COVID-19] outbreak a global pandemic. The spokesperson for WHO stated, "we are deeply concerned by both the alarming levels of spread and severity and the alarming levels of inaction."

On March 13, 2020, President Trump declared the ongoing Coronavirus Disease 2019 [COVID-19] pandemic of sufficient severity and magnitude to warrant emergency declaration for all states, tribes, territories, and the District of Columbia.

With this national declaration each state separately enacted guidelines to mitigate the spread of the COVID-19 novel virus. Between March 17th and April 3rd 34 of the 50 states enacted their individual respective 'stay at home' orders.

The national and local mainstream media, whether spoken, viewed or in print, had begun coverage of the COVID-19 virus on the first day rumors of the virus's exposure surfaced. There was an immediate obsession with the probability that the next major news event was about to occur.

The majority of the legacy and mainstream media news is, and always has, focused their reporting on negative headline stories involving death, pain, suffering, drama and all tragedies affecting mankind. Their reporting is devised to use bold scare tactics to influence the behavior of their followers, thus developing a magnetic fixation to them.

This excessive reporting on the media's hyperbole topic creates a craving in their followers to seek more information, with infinitely more explicit and graphic detail. The media goal is to create an image of fear and curiosity to last long after their coverage is over, to hold their follower's hostage until their next news cycle begins.

The media outlets are encouraged to continue to follow this time tested self-promoting tactic in order to gather more followers and increase their approval ratings. With higher approval ratings more advertisers, with more money, come to their doorsteps. The envisioned increased revenue stream encourages the mass media to continue their escalating hysteria type approach in reporting the news.

The COVID-19 pandemic had created a perfect platform for the media to commit all their resources to this one topic for the foreseeable future. Reporters writing, telecasters talking all ad nauseum redundantly, filling their readers and viewers frequently with speculative and misinformation, had a unilateral effect of spreading fear and uncertainty throughout our population.

When people are afraid, they don't function as they would normally, don't think and react in a typical manner, many freeze in-place, some panic. Fear causes many people to lose their creativity, individuality and are scared of obedience. With the media bombardment of COVID-19 coverage we had become a nation of fear, uncertainty, and unrest.

With the 'stay at home' orders in effect all non-essential businesses, those where more than a few people meet or shop, were immediately closed to the public. This included schools, gyms, churches, restaurants, office buildings, sporting events, etc. With a few exceptions, this immediate closing order covered all businesses except grocery stores, pharmacies, medical laboratories, and gas stations.

With each state regulating their own guidelines, some projected a reevaluation within 30 days, while others allowed 60 to 90 days to reconsider their 'stay at home' and business closing mandate.

School children were remotely, from their homes, virtually attending their school classes. The teachers were giving their structured class lessons to the students via their laptop computers.

The closing of schools created a major problem for many families particularly where both parents worked outside the home. With the schools closed and their children forced to study at home, many families had to make a decision on which parent would have to quit their job, abandon their career, and be at home with the children.

Additionally, the 'stay at home' order for many children was even more difficult for socioeconomically disadvantaged families. These families relied on breakfast, lunch and, in some cases, take home food, for their nourishment. In many cases the children were provided with aftercare at the schools, the time between when classes were completed for the day and the parents were off work.

When offices closed, turmoil prevailed. Both employers and employees were put in a perilous situation. The employers were trying to figure out how to continue to operate their business, without failure. The employees on the other hand were in fear of losing their jobs and thus their livelihood.

Many businesses were able to function with their employees working remotely from home. This was a good short-term fix for both employers and employees, but many of the office buildings housing the businesses would sit vacant, creating another set of problems.

Other businesses, such as restaurants and non-essential stores were closed. There were no options available for them. With no income and still overhead to cover, many small business owners were doomed to failure.

People were cautious, many were scared, and all were staying at home. With the travel ban and no place really to go, the streets were pretty much vacant. Life as we knew it had changed!

Linda and I, too, were cautious! We watched the televised daily updates on COVID to stay informed on the virus' progression in our country. We had always been very conscious of our healthy habits, but now we confirmed with each other that we were practicing them. When we went to the grocery store, we wore a clean cloth mask, washed our hands before and after each visit and kept space between us and the other shoppers.

Additionally, we consciously prepared and ate good nutritional healthy food. Finally, we took supplemental vitamins and minerals to enhance our immune system, hopefully avoiding any health debilitating deficiency.

On March 27, 2020, President Trump signed into law the CARES ACT, which was a $2.2 Trillion Dollar aid package. The bi-partisan legislation provided direct payments of $1,200.00 to most Americans, increased unemployment benefits, provided aid to small businesses and a massive loan fund for corporations.

During the first year of the coronavirus pandemic Three additional payments of $1,200.00 were paid to most adults and $500.00 per child, unemployment subsidies were continued and many businesses, both large and small were kept afloat.

In addition, the government provided a 180-day moratorium for renters and homeowners to avoid eviction and foreclosure. Also, there was additional financial support for hospitals, health care providers, state and local governments and schools and universities.

Between CARES ACT and other follow-up government actions, many financial concerns, and worries, in the short term, were abated. But all the Trillions of Dollars of financial support would substantially increase the debt of the Federal Government. Someday, someway this massive additional debt would have to be fiscally addressed.

New York was the hub of international travel, with people arriving from around the world traveling to other cities and countries. It was the city and state first affected by the novel coronavirus and thus became the epicenter for the incubation and spreading of the disease.

New York was the hardest hit city in the U.S. early recording 52,318 reported cases of COVID-19 with 428 deaths resulting from the pandemic. The city and state were so overrun by the pandemic that on March 28, 2020, President Trump ordered the USNS Comfort, a naval hospital ship with 1200 medical personnel aboard to New York. Its mission was to assist the crowded hospitals and abate anxiety in the people of New York. President Trump also ordered the construction of a 1,000-bed temporary hospital with the promise of adding three more of similar size, should the need arise.

Democrat Governor Andrew Cuomo of New York publicly thanked the president for his support but privately refused to use any aid, provided by the Republican President Trump. The charismatic and politically ambitious Governor of New York would make his own decisions on how best to manage the increasing health crisis in his state.

Instead of using the naval hospital ship and temporary hospital built for the overcrowded New York facilities, Governor Cuomo moved hundreds of COVID ill patients into nursing homes. The nursing home residents, many with preexisting health problems, were extremely vulnerable to the coronavirus disease. In one week, shortly after the transfer of the virus infected patients, 5,156 nursing home residents died from COVID-19. The weaker and more vulnerable nursing home residents could not fight off the strong invasive coronavirus.

In a few weeks of nonuse, the rejected naval hospital ship withdrew to a new assignment and the temporary hospital was dismantled. Ironically, the biased mainstream media coverage was focused against the controversial President Trump. It became obvious a national political battle was going to be fought at the expense and health of the American citizens.

On May 15th President Trump introduced "Operation Warp Speed" a public-private partnership initiated to facilitate and accelerate the development, manufacturing, and distribution of COVID 19 vaccines, therapeutics, and diagnostics. Operation Warp Speed [OWS] and five drug companies adopted several strategies for vaccine development while mitigating risks.

Trump allowed OWS and the drug companies to cut through the bureaucratic

"Red Tape" to fast track a vaccine that would be successful. Several clinical trials were run simultaneously to gather data on the safety and efficacy of their proposed product.

While the drug companies were working to develop a COVID-19 vaccine, individual tests, designed to detect the coronavirus, were being given to anyone wanting to be tested. These tests were available at most pharmacies and many specified drive-up locations. They were administered, at no charge, but many times the waiting lines were so long it took hours to get the test.

Ironically, the results of the test were not immediately available and could take up to three days to find out if the test results were positive or negative for the coronavirus. During that time, a tested person's affected status could change. Many people, out of fear, whether symptomatic or not, would frequently take the test.

Many states had begun adjusting their 'stay at home' orders, allowing their residents more public freedom. Some previously closed businesses, restaurants and gyms were opened at a reduced level of occupancy. In Minnesota, the 'stay at home' order was lifted on May 15th.

The angst in the American public from mainstream media's constant daily hype reporting of the increased spread of the coronavirus, hospitalizations and deaths was further exacerbated with the video-taped murder of George Floyd. On May 25th. Floyd, a frequent offender, and drug user was arrested outside a store in Minneapolis on suspicion of using a counterfeit $20.00 bill.

One of the four arresting officers, Derek Chauvin, a white police officer, pinned George Floyd, a black man, to the street pavement with his knee to Floyd's neck. Two other officers assisted Chauvin holding down the heavily drugged, former football player. Floyd, who was originally combative, now compliant, lay still while the fourth officer kept the gathering crowd from intervening.

After over eight minutes of Floyd's neck being pinned to the pavement an ambulance arrived with a paramedic. The paramedic actively attempted to resuscitate the now lifeless body of George Floyd.

The video of the white police officers murdering the helpless black man was viewed by the African American Community as a modern-day lynching. It loudly echoed police brutality and spoke to the reality of racial injustice. [This heinous act of white police brutality on a black man was equally abhorrent in the white community as well.]

For five days George Floyd's body was paraded from town to town with many Black speakers, politicians, and special interest groups ramping up racial division during his many casket-bearing processions. The mainstream media covered these daily well-orchestrated events, redundantly amplifying the many ways our country was divided by race.

Within hours of Floyd's death race related demonstrations began a slow brew, as both black and white sympathizers launched supportive protest marches in many metropolitan cities. Then like a match, striking a powder keg, mask wearing opportunists, looters, and petty criminals began breaking windows, looting stores, and setting cars on fire.

The peaceful demonstration protests had become out of control bloody riots!

As the deaths from the pandemic surged, so did the destruction from the increasingly violent riots. Citing "systemic racism" the out-of-control riots expanded into 47 states.

One of the main organizations instigating and promoting the protests, turned riots, was an organization known as Black Lives Matter [BLM]. This organization, BLM, garnered a lot of boot marching support from sympathizers of the oppressed.

For various reasons a lot of pressure was exerted on many major national corporations to financially support the BLM movement. Several of them, some coerced, hurriedly donated millions of dollars in support of a movement about which they knew very little. Many were being held hostage by their employees, customers of their business and others with ulterior motives.

Professionally designed and mass manufactured Black Lives Matter [BLM] signs were carried during protests, displayed in many residential yards and business locations in most cities around the country. Some businesses and residents were supporting the protest while others used the signs as a deterrent to protect their property from destruction.

Some anonymous individuals and organizations financed and developed a nationwide well-coordinated group of specialized protest-rioters. The well-funded and identically outfitted rebellious guerrillas were secretly moved, in new unmarked luxury buses and on private airplanes, from town to town and state to state in order to incite violence in the protesting cities.

This specialized highly trained mobilized hit and run agitating mercenaries created 90% of the violence committed during the riots. Their well-honed insurrectionist skills many times kept local less proficient undermanned peacekeeping police on the defensive as the mercenaries perpetuated their mission of civil unrest.

After several months of protesting and rioting, the social unrest movement began to subside. Order in our cities and communities began to return to near normal, but social statements had been made.

The murder of George Floyd and the resulting riots brought to light some major deficiencies in many municipal policing policies. Change was demanded. Change was needed. Change was coming!

On August 13th, the Food & Drug Administration [FDA] issued an emergency authorization for the vaccine introduced by the Pfizer Drug Company. Soon after Pfizer's approval, the Moderna and Johnson and Johnson vaccines were approved for production as well.

President Trump immediately ordered mass production of the coronavirus vaccines. His goal was to produce and distribute 300 million doses of the vaccine by January 2020.

During this time of the frightening growth of the coronavirus pandemic and the civil unrest perpetuated by the many daily riots, the build up to the 2020 U.S. Presidential election was beginning to unfold. On August 20th the Democratic National Convention, convening to select their presidential candidate, chose Joe Biden to oppose incumbent Republican Donald Trump.

During the early stages of the coronavirus pandemic, President Trump had acted quickly in following the advice of Dr. Anthony Fauci in closing the borders, setting up coronavirus preventive guidelines and creating Operation Warp Speed. Additionally, he attempted, a little erroneously, to convey a positive message that the pandemic would not last long. President Trump, frequently not wearing a mask, tried to tamp down the increasingly perpetuated fear many Americans were feeling.

Conversely, Joe Biden, spread 'Grim Reaper' type fear of the coronavirus pandemic in every message delivered. He claimed Trump had acted slowly in identifying and attacking the coronavirus, causing many unnecessary deaths of innocent Americans.

Biden, rarely seen in public, preferring to campaign from the well-decorated basement of his home, conveyed a strong subliminal message by always wearing a mouth and nose covered mask. He spoke softly articulating the message of cautious public movements and physical distancing. When directly addressing the coronavirus, Biden promised he would eradicate COVID-19 during his first year in office.

The two candidates had agreed to two televised presidential debates. The first debate with fractious back and forth demeaning personal character attacks quickly devolved into chaos.

The second debate, a month before the election, was cancelled when Trump was diagnosed with COVID-19 and hospitalized. Within three days Trump was back in the White House where he said, "Don't be afraid of COVID" Don't let it dominate your life".

Trump held smaller than usual outdoor rallies where supporters were asked to wear masks, some did not. His persona of being the bureaucratic outsider resonated with his supporters but had created a large target on his back. Many politicians and businesses, relying on 'special favors,' which Trump refused to accommodate, wanted him out of his leadership role.

Biden, portraying a grandfather-like figure, promising to unify the fragmented country, continued to campaign from his home. With over 35 years' experience in serving at different levels of the federal government, this gave Biden the insider backing of the incessant Trump threatened bureaucracy.

A few weeks after the hotly contested battle between Trump and Biden, when all the electorates were counted, the formal announcement was made; Joe

Biden had won the race to be the 46th President of the United States. The 2020 presidential election recorded a record number of votes: Joe Biden 81,266,358 to Donald Trump 74,225,839.

On December 15th, a little over a month after the presidential election, the first COVID-19 vaccine, Pfizer, was administered. With every professional scientist projecting at least 18 months to develop a viable vaccine, it took a committed group of their peers just seven short months to succeed. The move to contain and eradicate the COVID pandemic was under way.

The first priority groups of people to receive the vaccine were the 21 million health care workers and 3 million long term care facility residents. For months, the front-line health care workers had been pressed into service, working long hours and days without breaks, exposed to COVID infected patients and in life threatening hazardous conditions. Mental relief and physical health protection was now available to them.

At the end of 2020, the COVID-19 death count, calculated by the CDC, was 385,343 with a daily infection rate of approximately 90,000 people. Those alarming numbers scared the American public, channeling them into the waiting line for the COVID-19 Vaccine.

Linda and I, being in the highly affected age group, were eager to sign up for our first of two injections of the vaccine, hoping it would be Pfizer. On February 12, 2021, we were scheduled for our first injection, happy to discover it would be the Pfizer brand. A few weeks later we scheduled our second dose of the vaccine, hoping with these two inoculations and with our personal protection program we would stay coronavirus free.

Early in 2021 a new strain of the COVID-19 virus was discovered, labeled as the Delta variant. It was identified to be the predominant strain of the coronavirus. The new Delta variant spread faster, easier, and had become a more severe illness than the original strain of the coronavirus.

With the news of the new Delta variant, most people over 40 years old, rushed to schedule their vaccine inoculations. They wanted to be protected from this new strain of the coronavirus and prepare to get back to a more normal lifestyle.

By June 2021 approximately 60% of the U.S. population had received one dose of the vaccine. However, the rush to get the vaccine was beginning to taper off, with many people asserting their individual rights against getting it.

Mandates were issued by some businesses demanding their employees get the vaccines or be fired. Some Doctors, nurses, and long-term health care workers, who had worked tirelessly during the early stages of the pandemic, were fired for refusing to be vaccinated.

President Biden mandated all federal employees must be vaccinated or they would be fired. He later partially rescinded that order so the federal government could continue to function. However, his administration continued to press for enforcement of the vaccine mandates until the Supreme Court found Biden's

Mandates to be unconstitutional. The Supreme Court decision disallowed them from being implemented.

The commercial airlines industry mandated all staff must be vaccinated or they would be fired. One weekend the pilots and on-board staff staged a sick-in and, without notice, didn't show up for work. Their disguised protest stranded millions of airline passengers in terminals across the U.S. creating a nationwide travel interruption. The airline staff's point was made, and the airline's mandatory vaccine program was abandoned.

Many people in the U.S. had grown tired of being told what to do and how to live their daily lives. Those who were not lemmings began, in singular opposition, a resolute rebellion against the many politically motivated authoritarian rules.

Each individual State Governor, asserting 'States Rights' regulated the pandemic guidelines of their state. From the beginning of the coronavirus pandemic four states, Texas, Florida, Mississippi, and South Dakota, refused to issue statewide 'stay at home' orders. Six other states never went to lockdowns and didn't force businesses, churches or schools to close or demand citizens wear protective masks. Those Governors promoted and published good health guidelines for their residents to follow. They trusted the residents of their states to make good health decisions.

Some State Governors, similar to New York and California, created an 'absolute power' position in their states. They closed all places where people gathered, businesses, schools, places of worship, etc. They also promoted a 'tell-on your neighbors' contact tracing approach to supposedly control the coronavirus.

Most State Governors, however, took the middle of the road approach in protecting the health of the people in their state. They set guidelines, which were followed and increased or relaxed them as the pandemic threat evolved.

In 2020 most states mandated professional baseball, basketball, all university level, and other sports to be played without fans and spectators in stadiums and arenas. It was strangely odd seeing athletes competing maskless with off premise announcers and simulated crowd noise in the background.

In early 2021 as the COVID threat began to subside, along with the introduction of the vaccines, sports fans and spectators were impatiently waiting for the governmental authorities to announce the hollow and vacant arenas and stadiums would once again be open. Some state governments relaxed their lockdown mandates enough to allow organized sports to be played with a limited number of fans and spectators cheering for their favorite players and teams. While other states continued to impose strict lockdown mandates.

By the fall of 2021, many solitary resolute individuals began coming together displaying their disdain for the continued strong-armed politician's mandated programs. In several states, as many as 100,000 college football fans attended nationally televised open air stadium games refusing to wear face masks. They were cheering, laughing, and celebrating their new self-created freedom. Others would find their own self satisfying way to feel their release from political bondage.

In nationally televised speeches, President Biden loudly and brazenly chastised any person who had not been vaccinated as Un-American. He berated those who refused to follow his Pied-Piper unconstitutional mandates. Biden publicly drew a line between the vaxxed and unvaxxed, further dividing the American people he had promised to unite.

At a large car racing event a newsperson was interviewing the victor, when the crowd began to chant an obscenity aimed directly at Biden. The newsperson reworded the obscene protest chant, and the improvised version was embraced. The new version of the chant was so popular it became the lyrics of a recorded song. The revised chant was also replicated at many large public events.

People were tired of dictatorial politicians, quarantines, mandates, and mainstream media scare tactics. More and more people began to rebel against Anthony Fauci and the CDC, their ever-changing confusing statements of the effectiveness of the masks, the vaccines, etc.

For two years Linda and I had planned to have our 50th Wedding Anniversary celebration in Grand Cayman. We had envisioned our two Sons, Neil and Reid, their families along with a few friends enjoying a festive celebration on the beautiful white sandy seven-mile beach.

At the beginning of the pandemic the Cayman Islands, like the rest of the world, had closed its borders and international travel to non-residents. Grand Cayman, the main tourist Island, with approximately 30 thousand permanent residents, had only one hospital to serve the Commonwealth. To have the islands open to outsiders would have put an impossible strain on their limited medical facilities.

In early 2021, with the COVID pandemic starting to come more under control, we began to hope our 50th Anniversary plan to sing, dance and dine on the seven-mile beach would come to fruition. We called "Plantana," the condominium community we annually visited, to inquire about their post pandemic opening plans. Additionally, we began checking airlines to see if and when flights to Grand Cayman would resume.

The manager at the Plantana told us Grand Cayman was in the process of relaxing their isolation policy, but the condominium community was still closed. They encouraged us to check back with them in a month to get an update. With the island still closed, there was no need to inquire about non-existing flight schedules with the airlines.

Each month we checked with The Plantana for an update and every month they would tell us of more progressive relaxed visiting restrictions, but none would fully accommodate our 50th Anniversary plans. Finally in September, with our anniversary in October, we were told The Plantana was not going to open for guests until November for the busy Thanksgiving Holidays.

We called a few other condominium communities and hotels in Grand Cayman, with the same disappointing results. It appeared our Grand Romantic Idealistic 50th Anniversary plans were going to be postponed.

During our 50 years of marriage Linda and I had realized, on several occasions, it was good to have a Plan B. Our 50th Anniversary, while not ideal, was going to qualify as a Plan B option.

So, on October 16th, 2021, Linda and I enjoyed our day together looking at our wedding album photos, reminiscing about our early dating days, our wedding day and sharing several special memories of our time together. It was a fun, warm and most enjoyable trip down memory lane.

In the early evening, we put on our finest clothes and went to a nice luxurious restaurant. It was a quiet intimate setting where we had good service, a great meal and continued to share more of our favorite stories of our many years together.

Our 50th Anniversary celebration wasn't what we had planned or thought it would be, but our special day could not have turned out better. Fifty years earlier we stood by each other's side and on this most special day we were there for each other again.

In November 2021, the thirteenth variant, Omicron, of SARS-COV-2, the coronavirus that caused COVID-19, appeared in the United States. The Omicron variant quickly became the dominant coronavirus replacing the Delta variant in 98% of the cases reported.

The Omicron variant had evolved rapidly spreading with more cold and mild influenza-like symptoms. Fauci and the CDC said it would be quite likely everyone could contract the new strain, Omicron. Many people, they reported, may not even know they had the Omicron virus.

The persistent COVID-19 virus strains were not going away. Instead, they would continue to mutate into new, less life-threatening strains to go on through our country like the annual cold and influenza virus.

In March 1918, an influenza pandemic commonly known by the misnomer "Spanish Flu" or as the Great Influenza epidemic, was first documented in a U.S. Army cook in Kansas. It was caused by the H1N1 influenza A virus with genes of avian origin.

The influenza epidemic rapidly became an exceptionally deadly global threat to the international population infecting almost a third of the world's population or about 500 million people. The "Spanish Flu" virus killed 10% of those infected, an estimated 50 million worldwide. At the time there were no vaccines or antibiotics to protect against the deadliest flu epidemic in modern history.

In the United States from 1918 to 1920, with a population of approximately 103 million people, 675,000 died from the deadly influenza disease. The highest virus-related death rate occurred in predominantly healthy adults between ages 15 and 34.

The COVID-19 virus, while an extremely serious contagious disease, was less deadly than the 1918 pandemic with 1,103,517 deaths reported in the U.S. population of 331 million people. An early preliminary analysis revealed 70% of the reported COVID-19 deaths were in less healthy adults 70 years and older.

Of those less healthy adults who died from the coronavirus, most had two or more simultaneously present comorbidities. These comorbidities compromised the immune systems of the infected people adding to their suffering and ultimate death.

The most common reported comorbidities included cardiac disease, kidney disease, hypertension, lung disorders, cancer, diabetes, and obesity. With these immune weakening comorbidities, the COVID infected patients were less likely to be able to fight off the attacking coronavirus.

The singular most adversely affected group of people crippled by the COVID pandemic were the children and youth of America. When the pandemic began to spread most schools were immediately closed. Athletic and extra-curricular events were cancelled, interaction with children and youth, as a group, of any kind was prohibited.

Fear of the Petrie dish type disease spreading, often found in school age children, was distinguished before it could start. Children were forced into their homes, to simulate classroom study via on-line virtual learning programs.

The separation of children from their classmates, friends, extracurricular activities, and athletic groups created an acute sense of isolation. Unable to interact with their friends, see their smiles, share laughter with their peers and exchange embracing supportive hugs frequently created a sense of sadness and despair.

The COVID pandemic's effect on children's happiness had a devastating effect on the education and training of our youth. Academic grades went down and reports of an increase in children's mental illness went up.

The children and youth of America underperformed, fell behind in their academic studies, muted individual achievements, and muffled socialization skills. The whole new next generation of America's leaders was marginalized by their treatment through the fear of COVID.

In the fall of 2020, after receiving low incident reports of COVID in children and young people, the Governors in 26 states reopened their schools. However, they still limited their students to no personal physical contact and required social distancing. Very few extracurricular activities were offered.

The action taken by the Governors of the 26 states mirrored a report compiled by Michigan State University, showing children were at less risk for COVID-19. The study went on to reflect, decisions to have in person education were more tied to local political partisanship and union strength than to COVID severity. Instead of following science, states refusing to open their schools followed political science.

It took another year for the balance of the states to open their schools to their now academically regressed and socially deprived students. For many their world would never be the same.

The children and youth of America, particularly those in low income and disadvantaged demographics, ultimately lost at least two years of standard qualified learning. The actions of fear spreading, power seeking politicians, union leaders and greedy businesses were the ultimate culprits in the generational setback in school aged children. This travesty of isolating, essentially body binding, the children and youth of America was by far the largest most comprehensive sin against our society.

In 2023, over two years after the rush to blame COVID for the massive number of pandemic deaths, a more comprehensive study by the CDC revealed a more honest mortality assessment. Of those originally reported COVID deaths only 30% were actually directly caused by the coronavirus. This new report would indicate the actual number of COVID deaths would be about 331,055 or about half of the 1918 pandemic. Of the COVID deaths reported only 487 were children and youth ages 0-18 years. This was a huge and most troubling admission of overstatement by the CDC.

This horrendously overinflated admission by the CDC only added to the misinformation, misreporting, profiteering and fraud that had become commonplace during the COVID-19 pandemic. Niccolò Machiavelli said, "Never let a good crisis go to waste." The COVID-19 pandemic was a major crisis and many people, businesses, organizations, and government officials had used it to best their individual personal and financial interest.

One of the major issues surrounding COVID-19 reported cases was the way many hospitals, medical centers and other health care facilities reported the coronavirus deaths. The profit oriented medical facilities received more financial support, from the government, for treating patient coronavirus related deaths. Thus, the hospital, medical centers and health facilities reported any patient with fatal comorbidity issues, but had contracted the coronavirus, as having died from the pandemic disease. This misreporting brought more profit to the medical centers and more profit led to more misrepresented reporting of COVID deaths.

In the early stages of COVID many medical theories and commonly used drugs were discussed to fight the pandemic. One prescription drug, Ivermectin, known to have an effect on viruses, was being used by many doctors and nurses to fight the coronavirus.

The FDA went to battle, both through providing media misinformation and directly threatening suits, fines, dismissals, and revocation of medical and pharmaceutical licenses to anyone directly prescribing and dispensing Ivermectin. The FDA, more committed to engineering a new vaccine for the coronavirus, intimidated the believers in Ivermectin to discontinue their use of the drug.

Undaunted, a group partnered with American Frontline Nurses and My Free

Doctor treated more than 300,000 coronavirus patients with early Ivermectin. Only three of those ivermectin patients died.

Ultimately, the FDA, seeking more power and control, would go on to spend billions of dollars for a new vaccine when they had more than one inexpensive cure readably available. Frugal multipurpose remedies were not to be considered when it came to the misreporting NIH and CDC. The door had been opened for power seeking politicians, greedy businesses, and individuals to prey on the COVID panic driven population.

The pattern for profiting from the COVID-19 pandemic had been set. The federal government, having granted relief funding for people and businesses, had begun doling out life-support money with little to no oversight of the disbursements. Corporations looking to profit, and individual swindlers alike saw an opportunity in the coronavirus pandemic for financial enrichment.

The more sophisticated businesses and individuals, some fraudulently, syphoned off the lion's share of the available emergency federal funds. When the smaller businesses, many more directly affected by the lock-down pandemic, submitted documentation for federal support, they found there was no more funding available.

Small community and family-owned businesses providing non-essential services were forced to close at an alarming rate. It would take years for many communities to rebound and rebuild from the COVID pandemic.

The misreported COVID statistics, misinformation intentionally spread by the politicians and parroted, ad nauseum, through the mainstream media, perpetrated the greatest fraud, in recorded history. The people of the United States of America forced to live in isolation, practicing social distancing and wearing unneeded facial masks had been duped into becoming human lemmings.

This treachery of misinterpreting science for the benefit of individual power and profit is the largest stain on our supposed civilized informed society!

Our 50th Wedding Anniversary

It didn't seem like 48 then 49 years of marriage had passed as we began to develop a plan to celebrate our 50th Golden Wedding Anniversary.

Really, we had just briefly seen each other at a small gathering of college students talking about who knows what, but within 15 minutes she was gone, and I didn't even know her name. However, I did know her roommate and through her I connected with Linda Anderson.

Linda was very beautiful, with shoulder-length long dark hair, radiant complexion, and dressed in an upscale eclectic fashion. She was by far the most lovely and poised girl on the Ball State University campus. On our first date, mesmerized as I was, I realized she was extremely intelligent as well.

I guess there was something about me that caught her eye as she accepted my initial date request. We continued our date and time together the next day, into the next and so on until we became inseparable.

It seemed as though we were destined to be together, committed from the first moment we met, first smile between us, first word out of our mouth and first relationship sealing kiss. When we were together, we emitted a radiant glow to the world announcing we had not only an unbreakable bond but a seamless symbiotic connection, which would enhance the universe around us.

Now, all these years later, we were planning a time of remembrance, reflection, and celebration of our Fifty Years Together in Marriage. We wanted to bring our children and grandchildren together to share in this special commemoration of our commitment to each other.

We wanted to have a fun-filled celebration in a special place where our whole family had long lasting memories of happiness and joy. That place was Grand Cayman!

For years we, as a family, had traveled to Grand Cayman for 'fun in the sun' relaxation and SCUBA Diving. This was the place we agreed would bring us all together in a celebratory mood.

Linda, the family vacation planner, began putting a list together of all the things we needed to do to make this special event happen. Her list included checking airline flights and times, condominium reservations, finding a party planner in Grand Cayman, deciding on a restaurant for our commemorative dinner, etc.

Many of the things on her list were easily accessible and would not be difficult to schedule. The event planner, music, party on the beach, the many unknowns in a foreign country, would be a little more challenging.

We were happily moving forward with our big party on the beach plans when news of a new strain of a virus, COVID-19, was made public. Initially, we were wondering what was this new COVID-19 virus? Don't we get a new strain of the flu virus every year? This is February, our 50th anniversary celebration is in October. This COVID-19 should be gone, like all flu viruses, by spring. But it didn't!

The COVID-19 virus instead became a pandemic, spreading, infecting, and even killing some of the more vulnerable people it came in contact with. The coronavirus spread from town to town and country to country infecting many, in particular the elderly.

All travel abroad by ships and international flights were immediately cancelled!

The Caribbean Island of Grand Cayman, with a population of 30,000 residents, was a much-desired destination for several hundred thousand 'fun in the sun' guests each year. The island had only one hospital to provide the health care needs of their residents, so with the threatening coronavirus pandemic the government closed Grand Cayman to all non-residents.

At the present time and the foreseeable future, we were grounded, staying close to home, and placed in a wait and see mode.

Each month, March, April, May, June, and July, we checked with Plantana, the condominium community we had chosen for our celebration time in Grand Cayman. When we called, they would politely tell us nothing had changed in the island's isolation policy. Finally in August we received some hints Grand Cayman would soon be open to off island residents and some guests. But the 15 day after entry quarantine restrictions seemed onerous, which defeated the purpose of going to a beach resort in the first place.

Frustrations with the guest visiting guidelines continued, with no children being allowed on the island. Our 50th anniversary celebration became less likely to occur with each passing coronavirus update.

In September we received information the adult guest quarantine in Grand Cayman was to be lifted on October 14th. This was two days before our actual wedding anniversary, so Linda and I decided the two of us would go celebrate our 50th Anniversary together. We surmised at a later date, possibly in 2022, we could have our family together for a belated anniversary celebration.

With this national news release, we called the Plantana Condominium office to make reservations for two weeks of celebration, fun and relaxation. When the office manager answered the phone, we were told that while the island was supposedly open, they were not taking reservations until November. Additionally, we discovered since October was the slowest guest month of the year in GC, no other condominium communities and hotels were opening until November as well.

Since both Plan A and Plan B had not worked for us, we decided to stay at our home in Fishers, go out to eat in a nice restaurant and enjoy an evening together. Sometimes simple is best!

While this plan seemed to satisfy Linda, I wanted something better for her, for us. So, I called Margaret Hall, the lady who made special holiday event cakes for our family. For over forty years Margaret had made our holiday cakes, sometimes custom designed and uniquely prepared to fit the occasion we were celebrating.

I asked Margaret to use her creative skills to make a cake for us reflecting our 50th Anniversary celebration. This she was happy to do.

I then called our florist to order a nice floral arrangement for Linda. She loves beautiful flowers! I wanted to make this special occasion as memorable as I could for us both.

On October 16, 2021, Linda and I drove the 45-minute trip from Fishers to Muncie to pick up our, surprise to her, 50th Anniversary cake. When we returned home, I went to the florist to pick up her beautiful colorful floral bouquet. Both were pictures perfectly placed on the dining room table awaiting our private celebration.

In the late afternoon Linda and I sat on our living room sofa exchanging memories and reminiscing about the many great times we had over the years. We started with the time we first met, our first date, our wedding, honeymoon, first home, birth of Neil, then Reid. We talked, taking turns sharing the most wonderful times of our married lives.

Hours passed when we realized we needed to get ready to go out to our special restaurant. But, we hadn't yet opened our anniversary well-wishing cards to each other. When we simultaneously opened our mutual admiration cards, we realized we had both purchased the same card. Laughingly we enjoyed the fact there weren't a large selection of 50th Wedding Anniversary Cards and after 50 years of marriage we were thinking alike.

The enjoyable trip down memory lane conversation continued through our exquisite dinner. We complemented our fine meal with a nice dessert and left the restaurant feeling wonderfully full of food and fond memories.

After 50 years of marriage, it was amazing, almost unbelievable, that Linda and I have this everlasting unbreakable bond. We began 50 years ago to start a lifetime relationship, knowing the commitment we were making, but not being able to see the future. We had no way of knowing how strong together we would grow, how much better we would enhance each other's lives, the positive effect we would have on other people's lives and our community.

As a single person we were good. As a married couple our strength together was multiplied many times over!

We have shared many wonderful, honorable, and terrific accomplishments. We are so proud to have made the world a better place for many others.

The best part is, we aren't done!

Unauthorized Drive-In

As a small yet fairly athletic young boy, baseball had been my favorite participation sport. It had given me the opportunity to find a position to play with the bigger, more athletically gifted boys in our neighborhood.

The game of baseball became more prominent in my life when, in my seventh-grade Industrial arts, aka shop class, I constructed a crystal radio from various pieces and parts made available to me. This makeshift radio allowed me to travel to far-away places where I found a station broadcasting the Brooklyn Dodgers Baseball Games.

In 1955 I began listening to the Dodgers games with the great play-by-play commentator, Vin Scully. The line-up at that time included Jackie Robinson, the first Negro, Black, African American to play in the big leagues. Also, on the roster were greats Sandy Kofax, Don Drysdale, Gil Hodges, Duke Snider, Pee Wee Reese, Roy Campanella, and Junior Gilliam all, along with Robinson, were Hall of Famers.

In 1958 my beloved star laden Brooklyn Dodgers moved their team to Los Angeles, California. The two-hour time zone difference made it difficult for me to pick up and follow the Dodgers. The game summary and box scores were being reported a day later in our newspaper so my interest level in the Los Angeles team began to fade.

Enter the Cincinnati Reds as my new baseball team of interest. Established in 1869, the Reds, originally the Cincinnati Red Stockings, was baseball's first professional team. Since that time, the team's name has evolved to now, simply the Cincinnati Reds. By changing my allegiance to the Reds, I was now able to follow the day-to-day, play-by-play radio and television coverage of my favorite sport, baseball. Also occasionally, I was able to attend and thoroughly enjoy a game at the Reds ballpark in Cincinnati.

On August 24, 2023, I was sitting in the extended front room of our home at 11138 Easy Street in Fishers, Indiana. I was watching the Reds on TV playing a night game against the Arizona Diamondbacks in Phoenix. The Reds, a predominately young team, with many very exciting rookies, along with a few seasoned players, were vying for a playoff spot.

I had been closely following the young Reds, with great interest, hoping this year may be the one where they would finally break through the playoff drought. Bragging rights were on the line!

This game, a real pitcher's duel, was tied in the sixth inning, with neither team able to score a run. It was an exciting game with each team occasionally getting a man on base, but unable to get the player across Home Plate.

Being played in Phoenix, the game was three time zones from Indiana. This meant it was a late start time for me, but I wanted to watch as much of the game as I could. Finally, at 11:30 pm, with my score knotted at zip-zip, I decided to go to bed.

I shut off the light next to me, then the TV, and got up out of my full body friendly chair. I took one step to my right and KABOOM!

An ear splitting, body shattering Sonic Boom Concussion shook my now dark world. The concussion left me stunned but still standing trying to assess what had just happened. Adding to my confusion, the burglar alarm and the smoke detectors were automatically activated as well. The shrill continuous noise of both the burglar and smoke detector alarms created another challenge to reorienting myself.

The comfy room where I had just been watching the ball game was suddenly totally destroyed. It was obscure air filled with dark dense particles of dust and debris. I stood motionless trying to focus on what had just happened to me and my once peaceful surroundings.

Having been in Viet Nam experiencing the loud noise of artillery fire both coming in and going out I knew I was in a bad situation. This Sonic Boom Concussion, much closer, next to me was far greater than anything I had ever experienced. This, I instinctively knew, was a life changer!

For approximately 15 seconds I stood waiting for some clarity in my situation thinking to myself, stay calm, don't panic. All of my war time experiences, and SCUBA diver training raced through my brain. Breathe, Think, Act!

In those few seconds some of the dust and airborne particles of whatever had happened cleared enough for me to see. The pitch-dark room now had some light from the clear summer night in it, exposing some clues to my predicament. Through the sediment filled haze, I could see some leaves and some branches of a tree in the room.

A few seconds later I scanned to my left and first saw the black hood of a car, then the front bumper of it. I then realized a car had crashed into the room and was close enough to me that I could potentially reach over my mangled body friendly chair and touch it.

Alarming thoughts raced through my mind. How did a tree get into the room? How did a car get into our house?

I was hurt! I felt pain! I knew something very bad had happened to me, but I was erect. My immediate concern went to the person in the car.

I called out, "Are you okay?" I heard a moan and thought the driver was hurt, too. So, I called out again, "Are you okay?" No response. I called out once again with no response. I was concerned the driver was badly hurt or dead.

With the clear night light coming through the forced opening in the room I could begin to make more clarity of my situation. The tree, a beautiful 50-foot Maple tree, once my granddaughter's jungle gym, was blocking my path to get out of the room. There was no clear way to escape.

Barefooted, I stepped up on the broken glass covered sofa and carefully, gingerly managed to navigate my way to the door and safety.

When I reached the door I saw Linda, 30 feet across from the living room, holding a flashlight. I asked, "are you okay"? She said she was and asked me the same question. To which I replied I was.

I told her a car had just crashed into our house. I told her to call 911 to get help and repeated it one more time to ensure we were communicating with the same sense of urgency.

While she was calling for emergency assistance, I walked out our front door to the sidewalk connecting the driveway and the street in front of our home. I saw the rear end of the black car extending from the front room of our home.

With the front porch light from our neighbor's home, I could see multiple glints of glass, several large chunks of stone and debris in our yard. This yard, with sharp obstacles, was too much of an impediment for me, with bare feet, to approach the wrecked car. I didn't see or hear any movement coming from it, so I began to focus on me and my injuries.

Needing a complete assessment, I scanned my injured body. The left side of my body, having been fully exposed to the direct impact of the fallen maple tree and the wrecked black car, was a bloody mess.

I had a small wound on my forehead, my left forearm sliced like a peeled potato, the size of a buffalo's tongue, was loosely dangling down. The back of my left calf had a deep cut just below the back of the knee in my calf muscle. It was dripping blood leaving a distinct trail behind me. Two long brown burn marks, similar to being branded like a rancher's cow, scarred my left thigh. There were several smaller wounds, some cuts, and bruises, too numerous to count.

Our home is on a small curve at the end of a quarter mile straight-a-way. Not wanting the emergency vehicle to possibly drive by and not see me or the tragic scene, I walked to the end of our driveway and waited on the curb.

Within three minutes a police car, with a blaring siren and flashing lights came to a stop next to me. I quickly told him about the person in the car and he rushed to assess the situation. A minute later another police car arrived. The officer of the second car, seeing my injuries, escorted me to a large knee-high boulder and told me to sit down until the ambulance arrived.

A minute later the ambulance arrived. One of the EMT's immediately began assessing my wounds. For approximately 15 minutes he did a thorough scan of my body to see where I was injured, how badly I was hurt and trying to see if I might have any internal injuries. His main concern was the open wound on my arm and how to stabilize it until he could get me more formal medical treatment.

During this time approximately eight more police cars and two fire trucks arrived. After checking the inside of the car for an injured driver, who had disappeared, the police realized they were dealing with a hit-and-run crime scene.

The first policeman on the scene pulled Linda aside to interview her on what she had witnessed. During their conversation, the officer told Linda he had personally stopped the driver of the car for running a stop light approximately a mile from our home. When he approached the car to discuss the violation, the driver sped away, turning off his headlights to make his get-a-way. The driver had evaded him by making a quick turn down our road, Easy Street. With his headlights turned off, speeding down the quarter mile straight-a-way, the fleeing driver didn't see the curve in the road and had catapulted into our home.

The police brought in the K-9 team, activated an aerial drone while several police cars drove through the surrounding residential neighborhoods in an attempt to find the criminal culprit. All to no avail. The elusive, likely injured, driver somehow had fled the scene.

After his assessment, the EMT assisted me into the ambulance and sat me on the gurney. He was concerned about the open exposed wound on my arm and told me he was going to give me an injection stating, "This is going to hurt." I told him I was 'tough'! It wouldn't hurt me. And it didn't!

The EMT then made me lie down on the gurney and told the driver to get going. I heard the driver tell the EMT he was on his way to the nearest hospital emergency room. The EMT responded with an emphatic, "No!" We need to take him to Saint Vincent Trauma Center.

Within 15 minutes I was wheeled into the Saint Vincent Trauma Center and a private room. There I was hooked up to various devices monitoring my heart, pulse, and other life stabilizing machines.

The pain began to set in! I began requesting medication to deaden my senses to this now excruciating pain. None was administered! I soon realized I wasn't as tough as I thought.

Over the next couple of hours, nurses came in to check the devices connected to my body, but no medical attention was being given to me.

The only thing they did was to change the blood-soaked towel under my continually weeping leg. No one seemed to be in charge and no doctor appeared to be on duty.

During this time Linda and a few of the neighbors watched as the firemen sought a way to shore up the room in which I had been struck. They needed to keep the roof structure from collapsing. They also needed to extract the car to keep it from possibly catching on fire and destroying the rest of our home.

Ultimately, the firemen constructed a 4" X 4" column at the northeast corner of the severely damaged room. This temporary fix was sturdy enough to allow them to safely remove the culprit's car. With this effort complete, the car removed, they could safely back their firetruck away from our home. The firemen then put a large 4' X 8" sheet of plywood to cover the now exposed entry door into our home. With this completed, our home secured, Linda along with our neighbor, Leo Cropper, came to Saint Vincent's to be with me and advocate for my care.

About four hours after I had been admitted to the St. Vincent two physician practitioners came in and said they were going to stitch up the large open wound on my arm. Without properly cleaning it they administered a local pain killer and began to attempt to stitch up the buffalo tongue sized wound. With their slow unskilled movements, it was clear to me that they weren't sure about the procedure they were attempting to perform.

Outside my room, Linda, my advocate, supported by Leo, was protesting the procedure, telling anyone who would listen that my injured arm needed to be properly cleaned and a surgeon would be required to correctly close my complex wound.

Finally, an Orthopedic Surgeon arrived and took charge of the situation. He told the staff to schedule a surgical procedure for 3:00 pm later in the day to clean and properly secure all my wounds. An injection for pain relief was finally administered and I was able to relax.

In spite of the pain medication, it was an extremely restless night, with a lot of discomfort and no sleep. Around 9:00am I was told the Orthopedic Surgeon had moved my scheduled surgery from 3:00pm to 12:00-Noon.

I was relieved to get this much needed professional attention sooner, to my still weeping wounds. Additionally, I was anxious to get his professional opinion of their severity and the ultimate healing prognosis of my many injuries.

After getting the medical update and the time of my surgery, Linda went home to get a few hours of sleep. But, before taking time to relax, she called Neil. She relayed to him what had happened with the car crashing into our home and my medical condition. Neil told her he would call Reid and relay the information to him. Then said he and his fiancée, Taryn, would meet her at Saint Vincent's later in the day.

At about 6:30am Reid called Linda. He said he was looking at scheduled flight times from Phoenix and expected to be in Fishers later in the afternoon. It appeared all of Linda's and my support team was coordinated and in transit.

At 8:30am Linda called a special emergency construction company to come to our home and close up the two totally destroyed walls of the front room. She then called our insurance company to notify them of catastrophic damage to our home.

The amazingly quick and efficient emergency construction company arrived at 9:30am. They were met with a tree removal company that was hired by the Homeowners Association, of which we were members. The tree removal group engaged two chain saws to remove our once Great 50 Foot Maple Tree from inside our home.

With the tree removal operation under way, the emergency construction company began to seal off the front room from Mother Nature's seasonally destructive elements, and the little outdoor creatures looking for a new place to hide.

When Linda went outside to check on the construction and tree removal progress, she was amazed at the number of people that had come to look at our severely damaged home. Both sides of the street were lined with parked cars, their occupants walking along the sidewalk gawking at our skeletal front room. There were two media outlet trucks with video cameras and reporters speaking into handheld microphones, conveying our loss. Linda felt the frenzied scene had all the appearances of a carnival sideshow.

Around 11:30 am The Anesthesiologist came into my room and asked me if I was allergic to some things and sensitive to others and I told him, "No"! He explained the medication he was giving us and was prepared to calm any anxieties I may have had. I was experienced in this anesthesia procedure, so I told him I was okay with it.

A few minutes later the Orthopedic Surgeon came in to explain what he was going to do to clean and close my wounds. He said the one on my calf muscle and the other on my arm were deep complex wounds, but he had confidence he would be able surgically repair both, to my relief.

At 12:00-Noon I was wheeled into the surgery room, administered the anesthesia, and told to count backward from 100 down to? I didn't get very far. I lapsed into a quiet tranquil zone, where the surgeon could now perform his medical magic on my arm and leg.

What seemed like a moment later I was sitting up in a bed in the St. Vincent's recovery room. Whatever kind of anesthesia the doctor had given me had worn off; the pain medication was in full effect leaving me in a happy jovial mood.

While I was recovering, the surgeon met with Linda and told her everything went fine. His only concern was the large flap on my arm, which had been detached for a long time with no blood flow to it. He hoped it would reconnect and heal well enough that no skin graft would be required. He was very emphatic, the soft cast bandage on my arm must not get wet and no change to it be made to it until it was time to remove the stitches. At that time, we would know the level of success of the reconnection process.

A short while later Neil and Taryn arrived in time for me to be released from St Vincent. They along with Linda wheeled me out to our supportive neighbor, Leo's car for the ride home.

When we arrived home, I immediately wanted to see the interior of the boarded-up front room. The place where I had nearly lost my life. I asked Leo to help me do that. He went to his home, got to a pry bar, and started removing the nails from the sheet of plywood covering the entry.

Once done, we looked through the opening. With some daylight shining through the porous temporary construction, we could visibly make out some of the room damage. When I added my high intensity flashlight to the scene, I could fully see the devastation from which I had emerged.

The once colorful nicely appointed furniture was in pieces and parts. The six-foot tall armoire, which housed the desktop computer and printer was totally obliterated and unrecognizable. My favorite chair and table next to it was bent and broken. The sofa, on the far wall, while intact, was covered with debris and glass. The solid wood corner table next to the sofa had been driven deep into the drywall. All of the remnants of this catastrophic event had been pushed into a small heap waiting for a scoop shovel and a dumpster. Nothing was salvageable!

As I further scanned the wall above and around the sofa, I could see deep impressions in it from the many furniture and debris projectiles sent flying from the horrific crash. I took a moment to contemplate not only what I had just seen, but what I had actually lived through. It was indeed a miracle I had survived!

Painfully limping from the nerve damage in my left calf, I went outside. I wanted to see the route the car had taken to get from the road to the tree and ultimately inside our home. I was weak and still a little shaken but forced myself to walk out to the street to visualize the route taken by the offending car.

As I looked East to the quarter mile stretch of nice straight flat road approaching the curve to our home, I could visualize the car picking up speed, trying to elude the police. As the driver approached the curve at probably 80 to 100 miles per hour, without headlights, he failed to see the curve and went straight.

Two years after moving into our new home at 11138 Easy Street, we installed a Koi Pond. To facilitate this addition, we needed to build a three-foot high dirt mound where the road curved. This dirt mound served as the pinnacle of a faux natural scenic waterfall into the beautiful Koi Pond below.

Spaced along the top of the mound, protecting approaching car headlights from invading our exposed sunroom, we installed a few four-foot-high shrubs, a Spruce Tree and three River Birch Trees.

When the fleeing driver missed the curve and went straight, the height of the mound catapulted his car, fully airborne, over the shrubs slamming it down into our side yard. The out-of-control speeding car traveled another 30-feet before hitting the large Maple Tree on the East side of our home. The off center-force from hitting the Maple Tree spun his car fifty-feet north at a ninety-degree angle, which thrust the still fast-moving car into the northside of our front room.

From where I was standing, I could see the street sign the car had clipped, the damaged shrub it had catapulted and a large rock at the bottom of the mound, bearing a scar, where the car had landed. The surrounding ground was littered with black- and chrome-colored parts from the culprit's car.

After viewing this double whammy destructive scene, I was surprised our front room had not totally collapsed. Now, I felt like I had been blessed with two miracles.

Satisfied that I now knew what had happened the previous night, I limped over to our paver patio, sat down in a comfy lawn chair, put my injured leg up on a nice knee-high bean bag footrest and felt my body relax. The sun-drenched paver patio, overlooking the waterfall and Koi Pond, was to become my recuperating station for the next two months.

The next day I was inundated with calls from several media companies, including The Indianapolis Star, WXIN Television and WIBC, a popular local radio station. The drive-in crash was so devastating and unusual they wanted to interview me. To get the horrifying story from me, the survivor.

The media representatives came to our home, their cameras and microphones recording. They wanted to get the "big story of the day" to share it with their viewers and listeners. I politely walked them, step-by-step, through the intense nightmarish situation I had survived, showing them the rubble-filled front room, the high-flying scene from the road to our home and my many cuts, bruises, and stitches. Without fail each remarked, "they didn't know how I survived."

Cars continued to drive by. Some slowly. Some stopped, while some took phone-enabled photographs. Our once private serene homesite was being invaded. Our privacy was gone as well!

Over the next few days, while sitting outside in my recovery area, several of the neighbor children, along with their parents and grandparents came by to see how I was doing. Many had enjoyed visiting our Koi Pond, feeding the fish and now they were sharing their kindness with me. They brought get-well-wishing cards, crayons drawn pictures of the fish, some fresh baked goodies, and a colorful potted plant. They were all curious, but very kind. Their visits were uplifting!

The police officer who had pursued the eluding house wrecker, called to give us an update on their investigation. He told Linda only one vehicle collision airbag had been deployed, concluding the driver had been the only occupant in the car. He also said they found a driver's license on the front seat of the car and were investigating to see if it belonged to the driver and or owner of the car. He further stated they had taken fingerprints from the vehicle and were processing it for DNA as well. He promised to keep us updated on their investigation.

A few days later the officer called. He told us they had positively identified the driver of the car as Teigan Hunt, a resident of Fishers. They were awaiting some further evidence confirmation prior to issuing an arrest warrant for him.

This personal identification of the drive-in culprit, Teigan Hunt, created a curiosity, in Linda, to discover more information about him. To satisfy this curiosity, she opened her computer, entered his name in a record search and discovered some very disturbing criminal history on him.

Linda discovered, in Rantool, Illinois, in June 2021, eighteen-year-old Teigan Hunt robbed, at gunpoint, a 17-year-old of $30.00. The victim, after giving Hunt the money, created a diversion so he could get away to avoid potential bodily harm. The victim identified Teigan Hunt, who was arrested and charged with the crime. However, the charges against Hunt were dismissed when the 17-year-old died later that year. No cause of death was listed!

Less than a month after the first recorded armed robbery, on July 4, 2021, Teigan Hunt and another person perpetrated a drive-by shooting where five people were injured. Two of the five, a 15 -year-old and 7-year-old were taken to a hospital for treatment.

The prosecutor, unable to prove who fired the gun, wounding the five people, reduced the two Aggravated Battery with a Firearm charges against Teigan Hunt to a lower-level crime. On the lesser charge, Teigan Hunt was sentenced to three years in prison. He was released after serving 403 days.

In early August 2023, after relocating to Fishers, Teigan Hunt was arrested for being in possession of a firearm. He was released from jail on a Surety Bond, pending a formal Judicial Hearing. A few days later, on August 24, 2023, the convicted 20-year-old criminal, Teigan Hunt, while being pursued by the Fishers Police, recklessly drove his car into our home.

Discovering Teigan Hunt's criminal history along with the many guns related charges created a loss-benefit blessing for Linda and me. While this gun toting criminal had recklessly crashed his car into our home, Hunt could have emerged from his wrecked vehicle into our home. Quite probably, if that occurred, he would have had his gunslinging weapon with him. Then trying to elude his capture, Hunt could have threatened us, taken us hostage, shot at us or who knows what his deranged mind would have led him to commit. We had lost a room in our home, but we were still vertical.

On September 13, I had an appointment with the Orthopedic Clinic to remove the stitches from my arm and leg. With some apprehension, I went into the patient room to wait for the nurse to remove the soft cast and stitches from my arm. I was hoping to see and be told my arm wound was healing normally and wouldn't need a skin graft.

When the nurse removed the cast, she said, "Oh my" and paused for a few seconds, which seemed like an eternity, then said, "Oh, this looks great!" She then removed the stitches from my arm. With a sigh of relief, I felt like I had been given a reprieve from more surgeries, grief, and pain.

Next, the nurse removed the bandage from my leg, snipped it and extracted the stitches. The wound on the outside of my leg was scared and scabbed over, but I knew, internally, the deep wound to my calf muscle was a long way from reconnecting and regenerating my normal strength and balance stability.

She said my wounds looked good. She didn't, couldn't or wouldn't discuss the damage from my upper calf muscle to my little toe.

After my release from the hospital, my normal workout routine was squelched! I was told for a few weeks to not do more than some light stretching. My foot hurt when I put on a shoe, so most of the time I walked around barefoot. I didn't know what was causing all of the pain, so I set conservative limits on my exercise and stretching routines. I began walking short distances, but could not do the elliptical machine, which coordinated my arm, leg, and foot motion.

On October 23rd, I met with my orthopedic surgeon, in part, to get his assessment of my slow healing injuries. I was very apprehensive of the level of discomfort I was still feeling and the damage to my leg and foot. I had been slow to increase my physical activity, not wanting to do something to cause further injury to my body.

After reviewing my arm, leg and foot areas, the surgeon told me I was healing fine. He said, because there wasn't a lot of natural blood flow to the leg and foot area of my body, the healing process would be slower. He said the damaged nerve in my leg and foot was the major cause of my discomfort. He further told me it could take one to three years for the nerve to regenerate. As he was summarizing, the surgeon told me to exercise, walk and be active. This enhanced activity would increase my blood flow and the nerve would regenerate faster.

I took his advice and began phasing into my normal exercise routine. I increased my weightlifting, stretching, Pilates and Yoga routines. Additionally, I began playing disc golf again. On Thanksgiving Day, I walked the 3.1-mile Fishers YMCA Wishbone circuit. Although I still felt some discomfort, I pushed on!

On Thursday, November 2, 2023, my 80th Birthday, at 11:00 am, the Hamilton County Deputy Prosecutor, Ashley Thompson called me. She told me the police had just arrested Teigan Jazalero Zavon Hunt. The Hamilton County Prosecutor's Office sent me a copy of the formal charges against Hunt. They included five felony and two misdemeanor charges. His Surety Bond was set at $250,000.00, which, given his previous criminal record, in all likelihood would not be posted, so Teigan Hunt would be held in the Hamilton County Jail until his trial in March 2024.

The trial date, with some legal maneuvers, was changed to May 2024. On April 9, the Hamilton County Prosecutor called to say, with our permission, the prosecutor's office was offering Teigan Hunt a plea agreement deal. The agreement was for four years to be served, with three years at the Department of Corrections and one year on a work release program.

The plea deal, according to the prosecutor, would allow the State the cost of a trial while still securing a conviction. Linda and I, knowing this was a form of a sweetheart deal for the probable-for-life criminal Hunt, reluctantly agreed with the prosecutor to put this incident behind us and move forward.

After a lengthy discovery and settlement process with our insurance company, on November 16th a restoration company began the cleanup and renovation process of our destroyed front room. First, they had to clean out all the demolished former beautiful furniture and miscellaneous debris from the room. As they were hauling out the debris, we were pleasantly surprised to find no rodents had infiltrated the exposed openings.

When the clean-up was finished the framing, insulation, drywall and painting systematically followed. While we were happy with the progress being made, the fine dust and residue from the construction process hung in the air we were breathing and permeated every room of our home. As soon as it was dusted away more would return.

Additionally, the many construction workers almost daily coming in and out of our occupied home, occasionally needing to use our bathroom facilities, was very invasive.

The hopefully smooth-running improvement process was frequently interrupted while waiting for special ordered items such as the special ordered exterior stone and custom-made front window.

With all of the special-order delays, holiday interruptions, and other start-stop occurrences, the front room of our home was finally finished on March 29, 2024, eight months after it was almost totally destroyed.

During the construction time period Linda used the insurance settlement money, along with some of our funds, to purchase beautiful replacement furniture and accessories to enhance our newly renovated front room. When finished it looked elegant!

I have had a Great Life!

As of this writing, it's not over yet, but my life has had many ups and downs, twists and turns, makes and breaks, but my win-loss percentage is well over 50%. That positive percentage defines success, which excites me to say, "I have had a Great Life!"

There are many things I can attribute to my great life, beginning with my parents, who raised me in a loving, and caring home, setting a great moral, ethical, and religious foundation for me. My Mother, in particular, had a strong positive attitude about all aspects of life. Her positive guidance provided me with the impetus to adopt that approach for myself.

The positive approach to all the facets of my life was further enhanced when I met and married my wife, Linda. In our home, she created a warm, caring, humor filled and loving environment.

Linda, a voracious reader, and avid history researcher shared her ever expanding knowledge to move our family intellectually forward. She was instrumental in researching many new avenues of education to support both Neil and Reid in their academic studies.

Linda also arranged our many adventures filled with culturally enhancing SCUBA diving trips to 18 different countries. Planning well in advance of our trips, we were able to visit many remote towns and villages. In addition to exploring their underwater ecosystems, these trips were designed to enlighten our sons about how other people lived, their many differences in our collective lifestyles and to promote the concept of "giving back."

Additionally, several times a year, Linda shared her culinary master skills, preparing a wide variety of special holidays, family, friend, and business dinners in our home. Her always well-prepared varied menus enriched the creative palate testing by our many guests.

Linda was also very supportive of my ever-changing efforts in the world of business entrepreneurship. She always encouraged me in the growth and expansion of the many new business ventures I created. In addition, Linda added her personal touch of project enhancement and occasionally some mild yet much needed skepticism.

Growing up I was always very active, happy and gravitated toward people who said pleasant things, acted in positive ways toward other people, didn't raise their voices in anger, didn't argue and create unnecessary drama. Perhaps it was a little Utopian of me, but I liked happy, peaceful and tranquil surroundings. I am very much an environmental naturalist.

My formula for being happy and living a positive life has always been treating everyone and everything in my environmental world with 'Kindness and Respect.' I felt that by doing so that same level of courtesy would be returned to me. With things in the environment, I feel good with that philosophy. However, in the human world, some people don't always understand the 'Kindness and Respect Concept'; rather they consider it a personal weakness and take advantage of its extension. Nevertheless, I always tried to seek out the good in people.

I developed a "Positive Holistic Mantra for My Life," which included: I will ask God for blessings, direction, strength, and courage in all my endeavors. I will choose to be happy. I will be strong. I will bend but never break. In some way, I will attempt to make each day better. I will honor my body and mind. I will serve my fellow man. In honoring and practicing these 'personal tenets,' my life will be good!

I have always tried to say positive things about other people, believing; "if you don't have anything nice to say, it's best not to say anything at all." This includes talking about positive uplifting topics, rather than negative gossip and drama-based subjects.

Also, I focused on introducing positive images, readings and visited good stimulating learning places like churches, museums, and cultural centers. Most important to me was personally visiting the natural wonders of a serene environmental setting where my mind and body were one with Mother Nature.

My most memorable natural moments communing with the environment were enjoying a sunrise in Belize and a sunset in Australia.

During a brief visit to a remote jungle resort in Belize, one morning just before dawn I arose, walked to the edge of a tall grass hill overlooking a quiet tree filled valley, sat down, and waited for the beginning of a new day. Not a breeze was blowing or a sign of movement in my whole vista, just the most tranquil quiet moment I had ever felt.

As I sat in that moment the aura of the jungle morning began to change. Ever so quietly in the distance one solemn bird almost imperceptibly chirped. A brief second later another bird chirped, injecting its morning voice. Then another bird began to sing a few notes, and another with its lengthier melodic special singular voice and another until the whole jungle awakened around me, sounding like Mother Nature's largest most vibrant rhythmic symphonic presentation ever. It was truly majestic!

The sunset in Australia came on the evening of our much-anticipated introduction to a new century. While taking a break from our SCUBA diving adventure on the Great Barrier Reef, Neil, Reid, and I, along with a few of the diving staff, took a small dinghy to a tiny un-inhabited island for a quiet afternoon respite.

To pass the few hours of our visit we had indigenous hermit crab races, counted the Blue Footed Boobies and drank a couple of beers.

As the sun began to set on the warm sunny cloudless day, I looked in the distance to watch as it began to disappear, shadowing the bow of our SCUBA Diving Yacht. When the 20th Century's final glow began to fade, I observed several female turtles, instinctively returning to their innate nesting site, and cautiously swimming up to the fine white sandy beach of the Island to lay their eggs. It was a surreal way to end one century and begin another.

While I always appreciated and enjoyed my present-day experiences, I was forward thinking, looking around at things affecting my life and others, thinking how they could be improved and planning for the future. Restless, never really satisfied, being content with what was offered was not in my DNA.

Early on in my entrepreneurial career I coined the Phrase, "Make hindsight a thing of the past. Do it now!" I fervently believed, "actions speak louder than words" so I worked long hours to effect change in all my business activities attempting to stay one step ahead of the marketplace competition.

Change is good! Every day in my life, my environment, the city, and the world in which I live constantly changes being made, things simply evolving. In order to adjust to these changes, I tried to have an open mind to the ones relevant to me. The concept of accepting change, while I realized I was not always ahead of the curve, served me well.

Now, a different kind of change is coming into my life, an involuntary change. This change, like no other, will define the possible length, quality, and mental stability for the balance of my life.

As I began to come to terms with my 'advancing in Life,' I was acutely aware that many changes would inherently take place in my body and mind. Nothing I could ever do would change the evolution that occurs when a person, me included, ages. However, I felt, the mental and physical approach a person takes to their eventual outcome, death, can make a huge difference in the quality of life they may live.

I chose to be an active progressive participant in my advancing life changes. The changes I chose to focus on were diet, nutrition, exercise, positive mental activity, and overall holistic physical health. I had to keep in mind each day is different. Each day had to have meaning. I was committed to starting each day with a happy thought and a smile.

My diet and body nutrition required a commitment to discovering and researching good quality food with complementary ingredients. Then the food

214

would be prepared in a manner to best capture its nutritional value and consumed to effectively gain the most benefit from it.

To begin, Linda and I would shop at a variety of stores, finding the good to best quality food available to us. We were looking for food with all natural nutritional ingredients, avoiding the artificial colors, flavors and processed additives found in many food items offered for sale.

In my business office I had a sign which read; "Quality lasts long after price is forgotten." This philosophy carried on into my personal life as well, particularly where the quality of our food was concerned.

Linda loved to cook and prepared an amazing variety of meals for us. She was continuously looking for new recipes to mix up our menu, to take the boredom out of the food she prepared, which we ate. Consequently, we would frequently have a new twist on an existing recipe primarily for our evening meals.

We focused on having a well-balanced diet, which included fruits, vegetables, and proteins. I didn't keep a record of the number of calories, grams of protein or fat content; rather I mentally measured what I consumed and tried to balance my food intake to satisfy my individual taste and inherent dietary needs.

Good food in, equals a healthier body with good energy out!

My exercise routine has evolved tremendously over the past several years. Some adjustments were due to my physical inability to continue to do the things I had done for years, while others were voluntary, focusing on enhancing while protecting the good muscle quality and physical structure I had left.

On most days, at home, I prepared a cup of hot tea, rolled out my Yoga mat and for twenty minutes did a series of area focused and full body stretches. I incorporated a variety of stretches, some derived from Yoga and Pilates, while others were gleaned from years of watching and listening to successful physical trainers.

Many movements and stretches were focused on the small intricate connector muscles used to heighten the support of my larger muscles while facilitating the fluid motion of my active joints. In reality, all of my stretches were designed to keep my body well balanced, flexible, strong, with the emphasis on maintaining muscle elasticity with a fluid full body motion.

At the "Y," usually five days a week, I incorporated relative light weights when lifting, not trying to build muscle rather maintain what I had. I used some of their stationery equipment to sustain the range of motion I had rebuilt over the past few years.

Also, as I had learned in Pilates Power and Toys, I used the various pieces of PP&T equipment to challenge my movements, keep my senses balanced with increased heightened full body awareness. Finally, I used a stationary bike, elliptic machine, treadmill, and other high energy equipment to build and maintain my aerobic and cardio endurance.

I felt good full body elasticity, motion and strength added self-awareness, which would build and maintain my confidence to meet my many challenges ahead!

My mind and brain functions had, as I matured, gained self-awareness and confidence. I strongly veered toward a positive mental approach with all things I encountered. I always looked at the bright side of life!

Now, advancing into the fall and winter seasons of my life, it was more important to look to and have positive influences in my life!

Years earlier I had met two people, both approximately 30 to 40 years older than me. They would serve as role models for this advancing time period in my life.

Ed Ball was the son of one of the original founders of Ball Brothers glass manufacturing business, now Ball Corporation, an international company. He worked in various capacities in the family business and ultimately was Chairman of the Board of Directors. Ed was an avid physical fitness guru focusing on running and swimming. At age 65 he learned how to SCUBA dive. On Ed's 92nd birthday he dove into the depth of his age. The following year on his birthday he dove 62 feet to the Aquarium Reef Base in Key Largo, Florida. There he spent the day in their undersea science and education laboratory.

Additionally, Ed, after retiring from Ball Corporation, along with his wife Virginia, designed and built the Minnetrista Museum and Cultural Center in Muncie. The museum citing the evolutionary history of glass making in Muncie serves East Central Indiana with exhibits and programs for children, families, and adults.

At our semi-annual social gatherings Ed and I would discuss running races, his fund-raising swimming events and various SCUBA diving venues, bridging the 40-year age gap between us. He was always planning to do the next thing, perhaps checking off an item on his bucket list.

Phil Ball, no relation to Ed, was a local family physician, who practiced medicine until age 70, 30 years less than his father, Clay. As a hobby he wrote weekly humorous whimsical articles for the local newspaper under the pseudonym, Charles F. Coldwater, M.D. This fictitious identity wasn't directly connected to him for over 20 years. Once his true identity was discovered Phil spoke at many local and regional events regaling his audiences with humorous anecdotes from his make-believe memories of Middletown and Normal City, both pseudo references to Muncie.

Phil's business card read; Philip Ball, A.B., M.D., M. Sci., FACP, Muncie. Indiana. In addition, there were 49 other professions listed, some of which were; Mayor-for-Life of Normal City, Indiana, Internist Laureate [Indiana] 1992, Faith Healer, Specialist in Obfuscation, House calls Made, Equivocator, Con Artist, Poet Laureate [Indiana] 1992, Imposter, Gossip, Fraud, Ex-Communicated Presbyterian, Standup comic, Writer, Book Author, Columnist, Raconteur, Teller of Tales, Rumor Monger, Soothsayer, Fortune Teller, Stuffer of Fortune Cookies, etc. Outside of his profession as a local doctor and renowned poet, Phil did not take too many things seriously.

Phil continued writing his weekly edition for the Muncie newspaper until shortly before his death at 96 years of age. He, his wife, Esther, daughter, Susie and Linda and I met on several occasions, including their 70th wedding anniversary, over a glass of wine and dinner. Three years before his passing, Phil gave me a book of his whimsical memoirs as told to Charles F, Coldwater, M.D., and encouraged me to write my memoirs as well.

Both Ed and Phil, my mentors, found a way to stay relevant and live life with a meaningful purpose. These two words, 'Relevant and Purpose' were to become meaningful as well to me as I began to advance further in my life.

As a younger highly productive energetic person I was relevant in numerous ways including actively building my national footprint business, raising two gifted young boys, being involved in our church and community, etc. When my big business closed, my children started their own families. Linda and I moved to Fishers, In. I grasped many opportunities to be active and stay relevant.

Keeping in mind Ed, Phil, and many other people I knew and had read about, I realized, if I wanted a chance to live a longer, healthier and have a high quality of life, I had to stay relevant. I also had to continue to find positive influences in both people and places.

My mission to stay relevant came in a variety of ways. First and foremost, I had to make a mental commitment to do things that were meaningful to me. Second, in order to feel relevant, whatever I did needed to have the appearance of displaying a sense of accomplishment first to me and then to others. Third, I had to stay somewhat current with the evolutionary and generational changes occurring around me. Finally, whatever I chose to do, I could not allow myself to become 'Marginalized.' I had to be active, make a difference, be recognized!

In addition to staying relevant I knew I had to have a sense of purpose to my life. This sense of purpose, doing something, making a difference, will provide me with some mental enrichment and self-fulfillment.

My sense of purpose has always been to make things, something, anything better while serving others. By making things, such as roller skating, apartments, townhomes, and condominiums better, I was actually serving others. This creating, building, and developing always gave me a sense of accomplishment and fulfillment. To see a finished tangible product, something I had done making other people happy, gave me inner joy.

A few years after my big business closed, we were able to purchase 20 of the Muncie apartments. They were managed by one of my former staff but, through neglect, fell into a state of severe disrepair.

In 2009 I took over managing the 20 slovenly maintained units. The present residents had not been vetted, quality of employment had not appeared to be a factor, oversized and multiple household pets were destroying the interior living area, and some occupants were not even paying their monthly rent. The apartments were a disaster!

Immediately I evicted two non-paying freeloaders. Three other residents, who were abusing our property, were refused lease renewals.

When the new vacancies were listed for rent and inquiries made, I required a more stringent application and approval process. This approval process included former landlord evaluations, employment and income verification and a credit report from a national credit rating agency. At the time, these 20 apartments were our most valuable remaining asset. They were going to get my full undivided attention.

At the beginning of each year our new maintenance manager and I met to review our repair and replacement budget. We prepared a priority list of upgrades to bring the apartments to a higher standard of living. These annual changes would attract a better quality of residents, which would additionally allow us to raise our rental income.

Over the next ten years we were able to reinvest our excess revenue to totally renovate the interior and exterior of the apartments. These improvements allowed us the ability to continue to raise the rent and change the profile of the units, now referred to as Aspen/Snowmass Townhomes.

These former slovenly managed apartments had been turned into upscale high demand townhomes. During this ten-year period, the rent income had increased by 90%. This increase in revenue had a similar effect on the value of our assets. Additionally, the townhomes created a nice monthly income stream for Linda and me.

In 2018 Linda and I committed to a 10-year plan for the townhouses. During that time, we would continue to maintain and upgrade the properties to create a highly marketable asset. At the end of the ten-year period, we agreed to sell the Aspen/Snowmass Townhomes.

At which time we would reinvest the proceeds in another newer income producing venture? Hopefully, during the interim, I could show our now adult children the benefits of having someone working for them in their semi-retirement years, building equity for their next generation.

Managing and renovating the townhomes would give me a much-needed sense of purpose. It would also keep me relevant and insulate me from becoming marginalized. A truly winning situation!

As I progressed through the years at Fishers Y, I became aware some younger people were watching my workout regimen. The balancing and movements, such as squats, roll ups and roll overs, etc. on a bosu ball, yoga ball and foam roller learned from my former Power Pilates and Yoga Classes had caught their eyes.

Several 20–30-year younger people would voice their thoughts; they could not balance or do the many complex movements I did. However, as I explained to them; you can work on your large muscles, but it's the small connector ones that help you keep it all together.

Eventually some were encouraged enough to try the many balance and mat stretching techniques I did a few times each week. Those that tried actually did very well. They even added a few new movements of their own. This made me feel really good as I had now become a mentor as so many before had been to me.

Also, at the Y several people, some my age and many a little older, would come weekly to take the Silver Sneakers Class. They weren't in as good physical condition as I was, but they were there. Most walked into class while a few arrived with their supportive canes and walkers. Aided by a stationary chair they would stretch and contort their bodies. Always continuing to do their best! Never giving up! I was impressed!

As I continue to advance in my life, I know the Silver Sneakers will be my next progression. I had scaled down my workout regimen before, so I was sure, at some point, I could make this transition too.

I am so pleased with my life, the many adventures I have had, places I have gone, people I have met and accomplishments I have achieved. Early on in my life I committed to follow the laws of God and man. By doing so I was sure my path in life would be more rewarding, less stressful and with a better chance for happiness and success. That has truly been the outcome for me.

I have embraced my challenges, enjoyed my successes, and learned from my mistakes. I have been blessed with a healthy body and a sound mind. With the vessel God has given me I have done my best!

My happiest moments have been traveling with my family, Linda, Neil, and Reid, exploring the 18 countries we visited, embracing their cultures and SCUBA diving in the waters surrounding them. We learned so much about the many ways other people lived, worked, and thrived in their unique and very different environments. Lessons learned in school are one thing; our son's interacting with people in their own familiar surroundings was something special.

More recently many smiles have brightened my face and filled my heart with great pleasure while enjoying my grandchildren, Alex, Tristan Ethan and Evee. I have relished watching them at their many activities, looking at their happy interactive photos, but most importantly listening to their laughter.

I love interacting with them, listening to them, and imagining their future. With their parent's great nurturing skills, solid stable backgrounds, and their own personal accomplishments, they are creating a very positive developmental environment for Alex, Tristan, Ethan and Evee. Happily, and with great enthusiasm, the next generation is being prepared to be a positive influence in their society as well!

The single best sound I have ever heard is the laughter of children! Hearing this comfortable happy laughter always fills my heart with much joy. I love all the children of the world. They are our next generation, the future of the world, as we know it. God bless them all!

I have had a Great Life!

Random Thoughts for Reflection.

The BIG TEN are COMMANDMENTS!

LOVE is a Universal language!

Embrace change, It's coming!

You can't think outside the box if you stay inside the box!

If you don't have stories to tell you haven't lived life very well!

Love many, Trust few and always paddle your own canoe!

Make hindsight a thing of the past. Do it now!

Running uphill against the wind builds character!

Never Panic! When faced with a potential catastrophic situation, Stop, Think, Act!

Courage is The Great Separator!

Always set your expectations high!

Mother Nature is in control!

Keep your personal compass pointing forward!

Random acts of Kindness are the Best!

Think happy thoughts!

Decorate your mind with happy memories!

Breathe with intention!

Celebrate life!

Life is short-Plan for the long term!

Laugh every day!

The person who does more than expected will receive more than anticipated!

Embrace your parents...Ask your children if they're Okay...Ask if your Grandchildren are Okay...You will be Okay until the day you die as long as your family is okay.

Smile!

Printed in the United States
by Baker & Taylor Publisher Services